Queer Singapore

Queer Asia

The Queer Asia book series opens a space for monographs and anthologies in all disciplines focused on non-normative sexuality and gender cultures, identities and practices in Asia. Queer Studies and Queer Theory originated in and remain dominated by North American and European academic circles, and existing publishing has followed these tendencies. However, growing numbers of scholars inside and beyond Asia are producing work that challenges and corrects this imbalance. The Queer Asia book series—first of its kind in publishing—provides a valuable opportunity for developing and sustaining these initiatives.

Other Titles in the Queer Asia Series

Undercurrents: Queer Culture and Postcolonial Hong Kong
Helen Hok-Sze Leung

Obsession: Male Same-sex Relations in China, 1900–1950
Wenqing Kang

Philippine Gay Culture: Binabae to Bakla, Silahis to MSM
J. Neil C. Garcia

As Normal as Possible: Negotiating Sexuality and Gender in Mainland China and Hong Kong
Edited by Yau Ching

Queer Bangkok: 21st Century Markets, Media, and Rights
Edited by Peter A. Jackson

Falling into the Lesbi World
Evelyn Blackwood

Queer Politics and Sexual Modernity in Taiwan
Hans Tao-Ming Huang

Conditional Spaces: Hong Kong Lesbian Desires and Everyday Life
Denise Tse-Shang Tang

Contact Moments: The Politics of Intercultural Desire in Japanese Male-Queer Cultures
Katsuhiko Suganuma

Queer Singapore

Illiberal Citizenship and Mediated Cultures

Edited by
Audrey Yue and Jun Zubillaga-Pow

香港大學出版社
HONG KONG UNIVERSITY PRESS

Hong Kong University Press
14/F Hing Wai Centre
7 Tin Wan Praya Road
Aberdeen
Hong Kong
www.hkupress.org

ISBN 978-988-8139-33-0 *(Hardback)*
ISBN 978-988-8139-34-7 *(Paperback)*

British Library Cataloguing-in-Publication Data
A catalogue record for this book is available from the British Library.

10   9   8   7   6   5   4   3   2   1

Printed and bound by Liang Yu Printing Factory Ltd. in Hong Kong, China

Contents

Contributors   vii

Acknowledgements   xi

Introduction: Queer Singapore: A Critical Introduction   1
    Audrey Yue

Part 1 Cultural Citizenship and Queer Politics

1. How to Bring Singaporeans Up Straight (1960s–1990s)   29
    Aaron K. H. Ho

2. Enforcement of 377A: Entering the Twilight Zone   45
    Michael Hor

3. Sexual Vigilantes Invade Gender Spaces: Religion and Sexuality   59
in the AWARE Saga
    Laurence Wai-Teng Leong

4. "Oi, Recruit! Wake Up Your Idea!": Homosexuality and Cultural   71
Citizenship in the Singaporean Military
    Chris K. K. Tan

5. Transnational Lesbian Identities: Lessons from Singapore?   83
    Shawna Tang

6. Both Contagion and Cure: Queer Politics in the Global   97
City-State
    Simon Obendorf

Part 2 Queer Media Cultures

7. Photo Essay: A Brief History of Early Gay Venues in Singapore   117
    Roy Tan

8. The Negative Dialectics of Homonationalism, or Singapore   149
English Newspapers and Queer World-Making
    Jun Zubillaga-Pow

9.   Impossible Presence: Toward a Queer Singapore Cinema,   161
     1990s–2000s
     Kenneth Chan

10. The Kids Are *Not* All Right: The Curious Case of Sapphic   175
     Censorship in City-State Singapore
     Loretta Chen

11. "Singaporean by birth, Singaporean by faith": Queer Indians,   187
     Internet Technology, and the Reconfiguration of Sexual and
     National Identity
     Robert Phillips

12. "We're the gay company, as gay as it gets": The Social   197
     Enterprise of Fridae
     Audrey Yue

Notes   213
References   223
Index   251

Contributors

Kenneth Chan is Associate Professor of Film Studies at the University of Northern Colorado. He is the author of *Remade in Hollywood: The Global Chinese Presence in Transnational Chinese Cinemas* (Hong Kong University Press, 2009), and his work has also appeared in academic journals such as *Cinema Journal*, *Discourse*, and *Camera Obscura*. He chairs the International Advisory Board of the Asian Film Archive, Singapore, and is a member of the editorial board of *Journal of Chinese Cinemas*.

Loretta Chen is described by *Harper's Bazaar* as "a force of nature", *The Straits Times* labels her "a Rebel with a Twist" and a "Wild Thing" whilst *The Peak* calls her a "critical arts entrepreneur". This multi-hyphenated queer scholar-turned-director topped her Master's cohort at the prestigious Royal Holloway College, University of London and received her PhD from UCLA-NUS. She is currently Visiting Professor and Artist in Residence at University of Toronto, and Creative Director of 360 Productions. Her recent production, *The F Word* received an Amnesty International Freedom of Speech Award nomination. An active campaigner, she was elected as Nominated Member of Parliament and is the ambassador for The Body Shop, Hermes and Evian's outreach programmes. Loretta has also recently been honoured as one of Asia's *Most Inspiring Women*.

Aaron K. H. Ho teaches at SIM University and has published articles on gender, film and Victorian literature in journals like *Genders*, *The Oscholars*, and *General Themes in Literature*. As an editor of *Blame It on the Raging Hormones*, a novella on a gay teenager in Singapore, he wishes to promote literature to the people and, with the help of a few friends, runs a reading group, 'queerbookclub' (http://queerbookclub.wordpress.com). He is about to complete his dissertation on Darwin.

Michael Hor is Professor at the Faculty of Law, National University of Singapore where he has taught and researched in criminal law and constitutional due process for over 20 years. He studied law at the National University of Singapore before completing graduate degrees at the Universities of Oxford and Chicago.

Laurence Wai-Teng Leong received his PhD from University of California San Diego. He has been teaching in the Sociology Department, National University of Singapore, in modules such as Human Rights, Mass Media, and Sexuality.

Simon Obendorf is Senior Lecturer in International Relations at the University of Lincoln, United Kingdom. Educated at the University of Melbourne, he obtained degrees in politics and law, before completing a PhD in international relations. He has held academic positions in Australia, Singapore and the United Kingdom. Dr Obendorf's research utilises contemporary East and Southeast Asian materials to explore international theory and postcolonial futures. An Australian citizen, he is a founding member of the Melbourne-based Institute of Postcolonial Studies.

Robert Phillips received his PhD in sociocultural anthropology from the University of California, Irvine in 2008. He is currently a visiting lecturer in the Department of Anthropology at the University of Manitoba and is working on a monograph, based on his fieldwork, entitled "Little Pink Dot: Technology, Sexuality, and the Nation in Singapore".

Chris K. K. Tan received his PhD from the University of Illinois. He is Assistant Professor in the Department of Anthropology at Shandong University. As an anthropologist of the State, he studied the construction of cultural citizenship among Singaporean gay men for his dissertation. He currently researches the roles that the civil service plays in Singaporean state-formation.

Roy Tan is a medical practitioner with a passion for documenting Singapore's LGBT history. He started all the Singaporean LGBT-related articles in Wikipedia in 2005 and has amassed the most comprehensive collection of Singapore LGBT-related news broadcasts, documentaries and videos of local events on YouTube. Tan intended to organise Singapore's first gay pride parade at Hong Lim Park in 2008. This event later morphed into Pink Dot SG, a worldwide movement which "supports the freedom to love".

Shawna Tang is a PhD candidate at the Department of Sociology and Social Policy in the University of Sydney. She received her Master's degree in Sociology from the National University of Singapore. Her interest is in the convergence of postcolonial theory, transnational feminist critique and queer theory in engaging questions of modernity, globalisation, sexuality, gender, citizenship, state and nationalism.

Audrey Yue is Senior Lecturer in Cultural Studies at the University of Melbourne, Australia. She is the author of *Ann Hui's Song of the Exile* (2010) and co-editor of *AsiaPacifiQueer: Rethinking Genders and Sexualities* (2008), with Fran Martin, Peter Jackson and Mark McLelland, and *Mobile Cultures:*

New Media in Queer Asia (2003), with Chris Berry and Fran Martin. Her essays on queer Singapore appear in *International Journal of Cultural Policy, Feminist Media Studies, Circuits of Visibility: Gender and Transnational Media Cultures,* and *Creativity and Academic Activism: Instituting Cultural Studies.* She is currently Chief Investigator in three Australian Research Council funded projects on Asian Australian cinema, transnational large screens and multicultural arts governance.

Jun Zubillaga-Pow is a final-year PhD candidate in music research at King's College, London. His interdisciplinary work draws upon contemporary French theory and social reception. As a queer theorist, Jun has written on the concepts of the body, space and cinema in Singapore. In addition to two forthcoming volumes on Singapore's music history, Jun is currently working on the idea of homonationalism in a Singaporean context.

Acknowledgements

The genesis of this collection began in 2009 during Singapore's annual pride season, IndigNation, when Audrey Yue and Jun Zubillaga-Pow met and talked about the possibility of putting together a book that captures the new energies and voices that are emerging in the nation-state. In 2010 Audrey and Jun, together with the contributors whom we have invited, coaxed and almost harassed (!) to write an essay for this collection, came together for a seminar to further workshop the proposed topics and conceptual frames. This book reflects the combined voices of these scholars and activists, including many others whose voices have been folded seamlessly into these pages. They continue to play key roles together in the fight for recognition of LGBT rights in Singapore.

In particular, we would like to thank: Alex Au, Russell Heng and People Like Us for initiating the Rascals Prize that brought queer Singapore studies out into the open; Stuart Koe, Sylvia Tan and *Fridae* for making available their institutional knowledge and resources; Jack Yong and Shubankar Dam at the Singapore Management University for facilitating the workshop, and William Spurlin for additional commentaries during the workshop. Eileena Lee (RedQuEEn!) and Jean Chong (Sayoni) have also been queer comrades. The editors of the Queer Asia series—Chris Berry, Peter Jackson, Helen Hok-Sze Leung and John Erni—have been most supportive of the project from the beginning, for which we are grateful.

Audrey's work on queer Singapore has benefitted from the generosity of many colleagues, and she would like to thank, in particular, Meaghan Morris, Jacqueline Lo, Vicki Crowley and Kim So-young who have invited her to their conferences in Hong Kong, Canberra, Adelaide and Seoul, and provided most valuable feedback. Collaborations with Peter Jackson, Mark McLelland and Fran Martin on the AsiaPacifiQueer Network provided a foundational beginning that has also shaped the trajectory of this research. As always, Audrey remains indebted to Sandra Schneiderman for her constant support and love.

Introduction
Queer Singapore

A Critical Introduction

Audrey Yue

Introduction

Singapore remains one of the few countries in Asia that has yet to decriminalise homosexuality. Yet it has also been hailed by many as one of the new emerging gay capitals of Asia. This paradox has underpinned the telos of its postcolonial development, and rose to fore in 2007 when the penal code against same-sex intercourse was deliberated in parliament. The topic rekindled old grudges and a hoard of sentimental differences fomented in the public sphere. Some considered the episode an advancement of civil society through a new form of 'symbolic politics' (Chua, 2008) while others begrudged the acute deepening division among the vocal factions. After this provocative event, sexual politics have never been more divergent with opinions stretching from explicit blasphemy to *blasé* self-repression.

This collection of essays from a wide range of disciplines and perspectives aims to uncover the persistent affections borne by various segments of Singaporean society during and after this parliamentary discourse. It brings together original writings by established and emergent local scholars and activists. Focusing on issues concerning the political, economic, cultural, religious and legal frameworks, this is the first lengthy academic analysis on how contemporary queer Singapore has come to light against a contradictory backdrop of sexual repression and cultural liberalisation.

Theorisations of queer Singapore have emerged in recent years through three distinct streams. The first focuses on human rights, social movement and spatial politics to examine the repression of homosexuality, the rise of lesbian, gay, bisexual and transgender (LGBT) activism and its attendant impact on public culture (e.g. Heng, 2001; Leong, 1997; Lim, 2004; Tan, 2007). The second stream maps specific case studies of cultural productions in theatre, literature and popular culture (e.g. Chan, 2004, 2008; Lim, 2005a, 2005b; Yeoh, 2006). The third focus tracks public and media attitudes towards sexual acceptance (Detenber et al., 2007; Goh, 2008; Lim, 2002). Common to these studies is how the encounter with the State has created a different imaginary of homosexuality and sexual identity. They raise three factors implicit in the critical consideration of gay and lesbian studies about Singapore. While highlighting the illegality of homosexuality, they also reveal an emergent social movement, a prolific queer cultural milieu of production as well as an unusually high preoccupation with homosexual issues in mainstream media and its broader polity. These factors point to how queer Singapore has emerged through a specific geographical and historic set of conditions tied to the neoliberal regime of its postcolonial modernity. Key to this regime is the ambivalence of illiberal pragmatism. Although these theorisations engage the governance of the civil society, they do not explicitly consider how Singapore is also governed by the logic of illiberal pragmatics.

Illiberal pragmatism is characterised by the ambivalence between non-liberalism and neoliberalism, rationalism and irrationalism that governs the illegality of homosexuality in Singapore. Using the robust, pertinent and original framework of illiberal pragmatism, these essays aim to provide an updated and expansive coverage of the impact of homosexuality in Singapore's media cultures and political economy.

Illiberal pragmatism has underpinned the logic of neoliberal postcolonial development in Singapore (Chua, 1995, 1997, 2003). It has also enabled the cultural liberalisation of the creative economy so much so Singapore is more renowned globally as a gay rather than a creative city (Ross, 2009: 5). While illiberal pragmatics has facilitated the State regulation of social identity, it has also created new subjectivities for the new neoliberal economy (Ong, 2006). This treatise shows how new LGBT subjectivities have been fashioned in and through the governance of illiberal pragmatism, and how pragmatism is appropriated as a form of social and critical democratic action.

This framework locates the specificity of a critical queer Singapore approach that differentiates it from other queer Asian social movements and research methods. While Anglo-centric and homonormative studies have consistently fetishised the relationship between liberalism and the emancipation of same-sex sexual relations (see e.g. Frank and Meeneaney, 1999), the central rubrics underpinning queer Asian studies to date have been through social movement studies, media cultures or queer hybridity (see recent examples such as Martin et al. 2008; Leung, 2008; Martin, 2010). Most of these studies have also focused on the representation of queer identities in popular media cultures and everyday life. The approach taken in this volume departs from these studies. By using the framing of governmental policy to consider the regulation of illiberal pragmatism, contributors show how LGBT subjectivities and their attendant claims to representation and cultural production are produced in and through a logic of queer complicity that complicates the flow of oppositional resistance and grassroots appropriation.

In Singapore's multiracial state of five million people, four races—Chinese, Malay, Indian and Others (also known through its acronym, CMIO)—are officially recognized. The Chinese, making up 75 per cent of the population, maintains a hegemonic hold. This racial distribution is also evident across the local LGBT community where the default queer is the gay Chinese man. This book problematises this hegemony by queering its cultural history as well as including a diversity of non-Chinese gay perspectives from same-sex attracted Indian men and Malay lesbians.

In the last decade, the 'coming of age' of queer Singapore can be traced to three key events. While these events are explored in more critical detail in later chapters, the development of this unofficial LGBT public culture is significant to situating the context of contemporary queer Singapore. As the country does not permit the registration of social organisations, and the only place that allows public assembly and public speaking without a police permit is the Speaker's Corner in Hong Lim Park, an inner-city garden, the emergence of an unofficial public culture is a significant milestone that attests to how a queer social movement and consumer culture have flourished through illiberal pragmatism. Several rallies testify to this pattern.

1. Nation Parties: The first public LGBT party in 2001 was attended by 1500 people. The party coincided with Singapore's National Day on 9th August, a celebration of the independence of the postcolonial nation. The party-cum-protest addressed the exclusion of LGBTs from State recognition. By 2003, it had become a three-day event, attracting global media coverage to the power of the regional pink dollar. By 2004, over 8000 partygoers attended. Its success and high profile caught the ire of the State who quickly banned the party. The event moved to Phuket in Thailand at a beach resort booked exclusively for the occasion. The Nation Party was organised by Fridae, a Singapore-based gay web portal for personal ads and news (see Yue's chapter in this volume).

2. IndigNation: Singapore's LGBT annual pride season began in 2005 in the wake of the banning of the Nation Party. The season consists of a series of events including film festivals, readings, art and photographic exhibitions and plays hosted by individual groups coinciding with the country's National Day commemorations. The key organisers are People Like Us, an informal local gay and lesbian activist group that began in 1997 (with more than 2500 members on its email discussion list, SIGNel) and Fridae.

3. Pink Dot: The annual public rally began in 2009 when 2500 people, dressed in pink, gathered at Speakers' Corner in Hong Lim Park, to celebrate 'freedom to love' regardless of one's sexual orientation. In 2011, over 10,000 people attended the event sponsored by Google and promoted through *Time Out Singapore.* Notably, the colour of pink used

to brand the rally has two references: the pink identity card of Singapore and the pink triangle as a symbol for LGBT liberation.

These occasions exemplify how a range of practices—from activism, advocacy, queer consumption and media culture—are negotiated precariously in a country that still criminalises homosexuality. This book unravels this tactic of negotiation using the logic of illiberal pragmatism that has enabled the Singapore LGBT community to survive and thrive.

The LGBT community is expansive and diverse, comprising localized as well as globalised forms of sexual identity. For gay men, the most common parlance to describe one's sexual identity is 'gay', 'G' or 'on' (meaning: is he 'gay'?). For lesbians, it is 'L', 'butch' or '100 per cent' (two femmes). As 'queer' is not a term commonly used in the community, this book uses 'queer' in its title with two intentions: as an umbrella term for the diverse LGBT community, and; a critical tool to unsettle heteronormativity.

In recent years, the LGBT community has developed a distinct relationship with regional queer Asian centres, especially Thailand. Many trans-men and trans-women make trips to Bangkok for sex reassignment surgery (SRS). Despite Singapore's legal recognition of the transsexual status, many choose to go to Thailand for sex-change operations because it is cheaper and has more skilled doctors (see also Aizura, 2011). Phuket has also become a proxy destination for Singapore's gay parties after the banning of the Nation Party (see also Au, 2011). For queer Singaporeans, queer Asian centres in Taipei or Tokyo are viewed through almost the same global queer imaginary as San Francisco or Amsterdam, only they are cheaper to get to and closer. These places have established scenes and are marked by the history of their social movements. Thailand has a different resonance, which is more like Singapore. In the new millennium, Thai sexual cultures are driven by market capitalism (see Jackson, 2011), which has opened up a consumer culture for trans medical tourism and made it the ultimate destination for the gay circuit party. Rather than following in the telos of liberation and rights, the capitalist queer market that helped queer Bangkok flourish is also the same force that generated queer Singapore. Unlike Thailand where homosexuality has been decriminalised, this book shows how queer capitalism in Singapore quietly goes about its business by governing homosexuality through illiberal pragmatics.

Theorising Queer Singapore: Illiberal Pragmatics[1]

The ideology of pragmatism as the conceptual framework for postcolonial governance in Singapore has been a key theorisation in Singapore studies. Chua shows how pragmatism was conceived from the late 1960s to 1980s as "an ideology that embodies a vigorous economic development orientation that emphasises science and technology and centralised rational public administration as the fundamental basis for industralisation within a capitalist system, financed largely by multinational capital" (Chua, 1995: 59). This conceptual structure is evident not only in making domestic conditions favourable to foreign investments, but in all aspects of social life including the promotion of education as human capital, meritocracy, population policy, language and multiracialism. Pragmatism rationalises policy implementations as 'natural', 'necessary' and 'realistic'. As an ideology, it has enabled popular legitimacy: "in everyday language, [pragmatism] translates simply into 'being practical' in the sense of earning a living" (Chua, 1997: 131). Following Schein's (1997) application of "strategic pragmatism" within Singapore's cultural institutions, Low also points to how pragmatism is the "singular prerequisite" for the "political will to implement necessary changes … for continuous self-renewal to manage change and continuity" (Low, 2001: 437). The marked improvement in the material life of the population and the economic ascendency of the country as a developing nation to a global post-industrial metropolis in the last forty years has made it difficult to argue against the success of pragmatism.

Unique to Singapore's pragmatism is how governmental interventions are "contextual and instrumental" rather than "in principle"; that is, they are "discrete and discontinuous acts, in the sense that a particular intervention in a particular region of social life may radically alter the trajectory that an early intervention may have put in place" (Chua, 1995: 69), so that a rational intervention in one special area of social life may turn out to be quite irrational when the totality of social life is taken into question. These contradictions, evident and well documented in the policy and everyday domains of marriage, reproduction, language and education, highlight the ambivalence of pragmatism. Chua attributes such ambivalence in his formulation of a non-liberal democracy to a state where "the formal features of democratic electoral politics remain in place and intact" but is "thoroughly sceptical regarding the rationality of the ordinary citizen and unapologetically anti-liberal" (Chua, 1995: 185). Actions are rationalised as "pre-emptive interventions which 'ensure' the collective well-being, as measures of good government rather than abuses of individuals' rights" (Chua, 1997: 187). Central to pragmatism is thus the logic of illiberalism where implementations are potentially always liberal and non-liberal, rational and irrational. This ambivalence forms the foundation for the emergence of a queer Singapore, not one based on the Western post-Stonewall emancipation discourse of rights, but through the illiberal pragmatics of survival.

The following discussion demonstrates how this logic is evident in current discourses on homosexuality. These exchanges are scrutinised in detail because they present an account of the cultural and legal histories, practices and events that have shaped the current contexts of oppositional queer activism, and gay and lesbian lifestyle consumption. The first aim is to position a set of scholar-ships that can arguably be considered the emergent phase of queer Singapore studies. Written by a disparate group of international and local scholars, they engage historical laws and contemporary formations, and follow a rights-based approach to emancipation and cultural representation. The second and more significant aim here is to critically contextualise this milieu and show how these theorisations point to, yet fail to acknowledge, the illiberal prag-matics of governance.

The (Il)Legality of Contemporary Homosexuality

The prohibition of homosexuality is sustained by the British colonial legacy. Examining criminal law to show how sodomitical acts are charged under Section 377 (Unnatural Offences) and Section 377A (Outrages on Decency) of the Penal Code, Leong argues these laws lack human rights and "[appear] to be the last frontier in the Asian region for positive gay and lesbian develop-ments" (Leong, 1997: 142). While Leong's human rights model of emancipa-tion sits well in the chronology for the progressive post-Stonewall discourse on liberation, this model does not account for the illiberally pragmatic practices of gender variance and same-sex co-habitation that are legalised and subsidised in Singapore.

Since 1974, this country has led the region in gender reassignment surgery and conducted more than five hundred operations in government-funded hos-pitals.[2] Transgenders can legally change their gender identity, and in 1996, were permitted to marry legally. The logic of illiberal pragmatics shows how the institutionalisation of transgenderism does not honour the recognized tradition of indigenous transsexualism or the progressive claims of sexual minorities, but instead, reflects the governance of gender transgression as a disease that can be medically corrected and socially heteronormalised. The human rights model is unable to account for the opening up of an alternative expression of gender variance in a country that does not recognise homosexuality. This anomaly in the governance of sexuality is also evident in property law where same-sex couples were recently permitted to co-purchase cheaper, government-subsidised public housing. Although 80 per cent of the population resides in public housing, gays and lesbians have traditionally been excluded from such homeownership due to the hegemonic discourses of heteronormative domes-ticity and the proper family. By allowing a single person and/or groups of single people above a certain age group to legally apply and buy a public flat, the 'queering strategy' of the new housing policy has maintained sexual norms (Oswin, 2010) but has also unwittingly sanctioned the blossoming of new domestic non-heteronormative sexual partnerships. Rather than legitimating the interdependency of same-sex relationships, same-sex co-homeownership is a rational instrument introduced to alleviate the over-supply of public housing. Although same-sex relationships are not legally recognized, same-sex couples are now also able to make claims to the everyday intimacies of living together, domesticity and home ownership. These two developments show the anachronism of the laws that regulate homosexuality and the irrational logic by which homosexuality is governed.

Illiberal pragmatism is also evident in the development of the local gay political movement. Heng's (2001) activist account traces the development of the gay scene from the 1950s to the 1980s. In the 1950s the 'ah qua' was a commonly accepted sexual figure. The 'ah qua' is a local nativist transsexual who used to ply the sex trade in Bugis Street, an area in Chinatown that was an icon of the exotic Far East. In the 1970s the figure of the Westernised and English-language speaking 'Orchard Road queen' emerged when gay-friendly bars and discos opened in downtown Orchard Road and were frequented by Caucasian tourists. Heng categorises these figures as belonging to an emergent gay "scene" (Heng, 2001: 83). He shows how the gay community came about in the 1980s with economic affluence and societal liberalisation, and maps the rise of cruising against the increasing surveillance, entrapment and prosecution of homosexuality. In the late 1980s, the globalisation of AIDS, which led to the development of the non-governmental organisation Action for AIDS, provided a platform for gay activists to organise and mobilise. He examines the 1990s activism of a local gay group People Like Us (PLU) and traces its unsuccessful efforts to gain official group registration and attain political legitimacy. Heng warns of "coming out of the closet" in a country where "the relationship between homosexuals and the state will continue to have its share of suspicion and uncertainty" (Heng, 2001: 95). His self-reflexive account follows the progressive logic of Western gay liberation that traces the movement from scene to community towards an end-point of decriminalisation and recognition. By describing the two earlier figures as belonging to just "a gay scene which served their entertainment needs" and comparing them to "a (later) community with an identified purpose of improving the status and welfare of gay people" (Heng, 2001: 90), he attributes hierarchical values to the two different practices that equally sustain the vibrancy of gay lives. His trajectory follows the rights-based discourse cautioned by Warner (1999) and Seidman (2005) as normalising and assimilationist. By focusing on the fight for equal rights based on reforming the stigma of minority discrimination, Heng's account has unknowingly delegitimised the indigeneity of local gay sexuality. Meanwhile, heteronormativity and the effects of colonial and developmental capitalism on homosexuality, remain unchallenged. Although he acknowledges the territorialisation of homosexuality in the social and cultural spheres, he fails to locate these practices within the illiberal pragmatics of governance.

These irrational logics are evident in how the subterranean geography of homosexuality is produced in heteronormative spaces in Singapore. Lim (2004) examines the construction of homosexual practices through interventions in public debates, Internet publishing and public dance parties. Using interviews with gay activists and gay entrepreneurs, and juxtaposing these against print media debates on homosexuality, he argues: "the overt spatial expressions of homosexuality may be occurring, but that does not necessarily mean that homosexuals are accepted as part of 'mainstream' society ..., they are merely *tolerated*" (Lim, 2004: 1778, emphasis in original). Although he points to creative strategies of resistance, it is unclear what these strategies are and how exactly spatial tactics of resistance are enacted. What is clear in his analysis however, is the illiberal logic that underlies the production of subcultural homosexual spaces. While gay activists are not allowed to officially register gay and lesbian organisations, and gay Internet content is subjected to censorship, LGBTs can freely publish and access a global audience online, and organise carnivalesque public parties in real life. These contradictions between law and lore show how emergent LGBT expression is shaped by the neoliberal push towards entrepreneurship and digital literacy on the one hand, and non-liberal media surveillance and social control on the other.

Such illiberalisms are further explored in Tan's (2006) study of how the 'gay community' has been envisaged. Using two events—the first, in 2000, regarding the church's claim that "homosexuals can change", and the second, in 2003, regarding former Prime Minister Lee Kuan Yew's published comments endorsing the employment of openly gay civil servants, he shows how the gay community has been imagined through the views of the conservative majority that support the ideologies of family values, heterosexual social cohesion and neoliberal economic growth: "Through complex and dynamic ideological negotiations that take place within the broader and inherently contradictory trend of political and economic liberalisation, homosexuals are 'tentatively' interpellated as gay Singapore subjects who are part of a community that is rejected by an imaginary mainstream and yet grudgingly relied upon by a state anxious to appear sufficiently open-minded in order to attract global capital and talent" (Tan, 2006: 184). He further examines the gay community's reactions to these events on online forums and shows how a "siege mentality greatly helps in the processes of imagining this community into being" (Tan, 2006: 188). He criticises gay activists, in their struggle for equal rights, for portraying gay Singaporeans as civic minded and nationally patriotic, and colluding with the neoliberal discourse of economic creativity. He argues gay identities are formed not through the ideologies of social structures but "imaginatively formulated with strategic purpose within evolving discursive contexts" (Tan, 2006: 197). Tan's account clearly highlights the contradictions between the continued policing of homosexuality on the one hand, and economically driven social liberalisation on the other.

These discourses discussed above provide a contemporary backdrop to the (il)legality of homosexuality by inscribing an indigenous tradition of same-sex eroticism, accounting for the emergence of a rights-based social movement, and gesturing towards a neoliberal market agenda of economic reform and queer inclusion. Although they do not focus on the central role illiberal pragmatism plays in these transformations, these accounts highlight the country's irrational and ambivalent modes of governance.

The following text introduces the critical role of creative industries in augmenting the logic of illiberal pragmatism. Using gay literature, gay theatre and lesbian nightlife, readers can see how illiberal pragmatism is characterised by a disjunctive mode of displacement that has enabled local queer cultural productions to flourish.

Creative Queer Cultural Productions

Creative industries sell the business of the arts and culture by transforming arts and culture into services and commodities that add value to the economy. In 2002 Singapore published its policy blueprint, Creative Industries Development Strategy, for the new economy, detailing reforms in the clusters of arts and culture, media and design (Media Development Authority, 2002). This followed the release of Japan's Copyright White Paper developed to strengthen its intellectual property infrastructure (Ministry of Public Management, Home Affairs, Posts and Telecommunications, 2001). Since then, regional neighbours such as Indonesia, Hong Kong and Korea have also implemented policies to pursue their creative industries of copyright, cinema and information technology. All these reforms are characterised by a sectoral approach of cultural mapping (Global Alliance for Cultural Diversity, 2006: 6). Framed by the 'catch-up' thesis, this approach follows sectors identified in Western economies, uses universal statistics from global reports such as world and competitiveness yearbooks and models industries after influential studies by Florida (2002) and Howkins (2002). The normative use of these universal frameworks and empirical data, argue Gibson and Kong, "make[s] generalizations about the cultural economy ... where meaning[s] ... coalesce around singular, definitive interpretations" (Gibson and Kong, 2005: 549). In 2005, UNESCO introduced the second approach of 'cultural indigenisation' to frame the development of Asian creative industries by emphasizing how local communities are created through new networks of cultural industries that focus on participation and community-based development: "The industries in general are smaller and mobilize communities at a level that is closer to the grassroots than more traditional industry development" (UNESCO, 2005: 1). The 'cultural indigenisation' thesis incorporates culture into national development plans for the purpose of achieving "sustainable development" (ibid.).

While these two approaches support the economic rationale behind cultural liberalisation and queer inclusion, they inadequately account for the local specificities of creative queer cultural productions. The discourse of 'catch up' is problematic if it simply rehearses the post-Stonewall logic of progress and liberation; similarly, the discourse of 'sustainability' is also problematic if it is simply a nativist reaction to protect local cultures from global erosion. Catching up, as a process of belatedly speeding up, is also a process of what Derrida has called tele-technic dislocation (cited in Bhabha, 1999: ix). Catching up is thus a process that simultaneously provides access to and disrupts the essential temporality of the West. It unsettles the ontology of the native and its organic being-and-belonging of the nation. It entails "the move from organic temporality to disjunctive, displaced *acceleration*" (Bhabha, 1999: x, emphasis in original). This mode of disjunctive, displaced acceleration is evident in the queer productions of the recent creative and cultural industries. Using the industries of literature, theatre and entertainment, the following shows how the transsexual, the gay man and the butch have emerged as exemplary tropes for demonstrating this mode of displaced acceleration.

Disjunctive Acceleration: The Sister Transsexual and the Glocal Gay

Popular fiction has been one of the earliest cultural industries to examine homosexuality. More than ten novels have been locally published since the 1990s that examine the various themes of transsexuality, coming out, and living with HIV/AIDS. In 1990, Joash Moo published *Sisterhood: The Untold Story* based on his interviews with local transsexuals and transvestites. 'The sisterhood' is a collective term for local transgenders who call themselves 'sisters'. In the preface, Moo explains: "They are defined as 'transsexuals' or 'transvestites'. Transsexuals undergo surgery to change their gender. Transvestites dress up superficially to look like members of the opposite sex. They are not just 'gays'. Physically, they *are* men and women; psychologically they *are not*" (Moo, 1990: vii, emphases in original). The book traces the experiences of thirteen transgenders through the characters of lascivious prostitutes, effeminate soldiers and dandy undergraduate students. It details their ordeals of adolescent same-sex attraction, the shock of their sexual desire, the trauma of sex-change operations and the joys of marriage. The sequel, *Sisterhood: New Moons in San Francisco* (Moo, 1993), is a book—ended with an endorsement by Professor S.S. Ratnam, the surgeon and gynaecologist who performed the first sex-change operation in Singapore, and an acclaim by the local entertainment magazine guide, *8 Days*, claiming the book as the "[f]irst in local literary history to deal with the social phenomenon" (n.p.). These collections, published by Times Book International, a subsidiary of the conglomerate Fraser and Neave (and partially owned by the Singapore government's Temasek Holdings company), present personal portraits and inscribe an indigenous tradition of transsexuality that has only begun to be 'made present' as a result of the legality of gender reassignment surgery and the official support given to local writers to publish local stories. Here, the instrumental rationality of heteronormative incorporation that has endorsed and facilitated the medicalisation of gender reassignment has been disrupted by the rise and recognition of the transsexual as a gender deviant figure of 'both and not man and woman'. In doing so, the illiberal pragmatics of medical and literary modernisation have inadvertently produced the transsexual as a figure that negotiates not only the indigenous pre-gay and the Eurocentric post-queer (Jackson, 2001), but also the local modern. As a trope of disjunctive acceleration, the sister transsexual exemplifies this mode of displacement.

Two other seminal 'coming out' novels, Lee's *Peculiar Chris* (1992) and Koh's *Glass Cathedral* (1995), further show how the gay man has emerged as a critical site to challenge colonial heteronormativity. *Peculiar Chris* is the first novel to deal with the theme of 'coming out'. The author wrote the book when he was nineteen and in the army doing 'National Service' (NS). NS is a two-year compulsory government project aimed at training young men to fit the standards of national masculinity. *Glass Cathedral*, commended in the 1994 Singapore Literature Awards, centres around Colin's association with James, whose father is the director of a multi-national company. It explores Colin's initial infatuation with James' rebellious and alternative arts lifestyle, and his relationship with Norbet, a gay priest who encourages him to reconcile his sexuality with faith. Colin refuses the material trappings of James' gay lifestyle and chooses, instead, to work with street kids and prostitutes.

Yeoh (2006) examines these two novels against the genre of gay protest literature and within the contexts of national patriotism and the globalisation of queer. In particular, he focuses on how these texts offer queer subjects avenues to challenge and revise locally, nationally and globally endorsed models of masculinity. In *Peculiar Chris*, the gay characters exploit the physical rigour and surveillance of the army into "a means of queer networking": "In aesthetic terms, the physical rigors of NS produced masculine bodies in sync with global gay fashions" (Yeoh, 2006: 123). He further examines how the central protagonist, Chris, comes to terms with his sexual identity by comparing his different sexual encounters at underground beats, and with middle-class and straight-acting lovers, and shows how Chris' choice of the latter points to an imagined gay ideal that is similar to the dominant ideology of the nation. The world of gay domestic bliss, economic privilege, monogamy and family ties, compared to the underbelly of degeneracy, secrecy and guilt, have left "largely intact" the dominant Singapore values of "(r)ationality, order, meritocracy, elitism, family values and material comfort" (Yeoh, 2006: 127). In *Glass Cathedral*, Yeoh further shows how the novel "reinvigorate(s) the queer by insisting on a queer which is firmly embedded within the particulars of Singapore culture" (Yeoh, 2006: 130). Yeoh argues these two books display a "transgressive hybridity" where "the capacity of a hybrid, localized queer" can "trouble normative social categories" (Yeoh, 2006: 131).

Yeoh's transgressive hybridity highlights how the gay man has emerged in the logic of illiberalism as an effect of pragmatic complicity and performing conformity. Pragmatic complicity is the process of complying, in the sense of being practical, with the norms in order to 'fit in' and 'pass'. Performing conformity is also a similar process of enacting socially approved models so as to suit the norms of the hegemonic culture. While the rituals of both are similar, performing conformity points more specifically to the types of everyday rehearsals that are based on the assumption that the norms of the status quo are maintained through repetitions. Pragmatic complicity, on the other hand, does not emphasise the repetition of everyday rituals; rather, it singles out how forms of conduct are self-consciously altered by groups and/or individuals to accord with existing and/or new modes of governance.

Colin's work ethic, together with Chris' choice of economic privilege, domesticity, monogamy and family ties, resonate with the Asian values of communitarianism and neo-Confucianism. These signifiers show how the pragmatism of Singapore's performance principle has irrationally also created an environment where the non-liberal local gay discourse of catch-up has emerged to replicate the homonormative values of neoliberalism in the West. In this artifice, the logics of temporal and spatial progress that characterise queer liberation in the West are out of joint, unsettling the teleology of rights, recognition and liberation.

These modes of disjunctive acceleration and displacement are further evident in theatre. Theatre has the longest history of LGBT representations dating back to the 1980s. It is also the site where politics are explicitly contested, especially through censorship (Chua, 2004). Recently, the pressures of cultural liberalisation have made the government more secretive. Rather than front stage, censorship takes place in the 'back regions' of pre-production where companies regularly face the threat of defunding and scripts are subject to a higher degree of scrutiny (Chong, 2010). In spite of this censoring, theatre continues to receive the highest percentage of funding from the National Arts Council, over and above music, visual arts, dance, arts administration and literature (Chong, 2005). Non-profit companies such as The Necessary Stage, Action Theatre and Wild Rice are renowned for staging gay and lesbian themed plays, and playwrights such as Eleanor Wong, Ivan Heng and Alfian Sa'at have become local queer icons.

While Chong criticises how the government predominantly funds English-language plays as a strategy for asserting the country's global consciousness (Chong, 2005: 562), Lim (2005a) argues the use of English-language cannot simply be viewed as following the universalising strategies of Western culture. Lim examines the groundbreaking 2000 gay male theatrical production, *Asian Boys Vol. 1*, and shows how the colonial legacy of the figure of the Orientalist gay boy is recuperated and re-imagined through the diasporic and inter-Asian circuits of "Indian gods, Japanese pop icons, Chinese rickshawmen, *samsui* women, and Malay online chat addicts" (Lim, 2005a: 403). These different modalities of queer productions highlight what Lim suggests as the tactics of "glocalqueering", a process of revealing the "complex circuits of mobility that follow neither a model of bilateral cultural transmission (West to East and vice versa) nor a contextual study of national productions that attempts to locate a quintessential Singaporean queerness" (Lim, 2005a: 387). Although Lim calls these tactics "a set of pragmatic homoerotic practices with many inter-Asian and diasporic resonances" (Lim, 2005a: 404), he does not elaborate how pragmatism works as an instrumental logic for understanding this optic. West's philosophy of pragmatism is insightful here.

Redefining Pragmatism: Doing Gay, Doing Butch

West's philosophical conception of pragmatism differs from Chua's commonplace conception of pragmatism. The commonplace conception of pragmatism is evident from *The New Shorter Oxford English Dictionary*, where pragmatism is defined as "the truth of any assertion is to be evaluated from its practical consequences and its bearing on human interests" (1993 vol. 2: 2319). This popular definition emphasises 'getting things done or tackling difficulties in the most practical way', or a 'can do and whatever works' attitude. Westbrook cautions against this apparent conjunction between commonplace and philosophical pragmatism. He criticises the popular currency of the commonplace definition as "pragmatism at its worst" (Westbrook, 2005: x). West's pragmatism extends such commonplace definitions with a focus on social action and creative democracy.

Arising out of American philosophy drawn from the writings of Emerson, Peirce, James, Dewey and Rorty, pragmatism is a method that advocates how ideas are connected to action, theory and practice, which challenges the traditional belief that action comes after knowledge (De Waal, 2005: 4). Peirce's anti-Cartesianism and Dewey's engaged instrumentalism, for example, emphasise how experimentalism and experience constitute knowledge as a product of a situation that requires resolution. In *The American Evasion of Philosophy*, West highlights the radical potentials of pragmatism through its focus on "future-oriented instrumentalism", a preoccupation with the "materiality of language" and the evasion of an epistemology-centred philosophy (West, 1989: 5, 4). West points to how these distinctions have contemporary appeal because they share with postmodernism the scepticism about the fixity of truth. Their critical, destabilising and creative drives also have a moral and ethical emphasis on how power and social hierarchy can be transformed: "Its basic impulse is a plebian radicalism that fuels an antipatrician rebelliousness for the moral aim of enriching individuals and expanding democracy" (West, 1989: 5). Influenced by Marxism, African American social thought and liberation theology, he shares with Dewey a pragmatism that promotes "creative democracy by means of critical action and social action" (West, 1989: 212). West's pragmatism is less a philosophical inquiry concerned with the nature of knowledge and the fallibility of truth, and more about knowledge as a form of cultural criticism where meanings and solutions are put forward as a response to social crisis and problems. His pragmatism is 'prophetic' because he draws upon his Christian background to express the problems about black nihilism in America. Religion, however, is not a requisite for prophetic pragmatism:

> I have dubbed it 'prophetic' in that it harks back to Jewish and Christian traditions of prophets who brought urgent and compassionate critique to beat on the evils of their day. The mark of the prophet is to speak the truth in love with courage—come what may. Prophetic pragmatism proceeds from this impulse. It neither requires a religious foundation nor entails a religious perspective, yet prophetic pragmatism is compatible with certain religious outlooks (West, 1993: 233).

Mills criticises the casual synthesis between pragmatism and religion. He puts forth two interpretive solutions to understand this synthesis; the first comprising a thin "(theologically neutral kind) having universalist aspirations" and; the second, a thick "(religiously committed kind)" (Mills, 2001: 198). "For prophetic pragmatism to be taken as an interesting and viable contender," he suggests, "it must be taken in the religious sense" (Mills, 2001: 199). Wood argues this synthesis is not at all casual, but critical; it represents "the existential-ist issues of dread, despair, and death and the political concerns of democracy, equality, and justice" (Wood, 2000: 8). Putnam succinctly calls this synthesis of empowerment and engagement a form of "democratic faith" (Putnam, 2001: 35). Putnam's useful departure point is also echoed by Westbrook who describes West's prophetic pragmatism as a "reappropriation of pragmatism" (Westbrook, 2006: 202) that reconceptualises philosophy as a politically-engaged attempt to "transform linguistic, social, cultural, and political tradi-tions for the purposes of increasing the scope of individual development and democratic operations" (West, 1989: 230). West's prophetic pragmatism is thus located "in the everyday life experiences of ordinary people" and shares not only with Marxism's critique of class, but also Gramsci's praxis of the common sense and Foucault's operations of power (West, 1989: 213). Cowan elegantly summarises it as "a practical, engaged philosophy and a cultural commentary that attempts to explain America to itself" (Cowan, 2003: 55). Central here is its status as a "material force" for individuality and democracy, "a practice that has some potency and effect that makes a difference in the world" (West, 1989: 232).

These characteristics of pragmatism as a form of democratic faith that is action oriented, concerned with consequences, and possessing a dynamic position of social and cultural critique, is significant to extend the relevance of pragmatism to Singapore's creative queer cultural productions. Positioned in this context, the glocalqueering optic, a critical vision that queers the localizing processes of globalization, offered by Lim's gay boys can be further conceptualised not simply as a commonplace set of pragmatic moves under the governance of cultural liberalisation or the alliances created by the shared histories of cultural proximity and diasporic homelands, but a conscious mode of 'doing gay' that bears a commitment to challenging the shame of gay sex. Dowsett (2003) uses the term 'doing gay' to differentiate it from 'being gay'. 'Being gay' refers to the rights-based politics of fighting stigma and discrimination while 'doing gay' refers to fighting the shame that comes with gay sex. Following Warner's (1999) thesis that identity politics have resulted in the normalisation of gay men into mainstream culture through the erasure of sex, Dowsett argues identity politics can still be meaningful if it focuses on 'doing gay'. In Lim's accounts, the spectacle of the boys can be argued as potentially demonstrating this practice of 'doing gay'. Lim points to how these men follow the "global gay worlds featuring the homoerotic cult of male youth and urban male practices … (They) wear muscle tank tops with feather boas, use skincare and cosmetic products, work out at trendy gyms, and attend pride parades and circuit dance parties" (Lim, 2005b: 296). Although Lim contends they exploit the global gay aesthetic, depoliticise a homoerotic aesthetic, and share no affiliation with the local grassroots or a radical politics of sexuality, this chapter suggests that these men, in their visible sexualised body aesthetics, embody the self-fashioning ethics of 'doing gay'. By going to the gyms, dance clubs, and saunas, and participating in body cultivation, cruising and public sex, they reappropriate what have been shamed in the post-AIDS West as the decadent places and practices of gay sex. In the pre-AIDS era, these practices formed some of the central tenets of radical LGBT activism in the West. From the psychedelic trance of dance parties, the rites of cruising to the obsession with body building, they described the faith-like rituals of prophetic pragmatism by actualising the material practices of everyday life that connected faith to politics, art, literacy and economic

production. Queer activism in this context exemplified the rhetorical performance and social action of liberation theology (Herndl and Bauer, 2003). Warner
shows how, in the post-AIDS West, these practices have been disavowed by
the rights-based discourse through embracing the stigma of being gay but not
the shame of gay sex (Warner, 1999: 33). For gay men in Singapore, these reap-
propriated practices embody the most abject and the least reputable acts of
'doing gay', and in doing so, resonate with what Warner has described as the
ethics of a queer life, as a "special kind of sociability that holds queer culture
together" and a "relation to others" that begins by acknowledging the shame
of gay sex (Warner, 1999: 33). They also recall Foucault's ethics of care as a set
of self-fashioning practices designed to empower the self and engage the self
through knowledge in its conduct with others (Foucault, 1979). The ethics of
'doing gay' in this manner exposes the shame used by both the straight and gay
mainstream to repress gay identity; it focuses on the materiality of everyday
life experiences to emphasise how the self is governed through individual
cultivation, group management and official representation. As pragmatism, it
recognises the agency, choices and constraints by which groups construct their
self-presence and self-autonomy. This befits a consensual society like Singapore
that prides itself on the successful interpellation of its communitarian ideology
to socially discipline its population and self-regulate the individual. This section's final example of creative entertainment further demonstrates such pragmatics of 'doing butch' in the lesbian nightlife of Singapore.

Since 2001, Singapore's annual popular Butch Hunt competition has
instituted a new sensibility of 'doing butch'. Organised by Club Herstory, a
lesbian-owned events management company and an online lesbian portal,
these competitions have drawn hundreds of butches out of the closet and legitimated 'doing butch' as an embodied way of everyday life in the country. One
thousand six hundred people attended the first finals at Zouk, a well-known
dance club located in the Chinatown creative precinct. During the event contestants parade in a pageant, field questions on dating and romance, and pass
a skills test ranging from singing, kung fu, dancing to stand-up comedy. The
average age of the contestants is between nineteen and twenty-two.

Not all the contestants are outwardly 'masculine'. Some refer to themselves
as pretty boys, most sport the trendy Asian *bishonen* long hair, and very few
flex their pectoral muscles. They don hip-hop gear, smart suits and ties, leather
shoes, cowboy shirts or just plain street wear. They come from all walks of life;
university students, sales assistants, chefs, teachers and graphic designers.
Common to all is the breast binder. The breast binder is made out of DIY elastic
bands, bandages, duct tape or clear wraps, or professionally manufactured
spandex and Velcro-adjusted sports bras and tee-shirts in assorted colours pur-
chased on the Herstory website or at the events. The breast binder is not only *de*

rigueur among the contestants, but all young butches on the streets, in the clubs and at the bars. Unlike the older generation of butches who may wear a normal sports bra with a tee-shirt under a baggy shirt, these young butches flaunt the flat chest at every opportunity, with sleeveless tank tops or tight-fitting shirts. The competition has popularised the breast binder as the technology *par excellence* in the practice of 'doing butch' in Singapore. It has liberated the sexual shame associated with being butch.

Where 'doing gay' is directly related to the shame of gay sex, 'doing butch' is also directly related to the most abject and debased of lesbian gender, what Munt (1998) has theorised as the shame experienced by the butch. Munt describes such sexual shame through the butch's experience of her body, breasts, genitals and sexual behaviour, as well as her male impersonation as a "failed copy" (Munt, 1998: 5). She also locates the butch's fantasy of impermeability as a sad and brave act expended to fight the toil of maintaining her masculine body. Shame, Munt argues, "is the foundational moment in lesbian identity, ... (in) butch/femme identity" (Munt, 1998: 7). Unlike the macho bulldagger or stone butches in the West, the musculature of the Asian or Singaporean butch is more lithe and less slight. Breasts, rather than womanly hips, are the first external physiological signs of the butch's failure to pass and the beginning of her internalisation of shame. In these competitions and in the materiality of everyday life among the young butches, the spectre of the breast is reconstituted through the explicit use of the breast binder as a new signifier of 'doing butch'. 'Doing butch' recasts shame with a new agency, making it a source of empowerment and engagement, and a new material force for individuality and sexual democracy. As Gea reports on the 2006 competition, "On pageant nights, the sheer amount of lesbian visibility creates a palpable sense of excitement. One can almost sense a proud, unspoken declaration among the women who attend—a declaration along the lines of, 'I'm lesbian and proud of it!'" (Gea, 2006: np).

This critical discussion of how the cultural liberalisation of the creative economy has enabled the emergence of a uniquely local Singapore queer culture (characterised by the logic of illiberal pragmatics), also extends this logic with the philosophy of pragmatics as a method for critically instrumentalising creative democracy and social action. This section began by introducing the specificity of illiberal pragmatics within the developmental and postcolonial capitalist logic of Singapore. Illiberal pragmatism is characterised by the ambivalence between non-liberalism and neoliberalism, rationalism and irrationalism. It pointed to how this logic is evident in the contemporary (il)legal discourses of homosexuality in the country. It further showed how the new creative industries provided a fertile arena to consolidate this logic as central to the production of LGBT cultures in Singapore. It argued how a local Singaporean queer culture has been constituted, not as a result of the recognition of rights and liberation, but through the disjunctive acceleration caused by economic and cultural reforms. In the popular cultures of contemporary gay fiction, gay theatre and lesbian nightlife, the sister transsexual, the Asian Mardi Gras gay boy, and the tomboy butch have emerged as exemplary figures of this creative queer culture. In their reconstitution of pragmatism with democratic faith, cultural critique and social action, they have reclaimed the shame of their deviant homosexualities and localised new embodiments of doing queer.

The Book

Structured in two parts, the chapters in this book showcase a diverse range of methodologies ranging from textual and discourse analysis, policy review, archival studies and empirical research, across a range of case studies including history, literature, religion, law, military, print media, lesbian theatre, queer cinema, creative arts, social media and queer commerce. These chapters are written by scholars who have strong attachments to Singapore: most are Singaporean-born and bred, most work in Singapore universities or industries, and some live in the Singapore diasporas in the West while others have conducted longitudinal research in the country. Although these scholars have received their research training internationally—notably, the UK, USA and Australia—the critique they present in this book shows a localizing approach to Singapore queer studies. Beginning with engaged interventions in social and cultural institutions, and bringing critical theory to bear on the impacts of its practices, the chapters show how queer theory is mediated through localized sites and identities. Rather than writing from within queer theory, the chapters are positioned in distinct disciplinary fields—sociology, anthropology, legal studies, media communications, film and theatre studies, public relations and entrepreneurship studies. This multi-disciplinary framework reflects the emergent field of sexuality studies in the country. There are no gender programs in the universities, and the study of sexuality is introduced through course modules on human rights, media and cultural studies.

The first part examines how issues of access, equity and representation are articulated, contested and claimed through cultural citizenship. Chua (2007) suggests cultural citizenship exists in Singapore through the narrow form of political culturalism, a governmental process of steering participation through ethnic channels to promote multiracial harmony as a public good. This book extends this conceptualisation to suggest that for minority LGBT groups, cultural and creative industrial policy developments have extended the scope of political culturalism and facilitated the potential to make claims to cultural citizenship.

Cultural citizenship refers to the process of how different groups make claims to their right to a culture. As a result of the culturation of the modern economy and contemporary society, cultural understandings of citizenship have emerged to be concerned not only with "'formal' processes, such as who is entitled to vote and the maintenance of an active civil society, but crucially with whose cultural practices are disrespected, marginalised, stereotyped and rendered invisible" (Stevenson, 2003: 23). Advocating the use of cultural expression as a claim to public rights and culture, cultural citizenship addresses dominant exclusion and subordinate aspirations by focusing on the "redistribution of resources" and a politics of "recognition and responsiveness" (Rosaldo, 1999: 255). Through multiculturalism and cosmopolitanism, cultural citizenship is also a site for shaping common culture and providing the capacity for autonomy (Kymlicka, 1995). Cultural rights not only bring "a new breed of claims for unhindered representation, recognition without marginalisation, acceptance and integration without normalizing distortion," they also propagate a cultural identity and a lifestyle (Pakulski, 1997: 80). A dual process "of self-making and being made in relation to nation-states and transnational processes," it is shaped by "negotiating the often ambivalent and contested relations with the state and its hegemonic forms that establish the criteria of belonging within a national population and territory" (Ong, 1999: 262, 264). For LGBT communities in Singapore without the right to sexual citizenship, cultural citizenship is another arena to consider new ways of making claims to and contesting normative citizenship, and participation in national life. Precisely because citizenship is being reconstructed and reformulated in a neoliberal economy (Ong, 2006), cultural citizenship furnishes a rich site for the new oppositional and compliant subjectivities of the Singaporean LGBT communities. This framing provides a theoretical backdrop for illiberal pragmatics in a way that unravels the contradictions between rights and recognition, sexual repression and cultural liberalisation, everyday life and governance.

Aaron Ho's Foucauldian account of cultural and sexual history uses three case studies in public health, racial science and the aesthetic movement to compare Victorian Britain and postcolonial Singapore. He shows how government strategies enforcing compulsory heterosexuality are similar to those practised in Victorian Britain that posited homosexuality as a threat to the nation-state. He further surveys the pragmatic governance of compulsory heterosexual masculinity in the realms of politics, law, media and education, and argues such practices of regulation have resulted in the erasure of queer migrant history and denial of sexual citizenship.

Michael Hor provides a critical legal framework to discuss how the 377A Penal Code is retained as an ambivalent but pragmatic tool for minimising

risk and instigating fear. The Code, which criminalises an act of 'gross indecency' between males 'in public and private', and punishes the offence with
a two-year imprisonment, afflicts the spectre of everyday homosexual life.
Although the government assured the gay lobby in 2007 that there would be
no direct enforcement of this law, Hor shows how the Code is still applied to
judicial cases of selective passive enforcement. He surveys the period between
1995 and 2010 and considers why underage offences and public disturbances
are prosecuted under 377A rather than other constitutional laws that could be
used for fairer prosecutions. He reveals how prosecutorial discretion has led
to an ambiguous interpretation and application of 377A. This ambiguity, he
argues, reflects the pragmatic 'messiness' of liberalism and illiberalism that
surrounds the governance of homosexuality. While free to choose same-sex
partners, gays and lesbians are bound by a law that does not approve sexual
rights. The law, on the other hand, while pretending to ignore their presence,
nonetheless continues to thrive as 'a bad romance'.

Laurence Wai-Teng Leong provides a critical development of 'the AWARE
saga' to consider the intersections of sex, sexuality, religion and education. This
saga, as it is generally known in local parlance, refers to an event that took
place in 2009 when a group of women from the same church seized control of
AWARE, Singapore's premiere non-governmental organisation that advocates
and defends the rights of women. Developments revealed that the leaders
who led the coup were less concerned with the position of women than with
sexuality in general and homosexuality in particular. The saga culminated in
an extraordinary public meeting where 3000 women turned up and voted out
the coup leaders. Using media reporting, Leong shows how, in a country where
the State plays a major role in shaping the lives of the citizens, and where sex
comes under the purview of the State in the areas of criminal law and welfare
policy such as allocation of housing to heterosexual families, issues of sex and
sexuality are also regulated by 'moral entrepreneurs'. He further examines the
practices that surround the event as reflective of the liberal and illiberal nation-
state. Hailed as the coming of age of the modern civil society, this event saw
women from all walks of life come to fore and be heard. Through the gender
platform of a State-sanctioned women's organisation, minority sexual rights
were advocated as cultural rights. In its aftermath however, the State stopped
AWARE's delivery of sexuality education program in secondary schools. While
endorsing the rights of women to voice their diverse sexualities, it does not
condone the pedagogy of diverse sex and sexualities.

Chris Tan examines how the military is a 'prime site' for gay men to negotiate their cultural citizenship. Using anthropological fieldwork, he discusses the
life experiences of gay men serving in the National Service (NS). NS is compulsory for all Singapore male citizens; from the age of sixteen and a half, they are

required to serve full-time for two years, and after discharge from this period of active duty, remain in the reserve, and attend yearly training camps, until they are least forty years old. Tan compares the differences between gay soldiers who are open about their sexual identity and those who are not. He reveals the military as a site of masculine nationality and shows how marginalised gay soldiers appropriate its hegemony to create cultural belonging. Gay soldiers enact cultural citizenship by performing pragmatic belonging in a heterosexist, patriarchal and nationalist institution.

Shawna Tang examines how Singapore lesbians embody a transnational sexual identity that is 'a contradictory, complicit and contingent negotiation of the local and global'. She frames her ethnographic data against transnational feminist sexuality scholarship, and shows how working and middle-class lesbians negotiate the State's heteronormative regulation of sexuality. In sexual practices such as activism, coming out, and being in the closet, local lesbians construct sexual identity through the pragmatics of national ideologies that negotiate the dominant values of heterosexual family and meritocracy. Reproducing the postcolony's collusion with the colonial regulation of sexuality, lesbian identities are pragmatic processes of legitimating desire and selfhood.

Simon Obendorf uses international relations studies to examine the contradictions between the official representation of queer lifestyles in Singapore's narratives of global city developments, and the regulation of queer politics within the nation-state. Analysing foreign and public policies to consider how official discourses on the global city appropriate homosexuality to create Singapore as cosmopolitan, tolerant and open, Obendorf suggests these signifiers are also refuted in international diplomatic discourses of State sovereignty that linked homosexuality to 'compromised citizenship and threats to national security'. While the image of the global city is secured on the promotion of homosexuality, the construction of the nation-state depends on the continuing marginalisation and criminalisation of homosexuality: 'the tension between Singapore's status as both global city and nation-state [gives] rise to the government's illiberal and seemingly paradoxical regulation of Singaporean queer lives'. This contradiction between 'cure and contagion', he argues, has limited queer politics and empowerment.

Through each chapter's review of history, law, religion, education, the military, the creative economy and everyday life, we understand how the State has constructed an illiberal regime for governing homosexuality. Rather than directly enforcing 377A, it is pragmatically mobilised by the government to insinuate fear and shape compliant subjects. In such a regime, gays and lesbians make claims to cultural rather than sexual citizenships. Cultural citizenship claims are evident in the ways minority and diverse sexualities are articulated within the gender platforms of community organisations, and in the everyday negotiation of non-heteronormative identity within the family, the army and the nation-state. Rather than following emancipatory politics that aim to empower queer constituencies, these claims are life politics that empower queer individuals.

The second part shows how mediated cultures, as sites of cultural citizenship, have emerged in the city-state. Mediated cultures are critical intersections that express the politics of people, resources and power. This section traces Singapore's queer mediated culture through media networks, and examines the LGBT use of media, and the media's constitution of sexual identities.

The media has always been central in the shaping of Western and non-Western sexual cultures (e.g. Signorile, 1993; Martin et al., 2008). In Asia, the emergence of queer cultures since the mid-1990s was advanced by the Internet and its capacity to create virtual communities, link isolated individuals and bond collective identities (Berry et al., 2003). As suggested in the earlier section, the hub of this emergence, arguably, is the LGBT scene in Singapore, with its illiberal but pragmatic proliferation of queer cultural production, nightclub cultures and circuit parties, and new status as a destination for regional pink tourism (Price, 2003; Prystay, 2007).

Media in Singapore is highly regulated and predominantly State-owned (Ang and Yeo, 1998). With media globalization came increasing media regulation (Rodan, 2003). Singapore was the first country in the world to implement a nation-wide digital network: it was also one of the first to notoriously impose Internet censorship (Ang and Nadarajan, 1996; Lee, 2000). New media regulation followed old media's practices of policing sexually deviant content on television and radio, including news reporting on homosexuality through sensationalism and abjection (Goh, 2008). Despite tight State control, Singapore's marginal and underground LGBT's communities have also seized the media to challenge stereotypes, self-narrate identities and organise collectively (Tan, 2007; Yue, 2011). The second part of this book develops these practices by examining the newspaper reporting of homosexuality, the media censorship on LGBT content, the development of queer cinema, photography and subcultural gay spaces, the racialised sexual cyberculture and the rise of queer media entrepreneurship.

Roy Tan's photo essay provides illustration, histories and an ethnographic analysis of Singapore's gay meeting places. Mapping the urban sites of gay activity, and examining newspaper reports and institutional reactions, Tan plots the history of the city's gay urban geography. Creating 'a record of the collective local gay memory', Tan outlines the features which made particular sites exemplary for 'nocturnal gay cruising'. Examining attempts by Singaporean authorities to police and deter such activities—like installing lighting and police harassment—Tan points to the diminishing of Singapore's 'cruisy' locales. His essay portrays the waxing and waning of open-air meeting spots, saunas, clubs, bars and discos and speculates about differences between a history of restrictive practices exercised in these spaces, and the possibility of more permissive and empowered contemporary responses. Tan concludes that the use of social media such as Facebook will fuel the evolution of gay spaces in Singapore, marking a progression from the 'seedy' toward the 'mainstream'.

Exploring archives of a conservative English-language print media alongside the impact of a nationalist politics directed against homosexuals in Singapore, Jun Zubillaga-Pow uses a 'queer world-making' methodology in order to argue for a repositioning of 'queer lives and practices' within heteronormative public information systems. By using the National Library Board's digital archive of Singapore newspapers (1831–2006), Zubillaga-Pow's discussion highlights almost two hundred years of data dealing with LGBT-related news in Singapore. The discussion indicates how these largely negative reports become part of a national apparatus that seeks to regulate homonormativity. This governmental apparatus, Zubillaga-Pow suggests, works to position homosexuals as 'a priori anti-national'. Through an analysis of a number of news items, the chapter outlines dialectics between positive and negative homosexual genealogies in Singapore. Establishing an axis between a 'homonationalist' discourse and a 'world making' method, the writer argues that negative representations of the homosexual are being used as the impetus for nation-building, and that a useful response to this is a critical method which practically surveys and positions the genealogies of queer life in Singapore.

Kenneth Chan frames his analysis of Kan Lume and Loo Zihan's feature-length film *Solos* (2007) with a historical overview of the representation of queer sexualities in new Singaporean cinema. This approach also takes in the realities of the Penal Code Section 377A, arguing that not only do these repressive laws force queer sexualities to the margins of culture and society, but also that the State's censorship laws are a means by which it can reify 'the Asian value system's supposed rejection of queerness'. A close reading of *Solos* allows Chan to celebrate possibilities, but also lament the complicity, of representations of homosexuality in Singaporean cinema. By doing so, he emphasises the 'uneasy flexibility' which those in the film industry adopt in order to traverse the unstable morays of sexual acceptability, while they also attempt to make use of 'tactically opportune moments to push back and/or to resist the legal and political structures of heteronormative disciplining'. Chan takes this discussion a step further by suggesting that in the Singaporean context it is the very play between the national and transnational that makes the existence of a queer Singaporean cinema possible.

Loretta Chen examines Singapore's Media Development Authority's censorship of representations of lesbianism in film, music video, television and theatre. Her discussion juxtaposes the banning of Lisa Cholodenko's *The Kids*

Are All Right (2010), with fines imposed for the broadcast of the *Silly Child* music video, censure of episodes of the reality show *Cheaters*, and the restrictions placed upon the staging of the play *251*. Chen highlights the government surveillance and repression of portrayals of LGBT cultures and communities in Singapore by unpacking the ambiguities and contradictions underlying the censorship of these popular media forms. The discussion of the bans placed upon screening the award-winning film *The Kids Are All Right* suggests that positive depictions of lesbian relationships are restricted in favour of negative ones, a tactic designed to directly influence public opinion. At odds with the Singaporean authorities' prohibitive response to the music video *Silly Child*, Chen's reflection on this film reveals its apparent *anti*-lesbianism, thus highlighting an institutional 'inability to read lesbians'. Developing this argument, her chapter draws attention to the ambiguous legal status of lesbianism in Singapore and suggests that the administrative reactions to episodes of the program *Cheaters* and the play *251* point towards a deep unease regarding the representation of lesbianism in the performing arts. These media case studies are mobilised in order to support an argument concerning the fundamental flaws and indeterminacies inherent in the Singaporean censorship authority's approach to female homosexuality.

Interrogating racialised discourses in Singapore, Robert F. Phillips offers an analysis of queer Indian-Singaporeans' use of new and emerging communications technologies, outlining how these facilities have impacted upon developments in sexual and national identity. He examines the racialised discourses within the queer community and uses fieldwork data from interviews with 'self-identified queer Indian-Singaporean men' in order to explore issues related to wider concepts of race, sex and nation. Phillips considers the 'double minority status of queer Indian men in Singapore' and examines how these unique identities are part of a larger process of transnational diasporic identity formation. This perspective allows Phillips to shed light upon both sexual and national identity in Singapore. He also uses this nexus to investigate how a minority group 'use[s] the Internet as an alternative public sphere where they are able to construct and debate narratives of culture, identity, and national belonging', arguing that through the use of such technology queer Indian-Singaporean men complicate the relationship between sexual and national identity. Phillips highlights the importance of anonymity in online exchanges, which allows a virtual alternative for those uncomfortable in a physical public space. At the same time, technologies such as the Internet have allowed minority Singaporeans to transcend their national boundaries and interact in a transnational space of social exchange. Despite this move beyond national borders, Phillips' research shows how this process can actually contribute to a re-definition of the nation or home country itself. Queer Indian-Singaporean social interaction on the

Internet thus becomes the impetus for social change and a political contribution to the shifting ways in which Singapore is imagined.

Audrey Yue provides a critical examination of Fridae, the Singapore-based gay web portal. The chapter positions the aesthetics, activities and activism of Asia's largest online LGBT community forum within Singapore's culture of 'unofficial tolerance', and innovatively frames Fridae as a social movement with an entrepreneurial underpinning. This methodology offers a new way of approaching the content and consumption of gay social media, and means by which to understand the 'emergence of a gay social movement and queer entrepreneurship in a country where homosexuality is still illegal'. Yue argues that Fridae's blend of the social and the commercial taps into the neoliberal agenda of Singaporean culture and administration, and thus presents a 'model for the future of queer organisations in contemporary neoliberal economies'. Through its media, marketing and activist presence Fridae is able to contribute substantially to the development of gay social capital in Singapore and beyond. By establishing this new critical perspective, the discussion broadens the potential for scholarly engagements with gay and lesbian new media cultures and suggests that Fridae's 'illiberal yet pragmatic moral legitimacy' is a novel institutional mode that allows it to contribute to the visibility of gay cultures in an otherwise restrictive neoliberal environment.

All these chapters cover official and unofficial media, including archival gay photographs, mainstream newspapers, film, theatre, television and the Internet. They explore how local LGBT communities have thrived underground and above ground through pragmatic modes of resistance and complicity. From subcultural and abject beginnings to the national embrace of queer cinema and the global acclaim of social media, they show how contemporary queer Singapore has emerged as a self-aware, action-oriented and entrepreneurial culture that has worked within and twisted the illiberal logic of State control. Together, the chapters in this book provide a Singaporean queer critique of Asian neoliberalisms and build a platform for understanding the shaping of queer Asian futures.

Part 1

Cultural Citizenship and Queer Politics

1

How to Bring Singaporeans Up Straight (1960s–1990s)

Aaron K. H. Ho

Michel Foucault demonstrates, *inter alia*, two concepts pertinent to being queer in Singapore. *Discipline and Punish* (1995) uses Jeremy Bentham's panopticon as a metaphor for post-industrial civilization. Much like surveillance cameras in stores that prevent theft even though they may not even be switched on, a single warden at the centre of the panopticon, hidden from the prisoners' view, can watch over many inmates, installing fear and docility in them as they are never sure when they are being watched. The visibility of modern civilization, of having to study and work, of having a Facebook account, joining Facebook interest groups (Bear Project, Same-Sex Marriage, Gay Asia and the list goes on), of possessing a National Registration Identity Card (NRIC), allows institutions and individuals to stalk a person. Although much policing power is recumbent on institutions, we, who live in modern societies, partake in this surveillance and policing of other humans and at the same time, we, fearful of being watched, conform to societal *doxa*. We are both the police and the prisoners.

Knowledge is power and power is repressive but this dictatorship of knowledge-power is also perverse, productive and empowering for the oppressed, as Foucault continues his argument in *The History of Sexuality* (1990). Take the sensational, Victorian anti-sodomy trial of Oscar Wilde for example. Many gay Englishmen fled to Paris or Italy but many individuals who repressed their sexuality and believed they were the only deviants in the world found empowerment through group solidarity, identity and a name, 'homosexual'. In trying to repress homosexuality, agents of power—media, medical, legal and state— perversely magnify ideas they seek to repress; there is never such a thing as bad publicity. To Foucault, to be human is to be subjected to structures of power, that is, the construction of a selfhood is always dependent on times and conditions of power. Individuals can never be free from power and how it controls us although there are degrees of freedom of subjectivity within this internment. Following Foucault's line of thought, I want to examine postcolonial Singapore (1960s to 1990s) before the advent of any new media (Internet changes the dynamics of knowledge-power) and trace how Singapore institutions have made heterosexuality compulsory so as to answer the question of how human and free *all* Singaporeans are. The strategies that Singapore institutions employ are similar to colonial tactics used by the British Empire and these tools hold the key to the solution of many social problems in Singapore.

Neo-Victorian Singapore and the Erasure of Queer History

During the years 1867 to 1914, "a ban [on female prostitution] would also have encouraged homosexual prostitution which was fostered for many years by the importation of Hainanese boys" (Turnbull, 1989: 86). This cryptic reference to colonial homosexuality appears in only *one* sentence in the entire book of C. M. Turnbull's *A History of Singapore* although homosexual prostitution "was fostered for many years". Her inhibition contributes to Singapore institutions' constant erasure and rewriting of Singapore's queer history. Founded by Sir Stamford Raffles, an official for the East India Company, in 1819, Singapore was to be established mainly as an Empire's *entrepôt* between Europe and the East and had, at that time, only about 1,000 inhabitants (Turnbull, 1989: 5). Almost a hundred years later, by 1911, the population ballooned to 185,000 with men outnumbering women by ten to one (Turnbull, 1989: 95–6). In situations where there was a lack of women, men, regardless of their sexuality, had sex with other men. Intercourse between men in colonial Singapore was highly likely despite the lack of evidence. In a sense, unlike other already-populated colonies, most migrants came to Singapore, knowing that they would be dominated; they came to be willingly colonized. The demand for Hainanese boys as hustlers demonstrates that there was a homosexual desire amidst some impecunious migrants. The specificity of importing Hainanese boys is important in proving the migrants' sexuality. Hainanese men were (and still are) stereotyped to be tall and handsome with flawless complexion. The discerning eye for beautiful men of male migrants proves that they were not picking at scraps—there were no women; any hole would do—but even if they were, this activity merely validated the serosity of sexuality in relation to its spatiotemporal arrangements. If *entrepôt* is a metaphor for Singapore, then these labourers were seamen, seeking comfort in each other's arms. But such a history has been erased.

The erasure of queer history on the part of Singapore institutions is quite deliberate. Lee Kuan Yew (2005), the first Prime Minster (1965–1990), Senior Minister (1990–2004), Minister Mentor (2004 onwards), said in a 2005 speech, "I held [Ong Pang Boon, then-Minister for Home Affairs] back from trying to do the impossible—stop prostitution and gambling. I reminded him that from the founding of Singapore in 1819, seamen from the world looked for creature comforts when their ships were in Singapore harbour. So we left these red-light districts be." Since the founding of Singapore in 1819, there has been a history of homosexuality. Not only did the migrants have sex with Hainanese boys, seamen and soldiers in the Vietnam War looked for creature comforts (trans-vestites and transsexuals) at Bugis Street, an iconic space where drag queens and transsexuals solicited during the 1950s–1980s, when the soldiers came to Singapore for rest and relaxation. Yet in 1985, Bugis Street was bulldozed and forgotten. They did not leave these red-light districts be.

Singapore's history of robust heterosexual prostitution is enshrined and even winked at with a sense of pride, like the bragging of sexual prowess between heterosexual men, but queer existence on Bugis Street is quietly effaced. In today's imagination of young Singaporeans, Bugis Street is known for fashion-able, cheap buys, not its carnivalesque, nightly extravaganzas. As Alfian Sa'at, poet and playwright, suggests in his poetry book titled *A History of Amnesia* (2001), Singaporeans live with no history, or more accurately, they live with a postmodern history that is constantly erased, re-constructed, re-interpreted by institutions of power.

This rhetoric of silence, erasure and disavowal rings a bell because of its Victorian overtones. The uncanny resemblance of rhetoric between Victorian England (1837–1901) and early postcolonial Singapore can be mapped with reference to sex, sexuality and gender, as these cameos testify:

a.   **Victorian Syphilis v. HIV/AIDS in Singapore**. From the 1860s to the 1880s, in England, the Contagious Disease Acts allowed the police to detain and charge women, prostitutes or wives, within a certain radius of army camps. This law punished only women; no laws were made to regulate men. If a woman refused to undergo a painful and intrusive medical examination, she could be imprisoned indefinitely. Since there was no known cure for syphilis, the excruciating 'quack' treatments were potentially life-threatening, leading to kidney and liver dysfunction. Although both men and women had the disease, it was seen as a pun-ishment from God for the female's transgressions. As a group, both men and women were reluctant to see the doctor as the treatment was lengthy and because of the stigma of the disease. A hundred years later, in the 1980s, after profiteering from the sex trade during the Vietnam War, Bugis Street was demolished partly because of the fear that the transsexuals and transgenders might have contracted HIV/AIDS. Just as the spread of syphilis was inculpated only on the Victorian women, the Singapore government has constructed a myth that the disease is only associated with homosexuals and white people. This myth persisted even as late as 2004 when then-Senior Minister of State for Health, Dr. Balaji Sadasivan attributed the increase of HIV/AIDS to homosexual behaviour: Of homo-sexuals and "heterosexual men having casual sex in other countries … the gays are the bigger concern", that being despite the fact that more

heterosexuals than homosexuals contract HIV/AIDS. While in the
United States HIV/AID victims are vocal about their oppression (e.g. the
Silence=Death campaign), the Singaporean sufferers follow the Victorian
model that many self-righteous and religious people see the disease as a
punishment and attach great stigma to it.

b.   **Homosexuality, Eugenics and the Fall of the Empire**. In the 1890s, the
decline of the British Empire was linked to fears of degeneration and
homosexuality; it was believed that because the Empire was not producing enough masculine men to be administrators, the Empire could not
control its colonies. Francis Galton's study of eugenics, a term he coined
in 1883, urged gifted men and women to marry; he feared that the British
race would decline as capable people produce fewer offspring than the *hoi
polloi*. At this time, there was also an influx of immigrants, and the racist
Victorians believed that miscegenation might dilute the purity and supe-
riority of the English race. This unease about the racial and sexual 'other'
became enmeshed in the prevailing social attitudes and was immense.
A hundred years later, in the 1990s, Lee Kuan Yew championed 'Asian
values', which instructed Singaporeans to retain their racial, ethnic and
cultural values and not be influenced by corrupt morals from the West. In
the same vein as the fear of 'Other' in Victorian England, foreigners with
HIV/AIDS were banned from entering Singapore. At around the same
time, the government launched what Theresa Wong and Brenda Yeoh
(2003) call the "eugenics phase" from 1983 to 1986, which gave greater tax
relief to graduate than non-graduate mothers. As non-graduate women
had more children, the government feared that there would be a "gradual
lowering of quality of workforce", a fear inherited from the Victorians
(Wong and Yeoh, 2003: 8). Like racism and eugenics in Victorian England,
since the majority of graduate women were Chinese, "the implication
therefore was that Chinese should produce more children... [which
bears] eugenics, racial and discriminatory overtones" (Wong and Yeoh,
2003: 10).

c.   **Homosexuality, Effeminacy and Decadence**. Oscar Wilde was the leading
figure of Decadence, an aesthetic movement in the 1890s. Decadents
valued experience, regardless of morality of the acts. In Wilde's trial,
Lord Alfred Douglas, his lover, said, "To say that a man is an Oscar Wilde
is to say, well, that he is a pervert" (*The Times*, 1918). After Wilde's trials,
homosexuals were stereotyped as decadent, wicked, effeminate, perverse,
artistic, White and upper-class (Sinfield, 1994). Singapore inherited this
stereotype (or the rhetoric to oppress homosexuals) from the Victorians.
For instance, the wildly successful Nation Party (an annual rave party)
was banned because, as Dr. Sadasivan claimed, the event "allowed gays

from high prevalence societies to fraternize with local gay men, seeding the [HIV] infection in the local community" (2005).[1] Sadasivan's rhetoric, though specious, is brilliant because firstly, it links homosexuality with the West ("high prevalence societies") and disease and orgies which a conservative, unknowing Singaporean would condemn; and secondly, like Dick Hebdige's famous 1979 example of punks' appropriation of safety pins as earrings, when gay people dared to express themselves, the neoliberal, neo-Victorian State claimed they were decadent and clamped down on such behaviour; the safely pins which were at first appropriated as resistance by punks are now used as a reason for control by the government.

d. **Homosexuality, Silence, Shame, and the Immoral Other**. Although across all times and cultures same-sex action has always occurred, Victorians saw sodomy, as a "crime was first introduced into England about the year 1315, by a sect of heretics called Lollards; whose intent it was, among other most damnable doctrines, to subvert the Christian faith" (Holloway, 1813: 13). This view that the Other, not the Self, is always immoral and decadent is important in the construction of Victorian England. While homosexuality was quietly permitted in schools and even in Catholicism, it still remained, as Lord Douglas (1892) famously termed it, "the love that dare not speak its name". In E. M. Forster's *Maurice* (1993), the protagonist confesses his sexuality by claiming that "I'm an unspeakable of the Oscar Wilde sort" (159). The social stigma was imposing. Like Victorian England, homosexuality in Singapore has always been seen as an invasion and a corruption from the decadent West. Even as late as December 2007, the idea that homosexuality is a Western idea is presented in *The Morning After*, a 20-minute Singapore telemovie.[2] A boy comes out to his mother "so that you wouldn't blame the West for corrupting me" when he is about to leave for his studies in the States. In 1993, Wong Kan Sang, then-Minister for Foreign Affairs and current Deputy Prime Minster, said in a United Nations World Human Rights Conference in Vienna that "Homosexual rights are a Western issue" (as cited in Jackson, 2001: 8), which could either imply that gay Singaporeans have no human rights—because they are not humans?—or there are no such entities as gay Singaporeans. No such entities because the queer history has been erased and because, as we shall see later, there is an imposition of a compulsory heterosexuality. Singapore government's narrative of linking homosexuality with the West was so successful that in early gay scene of the 1950s to 1980s, many Singaporeans paired up only with Caucasians and/or migrated to Western countries (Heng, 2001: 82). From the 1960s to 1990s, homosexuals remained silent because to do so was to risk one's job and throw one's life away. In both Victorian England and postcolonial Singapore, homosexuality was linked to sickness, perversity, degeneration, shame, immorality, and the 'Other', all of which were/are seen as threats to the nation.

e. **Homosexuality and Literature**. The fears of *fin-de-siècle* England were accumulated into the figure of Bram Stoker's *Dracula* (1897) who is read metaphorically as a diseased, atavistic foreigner invading England to infect British women with syphilis. As Talia Schaffer (1994) tracks the genesis of the novel through Stoker's careful and elaborate erasure of Wilde-Stoker's homoerotic long-term relationship from his published and unpublished texts, such a monstrous figure is also a metaphor for the fear of homosexuality. Using this analogy, it is also possible to suggest that the indoctrination of Singapore was accumulated into Johann S. Lee's *Peculiar Chris* (1992), the first local gay novel. In the portrayal of all main gay characters as attractive, intelligent, moral and successful, Lee counteracts the ideology that homosexuals are degenerates yet at the same time, plays into the hands of the government in its definition of economical and genetic success. The dream of the protagonist to have children and a family reflects the conviction to 'Asian values'. Eventually the protagonist's boyfriend dies from HIV/AIDS because of a blood transfusion in Malaysia, not in efficient Singapore. Why should the boyfriend die? Or die of HIV/AIDS if the Singapore government's indoctrination wasn't so effective? In the end, the protagonist flies to England because homosexuality is associated with the West, not Singapore.

There are several reasons how Singapore has come to inherit a neo-Victorian policy towards sexual matters across time and space. Not only was Singapore fully established as a colony during Queen Victoria's reign, not only is the English-educated Lee one of the top law students at Cambridge University, implying that he knows British law and its historical law suits (such as Wilde's) better than most English, the demarcation between colonialism and postcolonialism is false and constructed because firstly, time is continuous and marking it as colonialism or postcolonialism is merely a convenient compartmentalization of what cannot be compartmentalized. As many scholars have already suggested, the postcolonial period is also a period of neo-imperialism. Besides, unlike other countries where upheavals signal a change of system, Singapore's independence in 1965 was relatively peaceful and granted by the British. Moreover, Hong Kong, which has a longer history of colonialism than Singapore, still retains Cantonese as its *lingua franca* but the uncritical adoption of the colonizers' tongue—English—in Singapore as the language of instruction in schools and for business, despite the island having a majority of Chinese immigrants and surrounded by Malay-speaking countries, confirms how unaware Singaporeans are of their neocolonial oppression. The yearly celebration of National Day on 9th August is not a parade of one's patriotism or even emancipation; it is a performance to bring into being the country's national identity.

Singaporean citizens inherited the English language, which means they inherit the phallogocentrism and self-deprecating colonialist otherness within the linguistic discourse, naturally deleterious to its national identity. Furthermore the colonizers trained Lee. As Frantz Fanon (1996) warns, the training of postcolonial bourgeoisie by Europeans is another form of neocolonial oppression. The other reason, and perhaps the most important, why Singapore bears such similarity to Victorian England is because Singaporeans inherited the English penal code, Section 377A. For instance, the "Unnatural Offences" of "Outrages of Decency" anti-sodomy law, a similar law ("Gross Indecency") that Wilde was indicted for, is still in operation. Such a law, of course, has much to do with cultural factors as well as religious mores for the Victorians. Edward Deacon wrote in 1831 in *Digest of the Criminal Law of England*, "Sodomy is that horrible sin against nature, and the ordinance of the Almighty, which the English Law most fitly describes as one not even to be named amongst Christians" (7). But this religious law is equally cultural as Matt Cook (2003) suggests of Henry Labouchere who wrote the "Gross Indecency" Act wanted to distance himself from "sodomites" such as Wilde who were frequenting the same clubs and theatres as he was. Singapore's laws have inherited the religious, self-righteousness and prudishness of the Victorian policy, and, like Foucault's prisoners, Singaporeans have tamed themselves to think like Victorians.

Law, language and Lee Kuan Yew, besides being on the 'right' side of binary, share a common love for rules, such as those that regulate Foucault's prisoners whose bodies are acted upon with devastating ramifications. But how did Singaporeans become so docile? Why weren't they as politically fervent as the Thais or Taiwanese? The psyche of the first migrants who came to make a living and to be dominated holds the key. This psyche is epitomized by two colloquial neologic words, *kiasu* (afraid to lose) and *kiasi* (afraid to die), etymologized from the *Hokkien* dialect that is used by most Singaporeans of all races. Because Singapore has no natural resources, its income is always dependent on trade and foreign investments. English is the *lingua franca* because it is the language of capitalism, and in the early post-independent years, 20 per cent of its gross national product came from Britain. (Similarly, the encouragement to speak Mandarin in recent years stems from Singapore's capitalist gains from China.) The language of survival and propagation, of *kiasu*-ism and *kiasi*-ism, drives Singapore; just as migrants in 1819 gave up their freedom, to be colonized and controlled, for a living, Singaporeans sacrifice political freedom and their narratives of subjectivity for money. Even as late as 2008 when Singapore has a stable and thriving economy, Lee Kuan Yew warned: "The Singapore opposition would ruin the wealthy city-state's achievement in five years if they ever gain power" (cited in *APF*, 2008). As Stuart Hall (2004) asserts, hegemony must be interminably produced by public acts of articulation. Similarly, as Antonio Gramsci (2000) points out, roughshod ruling alone will not do to win consent, the government generates endless narratives of solving economic crisis after crisis.

The narratives of survival and promulgation by the State are so efficacious that in a matter of forty short years of independence, Singapore has become one of the richest countries in the world.[3] The success of Singapore's economy and the effects of the narratives are written on the body. Where Singapore lacks in its natural resources, it provides a docile, productive and intelligent workforce to attract foreign investments (Grice and Drakais-Smith, 1985). This productive body is modeled after a masculinity of quiet strength, self-abnegation, obedience, discipline and social responsibility (Turnbull, 1989: 292; Holden, 2001). People who have risen from a working class background are much admired. When examining Cambridge-trained Lee Kuan Yew's autobiography, Philip Holden fails to note that these values are not merely very Chinese but also very Victorian. The influence on Singapore masculinity need not be mutually exclusive but to explain that the masculinity is Chinese is to fail to account that the Chinese were not homophobic. As Bert Hinsch notes in *Passions of the Cut Sleeves*, the earliest Western explorers to China deplored the prevalence of homosexuality (Hinsch, 1992: 2). The streets were rampant with boy prostitutes (like early Singapore with Hainanese boys) and everyone, from the poor to the rich, engaged in sodomy. If Singapore has modeled its basis on masculinity on the Chinese, then Singapore's brand of masculinity ought not to be homophobic and Singapore wouldn't resort to erase and rewrite its queer history. As I have traced earlier, Singapore's masculinity is closer to the Victorian's in that they both associate homosexuality with decadence, degeneration, and decline of a civilization. While Victorian homosexuals cannot produce or reproduce and were hence not productive and thus were blamed for bringing about the fall of the nation, Singaporean homosexuals, following the State narratives on promulgation and survival, can marry and have children. As Wah-Shan Chou (2000) argues in his book, *Tongzhi*, Chinese parents do not mind their children being homosexual as long as they have children to continue the family lineage. The fear and hatred of men, regardless of their sexuality, who didn't fit into Singapore masculinity was so totalizing that, for instance, long hair, which was seen as a sign of effeminacy, rebellion and decadence, was strongly discouraged. This was so regimentedly enforced that in 1984, even Kitaro, an award-winning New Age Japanese musician, was barred from entry into the city-state because of his long hair. In other words, Singaporeans, in the name of national survival, and amid the homosexual-degenerate ideology, were induced into what Adrienne Rich (1980) calls compulsory heterosexuality. Under such a regime, many gay men married or migrated.

In the above, we have established how and why Singapore is similar to Victorian England. In the following paragraphs, the discussion considers the full impact of such neo-Victorian masculinity on Singapore's citizens through governmental control of politics, legal systems, media, education and the military forces.

Structures of Power in Singapore

Like early Victorian politicians who deplored the universal suffrage of one vote per person, Minister Mentor Lee, in a sexist and heteronormative remark, suggested that "I'm convinced … that we would have a better system if we gave every *man* over the age of 40 who has a family two votes" (as cited in Zakaria, 1994. Emphasis in original). Like political classes in Victorian England in the Age of Reform (1830s–1840s) whose purpose was "to exercise control over the populace" (Wilson, 2002: 10), the People's Action Party (PAP), led by Lee, secured its power over Singapore politically, eradicating its rivals. Since Singapore's postcolonial independence, elections are held at least once every four years in order to satisfy the minimum criteria for a nation to be known as democratic. PAP had won every seat in the parliamentary democratic system until 1981 when J. B. Jeyaretnam triumphed in a by-election. Between 1981 and 2011, no more than four seats have been held by the opposition parties at each election. PAP's reign is moored due to several reasons. Firstly, since 1972, PAP has a history of suing its opponents to the point of bankruptcy. Jeyaretnam, a former judge, "has paid more than a million dollars to Lee Kuan Yew and other PAP litigants" (Singapore Democratic Party [SDP], 2009). In 2001, he declared bankruptcy and "under the law he will lose his seat in parliament and be barred from future elections" (SDP, 2009). Similarly, in 1993, Dr. Chee Soon Juan was not only prosecuted but also fired from his job at the National University of Singapore. Likewise, in 1997, Tang Liang Hong, a corporate lawyer, was persecuted and fled the country. Given the hostility to oppositional parties, it is little wonder that "in later years few aspiring politicians came forward except at the government's invitation" (Turnbull, 1989: 327). Furthermore, like Victorian Prime Ministers Edward Smith-Stanley and Benjamin Disraeli, to ensure PAP's victory, the PAP government gerrymanders, redraws boundaries and demands opposition parties to run in groups of four to six to win a constituency, in order to afford the PAP a high chance of forming a majority in the House of Commons. If Singaporeans do vote for the opposition, that particular constituency will be heavily penalized through diminished funding for upgrading infrastructure. From the 1960s to the 1990s, such political control was absolute.

As the preceding paragraph has established, there are no kangaroo courts in Singapore; the judges are always on the right side of the Law.[4] In 2008, the Singapore High Court ruled in the Lees' favour without going to trial when they sued the *Far Eastern Economic Review* (*FEER*), a monthly magazine, for defamation. In 2006, two years before the summary judgment, *FEER* was banned shortly after the article had surfaced.[5] "The government", Turnbull writes, "virtually controlled the mass media [before the digital age]" (1989: 308). In 1971, the editorial staff of *Nanyang Siang Pau*, a local Chinese newspaper, were arrested on charges of accepting money from communists; and other Chinese newspapers such as *Eastern Sun* and *Singapore Herald* were soon shut down. While Victorian publications were mostly self-regulated and self-censored, the Singapore's Newspaper and Printing Presses Act in 1974 (revised in 1978) further curtailed the freedom of publications, cumulating in the country being ranked 144th out of 173 countries in terms of press freedom (Reporters Without Borders, 2008). The media pie is chiefly divided into Singapore Press Holdings (SPH) for print and Mediacorp for television, both of which are State-owned statutory boards. In 1984, S. R. Nathan, a top civil servant, who later would become the President of Singapore in 1999, was appointed chairperson of SPH. Until 2011, SPH's chairperson was Tony Tan, former deputy Prime Minister and current President of Singapore. As for television, although Mediacorp is State-owned, the interactions between Mediacorp and the State render a simulacrum of democracy.[6] For example, the Media Development Authority (MDA), a department under the State, imposed a fine on MediaCorp for US$10,000, for airing an episode of *Find and Design*, which "normalises and promotes a gay lifestyle" and maintained that "[a] gay relationship should not be presented as an acceptable family unit" (MDA, 2008). If it is strange that a State-own corporation can be fined by a government agency, the message is clear: homosexuals are to remain as freaks. Books, newspapers, magazines, films, television and even the Internet are bound by censorship laws; before the democraticizing potential of the Internet, no narratives existed outside the State power. The legal and media control by the State was absolute.[7]

As the government has "declared its intention to use these means [i.e. media] to continue to inculcate national attitudes and political understanding", Lee insisted in 1966 that the "education system was adapted to mould a nation" (cited in Turnbull, 1989: 299). Joseph Bristow (1991) argues convincingly that boys' adventure stories that appeared at the latter half of the Victorian period were used to inculcate masculine values so that the boys would grow to become manly men of the Empire. However, in Singapore's case, the initiative was from the government and not from the concerned public. After more than forty years of moulding, the objectives of education in Singapore remain the same, as enunciated on the Ministry of Education's (MOE) website: "An educated

person is also someone who is responsible to his community and country"; s/
he is to be able to "appreciate the national constraints but see the opportunities" and to "think global [sic], but be rooted to Singapore" (MOE, 2009). Of
all the Ideological State Apparatus, Louis Althusser (1977) argues that education is the most inductive because of the sheer number of hours children spend
with authoritative figures of great power. Whether Althusser's claim is true or
not, the Singapore-Althussian State had "nearly 400 kindergartens" in 1988 for
children as young as four years old and all kindergarten "teachers had to be
PAP members, so that a popular service was combined with indoctrination"
(Turnbull, 1989: 308). Every weekday morning at about 7:30 a.m. for at least ten
years of their lives, school children sing the national anthem and, with right
fists over their left breasts, recite the *Pledge of Allegiance*. All schools are under
the jurisdiction of the State. Fanon would have been disappointed to learn
that intellectuals and professors in universities were not and are not given any
degree of freedom to shape the cultural identity. On the contrary, intellectuals
are especially suspect. The power of educational institutions controlled by the
State remains absolute.

But like British colonizers who used ideological apparatuses, such as scientific, legal, medical and educational discourses to prove the inferiority
of the colonized and homosexuals, and repressive violent measures to quell
rebellions—think of the brutal slaughtering of Indians in the Indian Mutiny
of 1857—Singapore too uses force. In 1963, 107 politicians and trade unionists
were arrested in Operation Cold Store under the Internal Security Act, effectively eradicating political competition for PAP. In 1987, Operation Spectrum
was launched, immuring twenty-two social activists on charges of Marxism.
Whether the 107 politicians and twenty-two activists were truly trying to usurp
power to turn Singapore into a communist state could not be known by the
citizens at that point of time because the newspapers, controlled by the government, printed several biased reports. The activists were released, after they
were psychologically and physically battered into 'confession', on the condition that they declared their 'crimes' on television. The city-state accumulated
so much power that when a chewing gum ban was enacted in 1992, nothing on
the part of the people could be done about it.

Under the State's discursive and repressive power, there was no interstice
that a queer person could come out and not be shamed; laws stood against him
or her. The demonstrations of power, both ideological and physical, affected
homosexuals as deterrent examples, which explains why as late as early 1996
when People Like Us (PLU), a gay support group, wanted to register with the
State as a society, the group could not even find "ten people willing to lend
their names to the registration process" in a country with three million people
(Heng, 2001: 89).

Ramifications of Neo-Victorian/Chinese Masculinity

The ramifications of imposing a compulsory heterosexuality and Chinese/ Victorian masculinity on Singaporeans are/were cataclysmic, affecting the bodies of homosexuals and everybody else. Groups that are deeply affected are the racial minorities, Malays, Indians and Others. The default national body was and is a Chinese male heterosexual, just as Lauren Berlant (2008) has argued in *The Female Complaint* that the implicit American subject is a White male heterosexual. But, as Berlant explains, living in a democratic and meritocratic society means that while "in practice the liberal political public sphere protects and privileges the 'persons' racial and gendered embodiment, one effect of these privileges is to appear to be without notable qualities while retaining cultural authority" (Berlant, 2008: 110). What Berlant means is that although on the surface, everyone appears equal, the Chinese Singaporeans still hold the power, and racial minorities are oppressed under a Chinese/neo-Victorian masculinity, an ideology that dare not speak its name in the name of racial harmony. For instance, Malays cannot hold high positions in the military. As then-Second Minister for Defence, Lee Hsien Loong, Lee Kuan Yew's son, explained in February 1987, the government did not want to put Malays in a conflicting position of choosing between his country and (Muslim) religion of the surrounding countries (as cited in Sa'at, 2008).

Racial minorities are not the only ones to suffer from the 1960s to the 1990s; even a heterosexual male citizen suffers. At birth, any disability would announce him as an inadequate citizen (Turnbull, 1989: 305). In school where "the object was to develop every child's economically useful capabilities to the full", where "the system offered tempting rewards but put great strains on talented youngsters and push the weak and less intelligent to the wall" (Turnbull, 1989: 301), and where "physical education was vigorously promoted … as a means to improve the health of the rising generation and to help build up a robust national defence force" (Turnbull, 1989: 305), any misstep in the Primary School Leaving Examination, Ordinary Level Cambridge Examination and the Advanced Level Cambridge Examination would render him a nonfeasance. Let's say that he had passed the exams with flying colours, he still had to complete two-and-a-half torturous years (reduced to two years in December 2004) of military conscription, an exercise in nation-building solidarity for *men* only.[8] At eighteen, he was not permitted legally to enter a cinema showing a movie with 'adult' themes but he could handle guns and kill people. The best years of his life were given to the country, spent in the armed forces. Before being drafted, he was subjected to a medical examination in which most gay men would deny their sexuality in a mandatory questionnaire because, although, in theory, the coming out is between the conscript and the Armed

Forces, the misgiving of missing out, based on rumours, groundless or not, on equal opportunities in public housing, employment and scholarships was and is extant. If he, as a heterosexual man, did not perform well in the Armed Forces, his chances at a scholarship despite his academic excellence were greatly reduced. His monthly salary as a corporal was S$60 (US$40) in the 1970s, S$150 (US$100) in the 1980s and $270 (US$180) in the 1990s. He bore it out: the incarceration and the cheap labour. Suppose he had performed well and managed a scholarship without being court-marshaled for the slightest breach, the major he chose at university was highly encouraged to be one that was useful to the country, medicine or engineering or science, even if it was his proclivity to study 'useless' subjects such as art or history. After his graduation, he served out his scholarship bond. He might have survived the helotry with his 2.2 children, a nice Toyota, a golden retriever and a five-room public housing flat that took him twenty years to pay. He had also better hoped that his children would and could and must repeat the increasingly pressurizing process. There was no reprieve; there was only constant striving.

What was the role of women in this regime of compulsory heterosexuality and Chinese/Victorian masculinity? As part of 50 per cent of the electorate, she voted for the PAP during the independent years but there was no female representative in parliament between 1970 and 1984 (Turnbull, 1989: 325–6). Her sexuality did not matter because she was and is merely a factory for making babies. When the government promoted the 'Stop at Two' reproduction campaign to prevent overpopulation and legislated abortion laws in 1972, she had to obey because, in addition to ensuring the survival of the nation, she would be fined for having more than two children, because nurses and doctors in the hospitals would pressurize her into having an abortion. Also people on the streets would glare at her family for not listening to the State, as if she had "committed a crime" (Turnbull, 1989: 304).[9] After the second child, the accouchement fees were increased significantly for each subsequent child and if she was a civil servant, there would be no maternity leave. If she agreed to be sterilized before the age of forty, not only would her child be given access to the best schools, she would have highest priority for public housing (Library of Congress, 1989). When this birth control campaign proved so successful that years before any projections about birth-rates ceasing to replenish death-rates, the government launched its "eugenics phase" from 1983 to 1986, giving more tax relief to graduate mothers. If she was less educated and under thirty years old, she would be rewarded with S$10,000 (US$6700) if she underwent a tubal ligation and had two or less children. Her body did not belong to her. Furthermore, as a woman, living in a neo-Victorian society with a rapidly increasing standard of living meant that she had to work to supplement the family income. Like in Victorian England, when she worked equal hours as her male counterparts, she received, until pay inequality was redressed in 1986, half their salary (Turnbull, 1989: 325). Her daily routine, after rising at 6 a.m., included a day's office or factory work. When she returned home at 5 p.m. to care for her children, she still had to cook dinner, mop the floor, do the laundry, wash the dishes, clean the flat, and supervise her children's homework while her husband watched TV and waited for freshly cut fruits. This was how a woman lived in a neo-Victorian/Chinese family. In fact, every Singaporean—men, women, Chinese, Malays, Indians, heterosexuals, and homosexuals—suffered under such a regime. Since no one could fit perfectly into the State's normative narrative of neo-Victorian model of compulsory heterosexuality and masculinity, everyone must already have been queer.

Conclusion: Neo-Sino Singapore?

This chapter begins with Foucault's thesis that we can never construct our selfhoods outside of power and examines whether Singaporeans could have their own subjectivities during the period 1960s–1990s. I approach the issue of Singaporeans' subjectivity by first noting the similarities between Singapore and the Victorian society through the tactics and rhetoric used by the two societies to oppress the (sexual) 'Other'. The multitude of reasons why Singapore became a neo-Victorian society has been explored in this chapter, including Singapore being fully established as an *entrepôt* during the Victorian period; Lee, the founding father, was the top student at Cambridge, the school of the colonizers; and English being the *lingua franca*. As to what the similarities between the two societies prove, Singaporeans have inherited the mindset of the Victorians, which I called neo-Victorian masculinity. The reason why neo-Victorian masculinity was so effectively propagated was because the structures of power—politics, law, education, and media—were in the complete control of the government. Therefore there was little or no resistance and subjugated Singaporeans could only think in one way because they were ignorant of alternatives. This chapter then goes on to demonstrate that this neo-Victorian masculinity oppressed and oppresses not only homosexuals, but also *every* Singaporean. In other words, for any (and every) Singaporean to gain his or her own selfhood, s/he must get rid of this ideology of neo-Victorian masculinity and nurture diversity.

The method to eradicate neo-Victorian masculinity is connected to the problems that contemporary Singapore faces. Firstly, in recent years, there has been a brain drain with Singaporeans migrating to Western English-speaking countries. Like homosexuals, these people migrate because they cannot identify with the State's narratives; being brought up in a neo-Victorian society, they naturally identify with the West. The metaphor of the *entrepôt* is still operational.

Secondly, Singaporeans are treated as inferior to elite foreigners. For instance, in 2008, Lee Kuan Yew assured an American gay professor, who was invited to head Singapore's and Southeast Asia's largest earth observatory, he would not face discrimination and could bring his partner to Singapore. The privilege, however, has not yet been extended to gay Singaporeans (Chang, 2009). Thirdly, given the rise of China, the increasing trend of neo-Sino-Singapore will just repeat the patterns of being neo-Victorian; Singaporeans will always lack a national identity. This chapter argues that Singapore is always attendant to other countries (to Victorian Britain and now to China), and therefore cannot build an identity of its own: following the homophobia Christian Victorians had, and with no sense of belonging, Singapore is always an appendage-like *entrepôt*.

In the light of larger, external forces, such as globalisation, the information freeways of the Internet and social media, combined with increasing numbers of students graduating from universities in the West present the Singapore government with a landscape that is increasingly difficult to control. This new wave means Singapore needs to make its own secular rules and allow its citizens the freedom to create their own narratives (so long as they don't infringe others' rights) so as to build a truly democratic society, based on justice and equality, regardless of race, language, religion, gender or sexuality. Such a transformation will still allow the country to maintain cordial working relations with other countries but inter-countries' politics shall not interfere with the intra-country politics; external politics should not be confused with nor influence internal politics. Because Singapore has been a neo-Victorian society, cautious Singapore politicians worry about their political status if they are to side with sexual minorities. The anticipated loss of electoral votes should not prevent politicians from doing what is fair and just. To say that 377A shouldn't be abolished due to the interests of an elusive 'conservative majority' is just a lame excuse. Singapore politicians have taken drastic and unpopular measures, such as the ban of chewing gum, and still held power. Besides, anti-discrimination laws usually precede the changing of mindsets, not the other way round. Every Singapore citizen deserves full happiness, prosperity and progress within the country's nationhood.

2

Enforcement of 377A

Entering the Twilight Zone

Michael Hor

I Don't Know How to Love Him

It is unusual that the government of Singapore, known in all other respects for its hard-headed rationality, should admit that official policy in a matter of public concern is "messy" (*Channel News Asia*, 2009); a state that has to be tolerated because it is the best that can be done under the circumstances. And that is precisely what the government has done in the context of the enforcement of the now famous, or infamous, section 377A of the *Penal Code* which criminalises an act of "gross indecency" between males "in public or private", punishing such an act with up to a maximum of 2 years imprisonment.[1] The terminology of "messiness" implies an appreciable degree of departure from common sense and logic. The purpose of this discussion shall be to probe and lay bare this mess, and then to ask if such a state of affairs is really the best that can be done.

The current position is, some would say, the misshapen offspring of governmental compromise most clearly articulated by Prime Minister Lee Hsien Loong in an attempt to broker peace (between the pro- and the anti-377A lobbies) at the culmination of an unprecedented public war of words over the criminalization of "gross indecency" between males (*Parliamentary Debates*, 2007):[2]

> They too must have a place in this society, and they too are entitled to their private lives ... They are free to lead their lives, free to pursue their social activities. But there are restraints and we do not approve of them actively promoting their lifestyles to others, or setting the tone for mainstream society. They live their lives. That is their personal life, it is their space .... We do not harass gays. The Government does not act as moral policemen. And we do not proactively enforce section 377A upon them.

There was therefore to be no harassment or "proactive" enforcement. But what exactly does that mean? If the substantive content of the criminal law as expressed in 377A is no longer the real guide of what one can do without criminal sanction, then it is only fair that a clear prosecutorial policy that is consistently adhered to should step in to fill the void. The rule of law, whatever that may mean in more controversial situations, demands that prosecution for a criminal offence must be reasonably predictable. By 2008, a technically more complete attempt to flesh out such a policy by the then Minister of Home Affairs, Wong Kan Seng, in Parliament (*Parliamentary Debates*, 2008) was articulated:

> Our basic approach ... is that the Police does not take active enforcement measures to seek out homosexual activities between consenting adults that take place in a private place with a view to prosecution.

Given this statement, it was now possible to tease out the discrete elements of the current enforcement policy—passive enforcement, consent, adults, and private place—in order to scrutinize the circumstances under which such a policy might conceivably allow a decision to prosecute someone for a 377A offence. Thus, this discussion will focus on the situation as it is now, after major amendments were made to enhance the sophistication of the definition of sexual offences in the Penal Code in 2008 (Section 375–377D).

That Boy's a Monster

Let us tackle the relatively uncontroversial matter of consent. No one would argue that the "space" to be accorded to homosexuals, or to anyone of whatever inclination, should extend to non-consensual activity. Is it then the case that it is either necessary or desirable that non-consensual homosexual activity should be prosecuted under 377A? There is at least one reported 1995 decision of a 377A prosecution in a purely non-consensual situation (*Ng Huat v Public Prosecutor*, 1995). A hospital radiographer was accused of touching the private parts of a patient who needed an X-ray of his injured hand. The radiographer had deceived the patient into thinking that it was part of the procedure. Whatever consent there might have been was vitiated by the misconception of the patient (Section 90(a)(ii)). The staff member was convicted and sentenced to 3 months' imprisonment. That this ought to be a criminal offence is not in doubt, but was there any need to use 377A? The obvious alternative is section 354 of the Penal Code, the use of force with intent to outrage modesty—an offence more collo-quially known as "molest" and also punishable with a maximum of two years imprisonment. If there was no necessity to use 377A, was there then any valid reason why it is to be preferred over outrage of modesty? I can think of none. Indeed the essence of outrage of modesty is the absence of consent; like the offence of rape, it is the absence of consent that transforms what is generally thought to be a pleasurable and legitimate activity into a serious offence. On the other hand, the essence of 377A is its "indecency", which the courts at the moment understand to be so regardless of consent. In terms of fair labeling, outrage of modesty, with its emphasis on the lack of consent, does seem to have been a superior alternative. Indeed it was unfortunate that the court did not accept the eminently reasonable alternative interpretation of 377A requiring both men to "cooperate" in the sexual act.

We will probably never know for sure why the prosecution chose 377A above outrage of modesty, but it is interesting to speculate on the potential reasons. I can think of two. First, is the temptation for prosecutorial authorities to look for the path of least resistance? Outrage of modesty is more difficult to prove because of the requirement of non-consent, so 377A would be easier to establish. If indeed the reason for prosecuting in the first place is non-consent, then it would be very wrong to prefer a 377A charge which would in effect prevent the court from adjudicating on the most important element of the case, that of non-consent. Secondly, and perhaps more speculatively, the aversion to outrage of modesty could have been because of another well-known decision, delivered the year before (*Public Prosecutor v Tan Boon Hock*, 1994). This earlier case had resulted in the then Chief Justice Yong Pung How rightfully pouring scorn over the prosecution of several men who had been enticed and entrapped into sexual activity by young male police officers pretending to be consenting parties. As the charge had been outrage of modesty, the apparently consenting police officers would render a conviction dubious indeed. It is again unfortunate that the court did not simply overturn the conviction, although it did the next best thing of reducing the sentence to a moderate fine. Yet if this were the reason for the use of 377A in the subsequent case, it would be nothing short of ludicrous that an earlier and patently wrongful use of outrage of modesty ought to prevent its rightful use in the later case.

It is heartening to note that there has since been no reported case where 377A has been used for purely non-consensual homosexual activity. We occasionally see outrage of modesty prosecutions for such situations (*Public Prosecutor v Teo Kern Yiam*, 2005), and it might well be safe to assume that the orientation-neutral provision of outrage of modesty satisfactorily deals with purely non-consensual offences without the need to recruit 377A. Indeed with the increased sophistication of sexual offence provisions after the Penal Code amendments of 2008, there is a smorgasbord to choose from: namely, if there is "penetration", Section 376 provides for sexual assault by penetration; secondly, if one of the partners is mentally disabled and induced, threatened or deceived into sexual activity, there is Section 376F. Like outrage of modesty, these offences are orientation-neutral and correctly place the emphasis of prosecution, proof, sentencing and labelling on the absence or inadequacy of consent. In which case, 377A surely ought to be operationally redundant.

You're Much Too Young, Boy

It is equally uncontroversial that sexual activity between an adult and someone who is too young ought to be prohibited, and the adult punished. The consent of the under-aged person is never an excuse or defence, although it may mitigate the punishment to be accorded. That is so for heterosexual, as for homosexual, activity. The offences of sexual penetration of a minor under sixteen (Section 376A), and of commercial sex with a minor under 18 (Section 376B) are orientation-neutral. They would be equally appropriate for a male homosexual, as for a female homosexual or any heterosexual activity. There is again no reason for recourse to 377A.

The apparent difficulty has been with sexual activity short of penetration involving a minor under sixteen. There is a clear record of recent prosecutions under 377A, for both consensual (*Public Prosecutor v Lim Beng Cheok*, 2003) and non-consensual (*Public Prosecutor v Adam bin Darsin*, 2000) underage sexual activity between males. There seems to be a distinct prosecutorial sentiment that 377A is still needed for this. Yet it has been argued rather convincingly and for some time by activists that existing offences under the Children and Young Person's Act (CYPA), and in particular Section 7 which prohibits the commission of obscene or indecent acts with anyone below the age of sixteen, is a perfectly satisfactory alternative.[3] Indeed, it is perhaps a superior one. Just as the use of outrage of modesty for non-consensual activity focuses the prosecution on absence of consent, the use of the CYPA concentrates the mind of the police, prosecutors and judges on the true evil that is to be dealt with—not the sexual orientation of the parties, as 377A would have it, but the involvement of someone who is deemed to be too young to understand the import and consequences of sexual activity.

There is some evidence that the prosecutorial authorities might be beginning to heed this suggestion. We see a number of very recent prosecutions under the CYPA where it would have been possible to prefer a charge under 377A (*Public Prosecutor v ZQ*, 2009; *Public Prosecutor v Soo Hwee Keong*, 2007; *Public Prosecutor v Amayapan Kodanpany*, 2010). Yet the practice is still confused, for we also see very recent 377A prosecutions for underage sex (*Public Prosecutor v Rahim bin Basron*, 2010; *Public Prosecutor v Chan Mun Chiong*, 2008). Is there a logic to these cases? One suspicion is that 377A is seen as the more "serious" charge in this situation, so presumably it is used when the prosecutorial authorities think that the circumstances are aggravated. The punishment regimen is, in one respect, more severe; 377A provides only for imprisonment and Section 7 of the CYPA has the option of a fine. But it would be odd for the prosecution to choose 377A for the purpose of depriving the sentencing court of the discretion of deciding whether or not the accused ought to be imprisoned.

Surely our judges cannot be so inept that they cannot be trusted with this very basic sentencing decision. Moreover, Section 7 of the CYPA now provides for enhanced punishment maxima for repeat offenders, whereas 377A carries a two year maximum no matter how many antecedents there might be. So logically, it is the CYPA which carries the more severe consequences, at least if one has repeat offending in mind.

The danger with continued use of 377A for underage sexual activity is demonstrated by the absorbing case of *Public Prosecutor v Chan Mun Chiong* (2008).[4] The accused had consensual oral sex with a male of sixteen years and three months in the cubicle of a public toilet in a shopping centre. When the accused wanted anal sex, his young partner refused. He then stalked the teenager who had to seek the assistance of a security officer, who in turn made a police report. Chan was found to be HIV positive; a condition which he knew he had but did not inform his partner of. He was charged under 377A, in addition to a separate offence related to non-disclosure of his medical condition. There are a few interesting aspects to this case, but we shall focus on the age issue. When asked to explain the 377A prosecution in Parliament, the Minister of Home Affairs said (*Parliamentary Debates*, 2008):

> The Public Prosecutor decided to charge the accused under Section 377A after taking into account all the facts and circumstances of the case, *including the complainant's age* and the fact that the offence had taken place in a public toilet.

There was no explicit mention of how the age of the complainant was relevant to the preferment of the 377A charge. He was patently above the age of sixteen, the threshold prescribed by the CYPA. If he had been a woman and the sexual activity had been heterosexual, there would have been no other charge apart from the HIV-related one. It is not easy to conceive of how his age could, even in part, have justified a 377A prosecution. Could it be that the prosecutorial policy is to use 377A even where one of the partners is above sixteen, if there are other aggravating factors? In another government press release in connection with a separate set of cases a few months later, the Attorney-General's Chambers declared:

> The Public Prosecutor will prosecute persons who exploit a young victim who is a minor, *irrespective of the gender* of the victim or whether the act was consensual. A young male victim, who is a minor, deserves to be accorded *the same protection* of the law as that given to a young female victim who is a minor.

This nearly contemporaneous explication of prosecutorial policy flatly contradicts the idea that 377A ought to be used against people who engage in sexual activity with someone who is perhaps a little over sixteen years of age. There is no equal recourse to any equivalent of 377A for either lesbian or heterosexual underage relationships. As the later declaration says, prosecutions must be irrespective of gender and the protection accorded to males and females must be the same—not more, not less. Could it be that in the intervening period between the HIV prosecution and the subsequent declaration of prosecutorial policy, the practice had changed? 377A prosecutions, with its focus on sexual orientation and not on age, bear with them a great potential to confuse decision-makers. Thus in the case of Chan Mun Chiong, it may well have lead them into the error of taking into consideration the age of the complainant. The 377A charge was eventually "taken into consideration", a technical phrase meaning that the accused admits to the offence, but is not convicted of it, although the court is to take it into consideration in sentencing.[5] A smidgen of consolation, but it is still wrong in principle.

The set of prosecutions which gave rise to the Attorney-General's 'media background brief' of 29 January 2009 itself is more than a little puzzling. A 15-year-old male had a string of consensual sexual encounters.[6] One of his accused partners pleaded guilty to a charge under 377A and was sentenced to four months' imprisonment. However, two others who had originally been charged under 377A subsequently pleaded guilty to a charge under the CYPA, each receiving three months' imprisonment (*The Straits Times*, 2009). We can only guess at why the charge was changed. The prosecution could have altered it unilaterally (perhaps heeding the call of activists to use the CYPA instead of 377A)[7] but this seems unlikely as the charge for the first accused was not similarly changed. A rather more sinister alternative is that the charge was reduced as a result of a plea bargain: a plea of guilt was exchanged for what was apparently assumed or perceived to have been the 'lesser' CYPA charge. Although I have explained that it is not easy to understand why the CYPA charge is necessarily, and objectively, less severe, it is possible that that is the perception. If this indeed was the case, the danger is that the original 377A charge may have been used as a bargaining tool, inviting the defendant to offer a plea of guilt to the 'lesser' CYPA charge. If these were the dynamics, it would have been a most unfortunate use of 377A. Charging decisions are properly made on the basis of mitigating or aggravating circumstances and without thought of bargaining prospects, and in this set of cases, there appears to have been no reason why an original charge under the CYPA would not have been suitable. The Attorney-General's declaration in connection with these set of cases correctly pronounces that prosecutorial decisions are to be made "irrespective of gender", and of course, if the 'victim' had been a female, there would have been no possibility of a charge under 377A.

We can safely conclude that while prosecutorial policies remain in a state of apparent flux, there is no legitimate or sensible reason why 377A is needed to deal with underage sexual activity. Indeed the possibility of 377A pros-ecutions for under-age activity brings in its train a host of unfortunate and illegitimate consequences.

Not in Public, Dear

Most societies have some conception of public decency and prohibit certain kinds of activity in public, which would be entirely lawful in private. We have a record of 377A prosecutions for homosexual activity in public.[8] Can it be that 377A is still required to protect public decency? Just as for non-consensual or underage sexual activity, 377A is a singularly inept tool to capture the evil to be contained, for it states quite explicitly that "gross indecency" is a crime whether it is in "private or public". Once again the prosecutorial mind is not directed towards the line between what can be done in private and what can be safely done in public. Nor is the court permitted to adjudicate the crucial issue—whether the offending conduct was committed "in public". Nor indeed is the denunciatory role of criminal law satisfactorily discharged by training its fire on the public nature of the activity. Do we have a better alternative? One would suspect that there is, for what indeed do the police do with non-homo-sexual sexual activity, or other acts of indecency, in public? Section 20 of the Miscellaneous Offences (Public Order and Nuisance) Act (MOPOA) punishes "[a]ny person who is found guilty of … indecent behaviour in any public road or in any public place or place of public amusement or resort, or in the immedi-ate vicinity of, or in, any court, public office, police station or place of worship" to a maximum fine of S$1000 or imprisonment not exceeding one month, or on a subsequent conviction to maximum fine of S$2000 or imprisonment not exceeding six months.

Unlike 377A, this is the offence which captures precisely what is being punished (and why)—indecent behavior, sexual or otherwise, which happens in a place with a strong public element. There are two sets of such places. The first is predicated with the qualifying word "public": any road, place, place of amusement or resort. It is not an offence if such a place is not public. The second set of places do not need an independent showing of being public: a court, public office, police station or place of worship. The rationale seems clear because for roads and other places in general, an unsuspecting member of public may chance upon the display and be subjected to something that would be embarrassing or offensive to him or her. Even if that member of the public knows that something indecent might be occurring in a public place, it would be unreasonable to inconvenience him or her by requiring a detour or change of destination to avoid the indecency. The second set of places is by definition public in nature, and they are all a venue of some solemn and important public function or other. Here it is not only that members of the public would be put to an unreasonable inconvenience, but the indecent behavior would detract from the solemnity and importance of the function being performed.

In the general scheme of events, these kinds of offences are low in the penal hierarchy and reports of such prosecutions are understandably rare. There is evidence of at least one instance in 2001 where a police raid on a gay sauna resulted in initial 377A charges, which were then reduced to MOPOA charges, to which the accused pleaded guilty and was fined S$600.[9] There is a real possibility that 377A has once again led the enforcement and prosecutorial authorities astray. If they had been thinking in terms of the MOPOA, the focus of the inquiry would be whether or not the sauna was a sufficiently public place to have attracted the MOPOA. This is how the prohibition is defined in the MOPOA:

> 'public place' means any place or premises to which at the material time the public or any section of the public has access, on payment or otherwise, as of right or by virtue of express or implied permission.

If they had concentrated on this, rather than on 377A, it would have occurred to them that there is at least a real question whether or not the sauna qualified as public place. A literal reading of the definition might indeed lead one to the conclusion that the sauna was a place where any member of the public has access, if he is willing to pay the fee. Yet a moment's thought will reveal that the literal reading does not seem to make sense. If we follow what I have suggested to be the rationale of public decency laws, then it ought to be a public place only if one of two alternative conditions are satisfied: first that an unsuspecting member of the public might stumble on sexual activity unaware, or second that a member of the public who is aware that he or she might see sexual activity, but for whom it would be unreasonable to expect him or her to take steps to avoid seeing it. So it is not mere 'access', but reasonable access. Presumably, gay saunas are not arranged such that someone stepping out of the street might chance upon sexual activity; there is likely to be some screening process, if only for the management to collect fees and to ensure that the customer knows what the establishment is about. There is little or no chance that someone would be caught unaware. There can be no question that it cannot be unacceptably inconvenient to expect a member of the public, knowing that the establishment is a gay sauna, to avoid entering it. It is in serious doubt whether the authorities applied its collective mind to the right questions, and the culprit could well have been 377A, which seems to say categorically that it is irrelevant whether it is in public or private. It is also unfortunate that the accused decided to plead guilty, but it could have been that they did not have a choice. It is possible that the charge was reduced from 377A to the MOPOA on the basis of the accused agreeing to plead guilty. If that indeed was the situation, 377A has worked evil at another level—it provided the opportunity for the prosecutorial authorities to use it as a bargaining position to buy a plea of guilt to the lesser charge,[10] thus avoiding a trial on the most crucial issue—whether or not the sexual activity concerned was public enough to violate public decency.

We return to the more recent prosecution of Chan Mun Chiong and recall the Ministerial explanation given for the use of 377A (*Parliamentary Debates*, 2008):

> The Public Prosecutor decided to charge the accused under Section 377A after taking into account all the facts and circumstances of the case, including the complainant's age and the fact that the offence had taken place in a public toilet.

Could it be that 377A had once again distracted the enforcement and prosecutorial authorities from the core issue—whether or not the sexual activity concerned had sufficiently violated public decency?[11] There is no doubt that any member of the public could well have entered the toilet, but the sexual activity did not happen in a place which could be seen or otherwise perceived as one passes the main toilet door; it took place in a locked cubicle, away from public view. A member of the public would have seen a locked door and probably assumed that other customary toileting activities were taking place. Even if the member of public had suspected that something else was going on, it would arguably not have been unreasonable to expect him to use another cubicle. There is at least a reasonable contention that a member of the public does not have access to a locked toilet cubicle. Again, if there had been audible evidence of sexual activity, the situation may again be different, but that was not the case at hand. Here is where there is a difference between the two sets of 'places' in the MOPOA. I would suggest that while a clear demonstration of a sufficient public element is required for the first set, there is no such need for the second. So long as such activity takes place in, for example, a place of worship, that is sufficient to engage public decency because of the solemn nature of the place. If indeed it is felt that public decency requires shopping centres to be elevated to the level of places of worship, then it is easy enough for the legislature to include them into the second set of places. Without addressing its collective mind to this matter, it is not easy to see why the venue of a public toilet is clearly relevant to prosecution. Once again, it may well have been 377A that may have led the prosecutorial authorities astray.

A similar theme emerges. Just as for non-consensual or underage sex, sexual activity in violation of public decency is well catered for by a more satisfactory alternative, the MOPOA, which is orientation-neutral and which focuses the mind of all concerned on the right thing—whether or not public decency has been violated. 377A is again unnecessary and indeed undesirable.

Top, Bottom or Versatile?

If we eliminate the variables we have already looked at—consent, age, and venue—because other more satisfactory provisions already deal with them, we are left with the core activity of adults engaging in consensual sex in private. Are there situations in which there is a conceivable need to prosecute for a 377A offence? If, as the Prime Minister has said, gays are "entitled to their private lives" and "free to pursue their social activities" (*Parliamentary Debates*, 2007)—conduct that presumably includes sexual activity—then how can it be a sensible policy that a 377A prosecution remains a possibility? The germ of such an eventuality may lie in the other portion of the Prime Minister's speech (*Parliamentary Debates*, 2007):

> We do not harass gays. The Government does not act as moral policemen. And we do not *proactively* enforce Section 377A on them.

Unfortunately, all the operative words here are too vague for anyone who is trying to decide how to behave without incurring penal consequences. The language of "proactive" enforcement gives rise to the possibility of non-proactive enforcement, which does not amount to harassment or the government trying to act as moral policemen. This naturally begs the question, what form may that enforcement take?

A few months later then Attorney-General Walter Woon was reported as saying (*The Straits Times*, 2008):

> As far as I am concerned, it is still against the law and we still prosecute if there's a need. The Prime Minister said that, if it's consensual between two adults, we are not going to go after them *if nobody complains* … In the case of 377A … we are prosecuting some cases, such as where you have an older man preying on young underage boys. If it's two consenting adults, technically it's an offence but, *if nobody complains*, the police aren't going to beat the bushes in the parks to spy on you. If somebody does complain, then the question is: Do we want to prosecute or do we just warn? Very often, we warn rather than prosecute.

How is the existence of a complaint relevant to a prosecutorial decision? Where two adult males engage in consensual sex in private, why should it matter if there is a complaint, perhaps by one of the parties or by someone else? One can think of a number of situations where a complaint might be lodged: a parent who cannot accept that an adult child is engaging in gay sex, a neighbour who does not like the idea of a gay couple living next door, a partner who feels that the other party has been cheating on him. If indeed gays are 'entitled' to their private lives, why can such complaints trigger a prosecution? It is equally difficult to understand the logic of the 'warn rather than prosecute' route, for what indeed does the police warn them against without infringing on their 'entitlement'? Indeed there has been no clear evidence in recent years where a prosecution has been brought under 377A just because of a complaint.

Perhaps then, the existence of a complaint is relevant, not for consensual activity between adults in private, but for homosexual activity that in some other way fails to fall within this class. As for underage sex, while it is often the case that the offence will be undetected without a complaint (as was the case for the sexually active 15-year-old), there ought surely be a duty to prosecute even if no one complains. But it is easily demonstrable that there is absolutely no need to use 377A for underage sex. One can imagine situations where the sexual activity is non-consensual but the prosecutorial policy is of non-prosecution unless the victim complains, especially if the violation is not of a serious nature. But in such situations, as we have seen, there is again no need for 377A. Similarly it might well be the prosecutorial policy that sexual activity in a technically public place—say in a heavily wooded part of a deserted forest in the middle of the night—ought not to be prosecuted unless there is a complaint. Perhaps this was the kind of situation which gave rise to the 'One Seven incident' (Au, 2010b). And if a decision is made not to prosecute, then it makes sense to issue a warning to the offenders. But yet again, there is patently no need to consider 377A when there is a perfectly acceptable alternative in the MOPOA.

We return to the ubiquitous case of Chan Mun Chiong. It will be recalled that this is the situation where the accused had consensual sex with a 16 year old in the toilet cubicle of a shopping centre without disclosing his HIV positive status. He was naturally charged under the *Infectious Diseases Act* (IDA) for failing to disclose his infectious medical condition that is not controversial.[12] But he was in addition charged under 377A. He eventually pleaded guilty to the IDA charge and had the 377A charge "taken into consideration". But why was he charged with 377A in the first place? The Minister explained (*Parliamentary Debates*, 2008):

> As to why he was charged under section 377A, our basic approach remains as stated by the Prime Minister during the debate on the Penal Code amendments in October last year, which is that the Police does not take active enforcement measures to seek out homosexual activities between consenting adults that take place in a private place with a view to prosecution. Mr Chan Mun Chiong's case, however, is not such a case. It is *not the result of active enforcement against him in a private place*. Mr Chan was investigated by the Police after *a report was lodged by a 16 year old male who had oral sex with him*. Thereafter, the Police referred the outcome of its investigation to the Attorney-General's Chambers. The Public Prosecutor decided to charge the accused under section 377A after taking into account *all the facts and circumstances* of the case, including the complainant's *age* and the fact that the offence had taken place in a *public toilet*.

We need to uncover what lies behind that convenient phrase, "all the facts and circumstances". I have discussed why the age of the complainant should have been irrelevant. I have also taken the view that if the evil was thought to be an offence to public decency, the right charge would have been under the MOPOA. It has also been argued that the lodgment of a complaint, valuable as it may have been to detection, should ultimately be irrelevant to prosecution. That it was not considered to be "active enforcement" probably means that police entrapment, which was once employed,[13] would no longer be so. It probably means that the police will normally act only when there is a complaint, although it seems unlikely that a complaint will be required if the police happen to stumble on, say, sexual activity in a public place, even if no one has complained. But even so, the charge ought to be one under the MOPOA, not 377A.

Thus stripped of everything else, the disquieting picture emerges that it might well be current prosecutorial policy to slap on a 377A charge where the prosecutorial authorities feel that the accused is concurrently guilty of some-thing else—in this case the IDA charge—just to 'throw the book' at the accused. If this is correct, then it is a mystery why the prosecutorial authorities think that this course of action is the right one to take. It is certainly hoped that this was not done in order to improve the bargaining power of the prosecution when it comes to plea bargain; that would be an illegitimate exercise of prosecutorial discretion. It is not easy to see what other legitimate reason there may have been. If the partner had been a woman and the circumstances were otherwise the same, the prosecution would not have had the option of piling on a 377A charge. Would that state of affairs—a single IDA charge—have been insufficient response? I think not. If that is so, then it must follow that the double charge in a gay sex situation is necessarily excessive.

Could there be a legitimate reason for double charging Chan Mun Chiong? What possible purpose could the 377A charge have served? If we accept, as the Prime Minister says we must, gays are entitled to their private lives, then the only sin committed here was non-disclosure of his HIV status; one adequately expiated by the IDA charge. Similarly, if it had been a problem with the venue, an additional MOPOA charge may not have been unreasonable. It does appear to be the case that nothing legitimate was served by the additional 377A charge.

Caught in a Bad Romance

At the end of the day we have failed to find any legitimate reason for the continued use of 377A, under any circumstances. That ought not to surprise us. The foundational speech by the Prime Minister which brokered the "*pax homosexualis*" of 2007 identified only one possible reason for the existence of the provision itself—the symbolic "signaling" that homosexuals are not to actively promote their "lifestyles" or to "set the tone" for mainstream society.[14] This was to be achieved by the mere existence of 377A, or perhaps the failure to repeal it, but not the enforcement of it. Any attempt to enforce it would inevitably violate the solemn assurance given in the same speech of the entitlement of gays to their private lives and social activities without being molested or threatened. Using 377A in non-consensual, underage or public circumstances is entirely unnecessary because of the existence of more satisfactory alternatives. In other words, choosing 377A over these other orientation-neutral offences do not in any way advance the only legitimate reason for the preservation of 377A—that of signaling that gays should not "promote their lifestyles" or "set the tone" for society, whatever that may mean. Deploying 377A as an additional charge against an accused person who may have committed another offence is illegitimate. A similar heterosexual offender is not subject to this burden. Similarly preferring a 377A charge as a bargaining tool in plea negotiations is illegitimate. The use of 377A in these situations is in no way relevant to the perceived symbolic need to respond to any promotion of homosexuality.

Indeed I think that a convincing case can be made out that *any* use of 377A is unconstitutional. In a recent and important decision, the Chief Justice had this to say about prosecutorial discretion (*Law Society of Singapore v Tan Guat Neo Phyllis*, 2007):

> The discretionary power to prosecute under the Constitution is not absolute. It must be exercised in good faith for the purpose it is intended, *i.e.*, to convict and punish offenders, *and not for an extraneous purpose*... In our view, the exercise of the prosecutorial discretion is subject to judicial review in two situations: first, where the prosecutorial power is abused, i.e., where it is exercised in bad faith for an extraneous purpose, and second, where its exercise contravenes constitutional protections and rights (for example, a discriminatory prosecution which results in an accused being *deprived of his right to equality* under the law and the equal protection of the law under Article 12 of the Constitution).

Simply, prosecuting anyone under 377A is unconstitutional for two reasons. First, he is subject to a 377A charge, when entirely suitable alternatives are available, for no rational reason and to serve no legitimate purpose. Second, he is discriminated against unfairly and unjustifiably when compared with another similar offender of heterosexual orientation against whom 377A is not an option.

I end with an interesting pronouncement concerning 377A by the Minister for Law, K Shanmugam on 5th July 2009. The actual transcript is not available, but it was reported by *Channel News Asia* (2010) as follows:

> He [Minister K Shanmugam] said: "We have the law. We say *it won't be enforced*. Is it totally clear? We, sometimes in these things, have to accept a

bit of messiness." [H]e said that while the government will not take the lead
in repealing the law, the legal courts in Singapore have the power to decide
how Section 377[A] is interpreted and applied.

If we must continue to have the bad romance with 377A, then the Minister has
said the only sensible thing there is to say: "it won't be enforced, is it totally
clear". Flirting with ideas like non-proactive or passive enforcement will only
create the opportunity for individual decision-makers to inject personal prejudices into the prosecutorial process and to go against the official policy of non-
harassment. The hint to the judiciary about having the power to interpret and
apply 377A is fascinating, but that is another story.[15] Surely the judiciary also
possesses the power and the duty to ensure that any attempt to use 377A is not
an unconstitutional exercise of prosecutorial discretion.

3

Sexual Vigilantes Invade Gender Spaces

Religion and Sexuality in the AWARE Saga

Laurence Wai-Teng Leong

In his comparison of Malaysia and Singapore, media scholar Cherian George (2006) noted that public discourse in Malaysia is much more vibrant and activist-oriented, correlated with democratic participation and grassroots social movements (Weiss, 2006). In contrast, public discourse in Singapore is somewhat muted and tame. Cherian George argued that this difference is not due to a stronger or more authoritarian State in Singapore that sets out-of-bound markers on speech; it is due to the poverty of civil society networks. There are not many non-governmental organizations (NGOs) in Singapore concerned with social issues such as human rights and social injustice. Many NGOs in Singapore are charitable bodies and faith-based foundations that have little to do with enlarging the democratic space for the citizens.

But in April 2009, a new consciousness about civil society was awakened by a war between two camps of women within a women's rights organisa-tion called AWARE (Association of Women for Action and Research). Gloating spectators would have enjoyed watching females mauling each other, pulling hair, scratching, biting, screaming and kicking. But the AWARE war was less facetious than an episode of female gladiators or female mud wrestlers: it was a battle over religion, sexuality, and the meaning of womanhood. A change of leadership in a women's organisation would hardly be newsworthy, but the allegiances of the new leaders was a cause for public concern because their conservative brand of Christianity brought many issues to the forefront: the role of religion in civil society, the place of LGBT in a women's organisation, sex education in schools, and civic participation in a State regime of pragmatic illiberalism. These issues fired the imagination and involvement of so many Singaporeans that far from being apathetic, they were galvanized to take part in the democratic process of affecting the course and direction of an NGO.

Founded in 1985, AWARE is an organisation tirelessly defending the rights of women against discrimination in the workplace, against domestic abuse at home, against under-representation in the political sphere, against misrepresen-tation in media imagery, and against any kind of marginalisation on the basis of gender (Lyons, 2004). The Singapore government signed the Convention on the Elimination of All Forms of Discrimination Against Women (CEDAW) in 1995, but the inadequacies of State action on behalf of women (e.g. quotas that limit the number of females accepted into medical school; disadvantages that single mothers face, etc.) have led AWARE to assume the watchdog role by filing a shadow report to the United Nations on what more needs to be done to improve the status of women in Singapore.

Over the years, AWARE has established a stronghold as the premier NGO in Singapore: it is an instantly recognisable brand name. Three of its leaders were Nominated Members of Parliament; many AWARE members are professionals with high-profile personalities and links to the political establishment. Indeed the common image-problem of AWARE has been the charge that it is elitist, run by a small circle of bourgeois women. This allegation is unfair because a small privileged social class can still work on issues generic to all women, such as workplace discrimination, violence against women, and sexual harassment. Moreover, much of the work done by AWARE members is voluntary, and often incurs the wrath of men, women and the State. For instance, the topic of domestic violence may be construed by some to be an intrusion into the realm of the private family (Narayanan, 2008). And in Singapore, the label "feminist" which is often hurled at AWARE members, carries negative connotations of misandry, frustrated spinsters and radical partisanship.

Since doing volunteer work on behalf of women demands much time, financial and emotional resources, many AWARE members have remained dormant: paying membership dues but absent in meetings and even less active in campaign drives. This state of affairs has provided a context for a leadership takeover by a new cadre of unknown women whose motivations were not immediately and publicly spelled out.

The dominant English newspaper, *The Straits Times*, scooped the story of AWARE's annual general meeting on 28 March 2009 when newcomers who had no experience in volunteering for AWARE took the limelight by capturing nine of twelve executive committee (Exco) posts (Wong, 2009a). Within a month, the new Exco members changed the locks of the AWARE headquarters, fired the manager who had been with AWARE for 15 years, and conspired to exclude old guard members from a press conference.

Three facets of this leadership coup were newsworthy:

a.   **Conflict among women**: the general rule about news media is that conflict provides audiences with a dramatic source of entertainment (Gilboa, 2002). In the AWARE case, conflict among women was even more attention-grabbing because of the potential nastiness of the outcome and the revelation that women are bitterly divided even in a women's advocacy group. The conflict between the old and new guard was characterised by the news reporters as "catfight" (Chua, 2009: 2) and as two camps "locking horns" (Basu, 2009a). A cartoon illustrating a commentary, "Dangerous Turns in Domestic Dispute", emphasised the word "war" within aWARe (Jacob, 2009).

b. **Stealth tactics of the new guard**: although the takeover of AWARE's key posts was democratic in procedure (secured through election), it was widely seen as an illegitimate coup and an usurpation of power because the change of leadership was an abrupt disjuncture rather than a smooth transition (Suhaimi, 2009a). Claire Nazar quit as president after eleven days and characterised the new Exco as "stormtroopers" who snubbed veteran AWARE members (*Sunday Times*, 2009). More importantly, the motivations for the takeover were not immediately transparent. The secrecy of the new guard provided the news media with cloak and dagger ingredients for a drama of intrigue and mystery. *The Straits Times* deputy editor Alan John (2009) titled his editorial, "Too Many Questions Left Unanswered" in light of the fact that the new president Ms Josie Lau had for weeks not offered a clear picture of her new team and of the direction of AWARE. Indeed Josie Lau's reluctance to open up to the public fuelled speculation of her intentions and agenda. The plot thickened in the wait for a resolution or denouement.

c. **Composition of the new guard**: the seizure of power perked interest about the nature of this group, in particular, their motivations to takeover AWARE, and their new blueprint, if any, to lead AWARE. Since Josie Lau and most of her team joined AWARE only two months before grabbing the leadership posts, *The Straits Times* reporters were puzzled by the paradox that these women had no past experience in civil society and yet saw the urgency in purging veterans of an established NGO.

From the media point of view, the three facets of the episode were in line with journalistic standards of asking when/what (conflict)? how (stealth)? and why (composition of newcomers)? Conflict and stealth are hallmarks of drama and entertainment that appealed to audiences (Shoemaker and Cohen, 2006). Gaps in information about the unknown newcomers offered opportunities for reporters to do investigative journalism (Pilger, 2004). The seizure of power in AWARE in other words was an ideal context for reporters to not only do a good story, but also probe deeper to unravel hidden agendas and connect pieces in a jigsaw puzzle.

The Straits Times reporters did background searches of the newcomers, and revealed that six of the new Exco members attended the Anglican Church of Our Saviour. The secretary of the new committee had written to *The Straits Times* forum in 2007, opposing the repeal of Section 377A of the Penal Code that criminalises sex between men. Josie Lau worked for Development Bank of

Singapore (DBS), which had publicly rebuked her for breach in the staff code of conduct because she had not sought prior approval for her external appointment as president of the new AWARE. Indeed she was embroiled in controversy in 2008 when she led the marketing team in DBS' credit card campaign that supported the evangelical Christian organisation Focus on the Family (Siow, 2008).

Further investigations revealed an extended network of family ties and church connections, all bound by an anti-gay stance. Focus on the Family, which Josie Lau championed, is known for its use of religious rhetoric to attack gays and lesbians (Burack, 2008; Cobb, 2006). Josie Lau's husband Dr. Alan Chin, an AWARE associate member, wrote in a 2007 *Straits Times* forum condemning gay lifestyles (Chin, 2007). Dr. Alan Chin's aunt, Dr. Thio Su Mien confessed at a press conference that she was the "Feminist Mentor" behind the takeover (Hussain, 2009). Dr. Thio Su Mien was once the dean of the Law Faculty, and her daughter Dr. Thio Li Ann, a law professor at the National University of Singapore, was a nominated Member of Parliament who argued successfully for the retention of the law that criminalises sex between men (section 377A).

The picture became clear that the novice Exco members and their supporters were born-again Christians who sought to cleanse what they saw as the corrupt sexuality that veteran AWARE members were said to tolerate or even embrace. This group constituted what Howard Becker (1963) calls "moral entrepreneurs": people who seek to persuade the whole society to follow their brand of ardently held moral beliefs. They are moral crusaders whose obsession with their own righteous sense of morality leads them to disregard the means by which the ends are to be achieved. Thus the takeover of AWARE by the novices with no background in civil society operations was marked by rambunctious shutting out of veterans, changing of locks, firing of seasoned staff, and passive-aggressive responses to media questions at press conferences.

At the core of the Thio Su Mien-Josie Lau's moral enterprise lay issues about sexuality. Thio Su Mien objected to several instances of what she characterised as AWARE's "gay turn" (Hussain, 2009):

(1) At its charity gala, AWARE screened a Taiwanese movie, *Spider Lilies* which is about women loving women. While then-president Constance Singam defended the movie as representing diversity and individual choice, Thio saw lesbianism as deviant sexuality.

(2) AWARE invited a Finnish gender activist who spoke about artificial insemination for women, which Thio said led to an endorsement of same-sex marriage.

(3) AWARE held a Mother's Day event in 2006, featuring lesbian-friendly mothers and lesbian daughters; Thio thought both groups of women were "out of sync" with how Mother's Day was conventionally celebrated.

(4) AWARE invited gay activist Alex Au to conduct health education on HIV and AIDS.

(5) preceding president Constance Singam reached out to include transgendered women into AWARE.

(6) AWARE mooted the idea of giving teenagers and foreign workers the rights to vote; and the proposal to give male members of AWARE the rights to vote was seen by Thio as a way of letting "homosexual activist men" in.

(7) AWARE initiated a sexuality education package in schools where pupils aged 12 to 18 were taught to accept homosexuality as a "neutral" rather than negative word, and to treat "pleasure", "fun", "orgasm" as positive words.

Thio's list of complaints about AWARE all struck at sexuality rather than women's status in society in terms of their disadvantage, discrimination, abuse or marginalisation—matters that AWARE has never lost sight of. Given the State policies that continue to stigmatise sexual minorities (Leong, 2008), AWARE's acceptance of lesbian, bisexual women, transgendered people and gays represented precisely the role of a civil society: to defend the weak and the vulnerable, and to transcend the limitations of the State. Rather than being a shadow, a replica or a microcosm of the State, an NGO ideally advances ahead of the state.

The moral fervour that drove Thio, Josie Lau and her team to raid an established NGO was founded on fundamentalist ideas that the Christian Right in America have championed (Burack, 2008; Cobb, 2006; Herman, 1998; Smith and Windes, 2000; Stein, 2001). Lines are drawn between normal and deviant sexuality, between the righteous and the sinned, and between good and evil. In this worldview, boundaries are zealously marked and guarded so that a singular and exclusive notion of woman and sexuality is maintained. Diversity, variety, inclusiveness are frowned upon not only because the apparent result of fuzzy chaos threatens the lines of their moral-cognitive frame, but also because embracing diversity is thought to have larger consequences like decline of the family and downfall of civilisation (Rubin, 2002). "Saving the family" is a rallying cry for moral entrepreneurs to resist and oppose the multiple permutations of gender, sexuality and household arrangements prevalent in urban, cosmopolitan settings (Baca Zinn et al., 2010).

American scholars have characterised the battle over gender, sexuality and the household as a "culture war" (Hunter, 1991; Escoffier, 1996). The meanings of womanhood, sexuality, and "the family" are heavily contested within debates about abortion, contraception, sex education, and the rights of sexual minorities. But in Singapore, why should the culture war as waged by Thio and Josie Lau take place in the context of a civil society organisation? Is a women's advocacy NGO the suitable platform for contesting sexual intimacies or pushing moral agendas? Why not set up a women's religious organisation that would be more transparent about defending a monolithic vision of womanhood and sexuality?

As conflict always means schisms, letters to *The Straits Times* forums reflected support and opposition to the AWARE takeover. Since the investigative reporters of *The Straits Times* had already unearthed the religious and family connections of the novice Exco members, one issue of major public concern was the role of religion in civil society. Should religion inform, guide, or infiltrate civil society? Given a State that imposes out-of-bounds limits on discussion of race and religion in Singapore, and any interfaith dialogue is not likely to succeed, which religion would preside over which civil society organisations? Why should the Christian faith dominate a women's organisation when in fact the demographic majority in Singapore are Buddhists/Taoists?

Meanwhile the founding mothers of AWARE were not content to watch their baby snatched by moral vigilantes. Veterans created an online petition to "Save AWARE" opposing the novice leadership (Chan, 2009). Membership of AWARE soared from 300 to 3,000. An extraordinary general meeting (EOGM) was called to consider a vote of no confidence in the new Exco. More than three thousand people attended the meeting on 2nd May 2009 at the Suntec City, Hall 402, a large convention venue normally meant for commercial exhibits. Taunts and angry voices, booing and jeers were hurled at the novice Exco. After seven hours of drama, the results were announced that 1,414 (as against 761) voted to oust the novice Exco (Wong, 2009b; Basu, 2009b).

The victory of reclaiming AWARE was due in a large part to media coverage that literally made people aware of the issues about religion, civil society and sexuality (Chan, 2009), and that galvanized people into civic participation. Men came in droves to give moral support to women at the convention centre (they were not allowed to vote) (Yong, 2009). Among the 65 per cent of AWARE members who voted against the new Exco, there were: (a) women who were long-time members regretful of their apathy that led to the undesirable takeover; (b) women who were anxious that twenty-five years of struggle to dignify women would be dismissed by moral vigilantes bent on pushing moral agendas; (c) women who felt that religion in general and Christianity in particular have no part in civil society NGOs; (d) women who were lesbian, bisexual or friendly towards sexual minorities, hurt by Thio's vitriolic remarks about lesbians as "sexually challenged women" (Thio, 2009); and (e) women who felt one or more of the above (Teo and Soh, 2009; Yong, 2009).

Social good is sometimes born out of social conflict. The AWARE tussle has positive outcomes. Firstly, civic participation was alive and well in Singapore. The stereotype of the average Singaporean as apathetic was disproved by the passion that moved people to vote against what they felt was unjust, improper, or illegitimate. AWARE has significantly increased its profile and in membership, demonstrating that people with convictions were able to come together to defend civil society (Ang, 2009).

Secondly, the battle lines clarified that many people wanted civil society organisations to be secular. Earlier, Derek Hong, senior pastor of the Church of Our Saviour instigated his congregation to support Josie Lau's team at AWARE: "It's not a crusade against the people but there's a line that God has drawn for us, and we don't want our nation crossing that line" (Suhaimi, 2009b). However, the president of the National Council of Churches of Singapore, John Chew, had to intervene with a statement that the umbrella Christian body did not condone church involvement in the AWARE affair (Hussain and Wong, 2009).

Thirdly, the AWARE episode demonstrated that pluralism is part of the democratic process. The AWARE veterans embraced diversity and took an inclusive stance: women who sought help were not turned down if they were lesbian, if they wanted abortion, if they were unmarried mother or if they were from ethnic or national minorities. On the other hand, the novice Exco were uniformly of the same ethnic group (Chinese), belonged to the same church, and did not want to give foreigners the right to vote in AWARE. Their vigilante and stealth tactics betrayed the styles typical of authoritarianism, self-righteousness and lack of transparency.

Fourthly, the mass media in Singapore, particularly *The Straits Times*, had done a good job in laying bare the issues about civil society, religion, gender and sexuality. It is a common idea that the local newspapers in Singapore serve as the mouthpiece of the dominant political party, and this image has dented the credibility of local news (Tan, 1990). However, in the case of a civil society (an arena that does not directly implicate any dominant political party), *The Straits Times* reporters are free to cover the issues, do exposés and unearth conflicts. And to that extent, *The Straits Times* played a big role in reinvigorating this civil society.

But once people were mobilised into action, joining AWARE, attending the Extra Ordinary General Meeting (EOGM), voting out the novice Exco group and reinstating the veterans back into power, the losers in the aftermath of the battle (i.e. the novice group) blamed the media for causing their eviction. Thio Li-Ann complained that the media were biased towards veterans and did not represent a diverse range of views. The losers sent emails to Members of Parliament, one of whom (Sin Boon Ann) raised the issue in parliament, accusing the press of polarising Singapore by using religion to frame the AWARE issue. Allegations were made that *The Straits Times* favoured some religions against others in this media coverage (Han, 2009). There was also "an organised campaign to discredit the media, with mass emails being sent, including to Reach, the government feedback portal" (Han, 2009).

In the face of these accusations of media bias, *The Straits Times* editor Han Fook Kwang (2009) defended the professionalism of his team of reporters, arguing that internal processes of fact-checking, editing and reviewing were all duly exercised in the coverage of the AWARE tussle. Against allegations of hidden agendas of the media, Han wrote, "The personal attacks against the integrity of our journalists sadden me because they show the vindictiveness of our critics and the length to which they are prepared to go to attack our professionalism."

Because conflict involves camps and sides, it is impossible to be completely neutral. Indeed the claim to neutrality is often disingenuous. Bishop Desmond Tutu has said, "If you are neutral in situations of injustice, you have chosen the side of the oppressor. If an elephant has its foot on the tail of the mouse and you say that you are neutral, the mouse will not appreciate your neutrality" (Quigley, 2003: 8).

The Straits Times coverage of the AWARE conflict appeared to critics to be biased towards the veterans not because of the privileging of the veterans' voices, but because the silence of the novices spoke volumes. The unknown, inexperienced leaders who had taken over a prominent NGO had refused to explain to the public about themselves, their goals, and their vision. Reporters who called, emailed and contacted the novice members only encountered a stonewall of silence (John, 2009). The secrecy that surrounded the leadership grab merely fuelled suspicions that the novices did have hidden agendas.

Those hidden agendas were confirmed at a press conference on 23 April when Thio Su Mien came out of the closet of secrecy to confess her involvement in sparking the leadership takeover. Her issues with sexuality boiled down to her objections to the liberal direction AWARE had taken: moral relativism, diversity, pluralism, inclusiveness, acceptance, fluidity of gender, sexuality and family were all frowned upon by her and Josie's team. And so their agenda was to fix that.

These revelations did not win the sympathy of the public majority—as measured by the letters to the media (Govindan, 2009; Serrenti, 2009; Yeo, 2009; Sum, 2009; Holden, 2009). Earlier, the shutting out of veterans, the secrecy, lack of transparency—all these already undermined their legitimacy of leadership. Thio's coming clean about the moral enterprise behind the usurpation of power merely added strength to the public fury against the takeover. The tabloid news, *The New Paper* (2009), ran a headline, "Most Hated: Feminist Mentor No More", and reported that at the EOGM, the loudest jeers were reserved for her. Subsequently, T-shirts were made to mock at her and other novice Exco members (Tan, 2009).

Although the Thio-Lau team lost the battle over leadership and legitimacy, they did not completely lose all that had been at stake. Their moral enterprise which privileged a monotheistic version of a mono-type of sexuality (i.e. heteronormativity with zero-tolerance for alternative forms) had an impact on sexuality education in schools. Since 2007, AWARE has initiated sexual education programmes in eleven secondary schools, run for small groups of students selected by their teachers and with the consent of their parents. About 500 students, mostly girls, have attended the workshops. Topics covered sexually transmitted diseases, HIV, contraceptives, sexual harassment, negotiation skills to resist peer pressure, coming to terms with one's sexual quotient, body image, eating disorders, teenage pregnancies, etc. (Vasundhra, 2009). The Thio-Lau team felt that AWARE's approach was too lax about sexual experimentation and use of contraceptives, and that it promoted homosexuality, and consequently threatened "family values".

Initially the Ministry of Education (MOE) reported that there was no negative feedback from students or parents regarding the sexuality education programmes (Tan, 2009; Sum, 2009). But weeks later after receiving 1,300 online petitions against AWARE's programme (Tan, 2009a), the MOE suspended the programmes and announced on its website that "MOE and the schools do not promote alternative lifestyles to our students. MOE's framework for sexuality education reflects the mainstream views and values of Singapore society, where the social norm consists of the married heterosexual family unit" (MOE, 2009a; Othman, 2009).

The casualty of the AWARE wars is less the Thio-Lau team (because their lives continue with the support and the blessings of their Christian church) than sex education in schools. Sexuality has become a dangerous minefield where the MOE now treads cautiously to avoid the wrath of moral entrepreneurs. Whereas in England, the British government has ruled that sex education should be a compulsory subject in primary and secondary schools (except faith schools) (Garner, 2009), in Singapore sex education is now banished to clinical biology classes. Studies have found that in America, states that do not offer sex education record high rates of sexually transmitted diseases, teenage pregnancies and dysfunctional families (Talbot, 2008; Cahn and Cabone, 2010).

In Singapore, rates of teenage sexual activities are high. According to Singapore police records, cases of "statutory rape" (where females aged 12–14 have consensual sexual intercourse with males) increased from 38 cases in 2006 to 57 in 2007, to 61 in 2008 and 83 in 2009 (2010). The combined total of "statutory rape" and "carnal connection" cases (where females aged 14–16 have consensual sexual intercourse) rose from 216 in 2007 to 310 in 2008 (2009b). Medical reports reveal that in 2008, 791 teenagers were diagnosed with sexually transmitted infections (STI), more than three times the 238 cases in

2002. As of August 2009, the number was 526 (Sudderuddin, 2009a). Among young adults between 20 to 30 years old, the STI rate per 100,000 population increased by 67 per cent, from 270 in 2000 to 451 in 2008. Among people below 20 years old, the rate more than doubled from 61 per 100,000 population in 2000 to 133 in 2008 (*The Straits Times*, 2010). All these rising figures imply that many teenagers engage in sex in spite of the lack of sex education in schools, and in total oblivion to the abstinence messages exhorted by moral entrepreneurs.

There is then clearly a disjuncture between what adults preach and what teenagers actually do. Moral entrepreneurs may be driven by their religious passion to seize control of an NGO in a desperate attempt to impose their brand of moral order to a rapidly changing, potentially chaotic world. But this kind of moral enterprise tells us more about these people than about the subjects that they ostensibly target. They may have their own psychological or spiritual demons to cast, and so asserting "family values" and a monolithic kind of sexuality functions to make them feel good about their own "breastplate of righteousness" (Humphreys, 1970).

Moreover, most moral entrepreneurs are middle-class people who associate themselves with a limited or even provincial circle of like-minded people. Seldom do they have contact with people of other classes and social stripes like ethnicity, bohemian orientations, and underdogs. It is therefore not surprising that their moral rhetoric is pitched at a level disconnected from the grass roots experience: teenagers will continue to have sex, there will always be gays and lesbians, and multiple forms of intimacy will be defended by people who champion the right to privacy and democratic choice.

Thanks to the media, the AWARE episode has opened up a range of issues: moral entrepreneurship, religion, sexuality, civil society, media, transparency and legitimacy. In the context of pragmatic illiberalism, where race and religion are constructed by the Singapore State as potentially fractious issues upon which "out of bounds" markers have been placed, a group of Christian women who seized control of an NGO had to hide their agendas and not make their motivations known. But unmistakably, religious fervour provided the basis for their moral enterprise to banish queer sexuality from Singapore. This obsession with sex eclipsed gender issues: improving the status and lives of women in Singapore was sidelined by the agenda to purge AWARE of its liberal approach toward sexuality.

Even after the public defeat of returning the leadership posts back to the veterans, the moral entrepreneurs were not content to let the issue of sexuality rest. They turned to the State (the Ministry of Education), playing the card of pragmatic illiberalism, to attack AWARE's sexuality education programmes for being too liberal and accepting of queer sexualities. As a result of such pressure tactics, the Ministry of Education (MOE) suspended external providers of sexuality education modules and AWARE withdrew its programmes in February 2010. Today, positive approaches to the treatment of queers are now removed from sex education programmes in schools. Policy officials at the MOE tread sex education with great caution: parents are assured that MOE does not 'promote' homosexuality, and students are reminded that homosexual acts are still illegal (MOE, 2009b). These kinds of contexts make it difficult for teenage students to find sexual acceptance of self and others, and subject them to the threat of bullying in schools (Chan P., 2010).

The AWARE saga has strengthened civil society as the women's NGO rearticulated itself as secular, pluralistic and inclusive, and the interested public were mobilised in the democratic process of participation and engagement. Arguably, the casualties of the tussle between a group of Christian women and veteran leaders are teenagers who, deprived of secular and informed sexual education programmes, will have to learn sex not through parents or teachers, but on their own, in real and virtual spaces (Quek and Spykerman, 2009; Toh and Thomas, 2010; Chong, 2010). And the queer teens among this group will continue to struggle with their sense of being in an environment that treats homosexuality as illegal and queers as "deviants" (Chan L.G., 2009).

4

"Oi, Recruit! Wake Up Your Idea!"

Homosexuality and Cultural Citizenship in the Singaporean Military

Chris K. K. Tan

Introduction

In this chapter, I shall examine gay life experiences in another fundamental pillar of Singaporean society—the military. Since 1967, all able-bodied male citizens are legally obliged to serve their National Service (NS) upon reaching the age of 16½ years. Enlistees perform a minimum of two years' full-time duty, followed by ten more years in the part-time reserves. NS aims to instill national loyalty despite Singapore's severe geopolitical vulnerabilities. Both the universality of NS and the transmission of national values make NS a prime citizen-making site. Gay men must also serve NS as homosexuality does not excuse them. How then do they serve in the strongly heteronormative military? How do their experiences inform our understanding of Singaporean citizenship?

Drawing upon both the idea of cultural citizenship and my dissertational fieldwork, I argue that the sense of national belonging in Singapore differs from previous conceptualizations of cultural citizenship as largely top-down (Ong, 1996) or bottom-up (Rosaldo, 1994) processes. Rather, the State determines the contours of cultural citizenship and citizens react only when the strictures work against their interests. The military exemplifies this passively driven negotiation. Although many gay men consider the military an abusive and wasteful organization, others see it as the nation-building experience *par excellence*. Its emphasis on quantifiable test results means that gay soldiers need not come out—and most do not. Yet, those who do (even flamboyantly so) will find much manoeuvering room *if* they satisfy stringent standards of physical fitness. This flexibility highlights the possibilities and limits of NS as a citizen-making site.

Legal and Cultural Citizenship

Before I discuss cultural citizenship theory, it must be first distinguished from legal citizenship. In his seminal essay that analyzes the development of British legal citizenship from the eighteenth to the twentieth century, Marshall (1950) asserts that a full citizen must possess civil, political and social rights. He further links this possession to social class. This definition reveals a number of modern citizenship's key characteristics. Firstly, legal citizenship is inherently exclusive. Typically, States grant membership only to individuals who satisfy their membership criteria. Secondly, States bestow citizenship arbitrarily. For instance, an individual becomes a Singaporean simply because his or her parents are themselves citizens. Lastly, citizenship buffers against the material and social inequalities that capitalist societies unavoidably produce. Seeking to maximize profits, the capitalistic market place provides little against unemployment, work-related injuries and illnesses, old age, an individual's social (ir)relevance, and other vagaries of life that a worker must inevitably endure. The redistribution of rights and material wealth implicit in citizenship offsets the negative consequences of an unregulated market (Turner, 2009).

While acknowledging the utility of Marshall's theory, scholars also criticize it on several grounds. Firstly, Marshall neither analyzed coherently and consistently the causal mechanisms (e.g. ethnic discontent in the United States) that produced an expansion of citizenship (Alexander, 2006) nor explained the variance of citizenship forms across different historical trajectories. Secondly, he said little about citizen duties and obligations. He assumed a passive citizenry that the State protects from the market's uncertainties through a system of universal social rights, but did not question how these social rights transform from mere formal claims to effective forms of entitlement (Turner, 2009). Thirdly, critics question how much modern citizenship buffers against the free market's vagaries, arguing that it has neither altered the basic structures of capitalistic inequalities (Mann, 1987) nor improved the social position of women (Siim, 2000). Lastly, legal citizenship maps national belonging directly onto membership in nation-states. Such a theoretical framing no longer suffices in a world of rapid cross-border flows of people, capital and information. Scholars now see citizenship as a set of socio-cultural processes rather than simply a political status or a juridical contract of rights, entitlements and obligations between individuals and the State (Shafir, 1998). Lister (1998), Williams (1991) and other feminists and critical race theorists complicate the notion of universal citizenship further by highlighting the inflections that race, gender, class, sexuality and other categories of difference make upon one's understanding of citizenship.

Despite Marshall's critics, we should not dismiss legal citizenship as either a static category or simply a status whose conferring depends on the fulfillment of certain legal requirements. A nation-state's cultural values and aspirations inform the legal criteria and opinions concerning membership in that entity. As the values and aspirations change over time, so do the criteria and opinions (Daniels, 2005). This historical mutability also identifies citizenship as central to the studies of governmentality by focusing on the constitution of the human subject *vis-à-vis* itself and constellations of power (Donzelot, 1979).

Cultural citizenship, in contrast, refers to the extra-legal emotional ties that bind one to his or her country. Within anthropology, two scholars contribute significantly to the development of cultural citizenship studies. Working among Latinos in the United States, Rosaldo (1994) envisioned citizenship as a people-driven and continually expanding process of inclusion and enfranchisement. To him,

> cultural citizenship refers to the right to be different (in terms of race, ethnicity, or native language) with respect to the norms of the dominant national community, without compromising one's right to belong, in the sense of participating in the nation-state's democratic processes (Rosaldo, 1994: 57).

Ong (1999) critiques Rosaldo for privileging the agency of subordinated groups too much. Indeed, voluntary grassroots associations may hinder the development of inclusive, participatory social relations just as well as fostering them (Hefner, 2001). Ong (1996) takes a more top-down approach and treats cultural citizenship as a process of subject formation where civil institutions socialize newcomers and integrate them into the nation-state. She demonstrates a primary concern with the regimes of governmentality in her study of flexible citizenship practices among Hong Kong elites (Ong, 1999). However, neither Rosaldo nor Ong conceive of dominant majorities and their qualitative citizenship. Referring to Fijian and Malaysian "natives", Daniels (2005: 8) notes that:

> although members of such groups are conventionally thought to be the default citizen-members of national communities, they may also develop a sense of second-class citizenship or marginalized first class citizenship due to particular social and political policies or processes.

Hence, full membership in a dominant group does not automatically guarantee cultural belonging.

The Singapore Armed Forces

In Singapore, the military presents a prime site where gay men negotiate their cultural citizenship. The State demands military service ostensibly to deter would-be invaders. As a major requirement of their legal citizenship, all able-bodied male citizens must serve at least two years when they turn 16½. Women and first-generation citizens are exempted, but they may volunteer. Conscripts serve mainly in one of the army's military formations, although a smaller number serve in the navy, the air force, the police or the civil defense force instead. After they are discharged from full-time service, they are still obliged to serve on a part-time basis. Until they reach the stipulated age for full military discharge (i.e. forty for non-commissioned officers and fifty for commissioned ones), they must also serve a maximum of forty days a year for ten years in the reserves. These ten years need not be consecutive. Reservist soldiers attend in-camp training sessions that purportedly keep their military skills honed and updated. Depending on the part of the training cycle a reservist unit has advanced to, these sessions can range from 'low-key' activities that last about a week or less (e.g. live-firing at ranges and technical skills refresher courses) to 'high-key' ones that last a month or more (typically full-blown military exercises held either locally or overseas). Medically fit reservist soldiers must also take an annual physical fitness test that consists of a standing broad jump, chin-ups, sit-ups, a shuttle run and a 2.4 km run. Those who pass receive monetary rewards that vary according to the quality of their passes. Failures must attend remedial physical training that can last up to two months.

With so many men serving their military duty every year, NS makes a significant impact on Singaporean everyday life. Full-time soldiers delay their entry into the working world or the university. Reservist ones must rearrange their daily schedules to accommodate their in-camp and physical fitness training. Linguistically, many terms of the colloquial variety of Singaporean English called 'Singlish' also originated as military lingo. For instance, the titular imperative of this chapter *wake up your idea* reminds the addressed to stop whatever he is planning and return to reality. Sergeants often use it to berate new recruits into falling in line with existing practices. More importantly, the ubiquity of NS also prompts a critical question: does NS generate a sense of national belonging among the recruits?

Being a Gay Soldier

As part of my dissertational fieldwork on cultural citizenship among Singaporean gay men that I conducted from August 2007 to January 2009, I interviewed twenty-nine men. All but one of them was Chinese; the exception being Malay. Twenty-six self-identify as gay and three as straight. Most of them were in their late 20s to mid-30s at the time of the interviews, although a small number was older. The majority also reported middle-class backgrounds, albeit to different degrees. When I asked my informants what they thought of NS, they professed mixed attitudes towards it even as they acknowledged its national importance. For example, David perceives the military as severely mismanaged:

> In my case, hated it. Waste of time. I got to see how badly the army is managed. It just boggles me how badly the army is run. I mean, the admin is so slow. I mean, they lose documents.

Conscripts only serve two years, so they need not be conscientious about their supposed national duty. Knowing that conscripts can at most attain only a certain rank (usually Third Sergeant) and that they wield little influence as individuals, more senior officers sometimes exploit them. When I served my NS, my unit would occasionally run outside our camp and sing songs along the way to boost our morale. During one such run, my commanding officer pondered loudly why he could not hear my company sing. Later that evening, my sergeant major ordered the entire company to stay back for another two hours that Saturday to sing. At that time, conscripts stayed in most of the week and went home for the weekend only on Saturdays at noon. Naturally, we read the singing order as unfair punishment for something that hardly counted as an offence, and as the sergeant major's overt attempt to curry the commanding officer's favours at our expense. The subsequent loud protests changed the sergeant major's mind. We still had to sing, but we did so on Saturday morning. This left our departure time unaffected.

Despite the military's manpower abuses, other consultants thought of their NS experiences in positive terms. The rigorous military training readied them for the working world, they claimed, by instilling maturity and self-discipline. Brian intimated, "It change[s] a person ... Discipline-wise, I think it does help a lot ... It also teaches you to listen to your superiors ... It prepares you for work where you'll be under somebody. Even if you don't like the person, you'll still have to do it, which is what the outside world is going to be." Ah Ren, a straight consultant, conceives of NS as a crucial component in the nation-building process:

> I think that National Service becomes a defining sense of national identity, not because the government intends it to be so ... but because of the very processes of being stripped away of everything and being sent together to serve with other people [with nothing but] your shirt and your nationality. I think [it] forces you to investigate your nationality and bond with the people you're serving with, 'cos it's mutual suffering *lah* ... [Here in] Singapore, we talk about the four main races [of] Chinese, Malay, Indians [and] Others ... we talk about languages, we talk about respect for religion and a few other things, and you go into the army, there're many people who have never met anybody outside of their religion, their ethnic group, their social class. Most of the time, the army is the first time you actually do [meet others]. You become Singaporean because then you really see Singapore ... If I randomly picked [men] off the street and threw them together, you could not get a better sample of what National Service is like other than that.

In fact, NS acts as Singapore's great social equalizer by forcing recruits from different ethnic and social backgrounds to live, train, work and suffer together. One afternoon, I chatted with Chor Pharn and his long-term partner David over lunch. David referred to Chor Pharn as a "white horse", i.e. someone

from a background privileged enough (usually, but not always, due to political connections) to warrant such special treatment as deliberate deployment
in easy, desk-bound positions. Indeed, Chor Pharn revealed he served NS as a
navy clerk and he was never recalled for reservist training. When I asked him
whether he thought of NS as a worthy endeavour, he replied with a chuckle:

> This is funny, because after David said I was a 'white horse' and everything,
> I would say this is a good thing because—this is so ironical—I didn't really
> find many chances to interact with a whole swath of Singapore society. Oh
> dear, this is so funny. This is like let-them-eat-cake Marie Antoinette, right?
> But I do remember my [basic military training] with great affection, because
> I met bums. I met so many of what you'd call people who were never up
> to anything useful or good or productive. But they were interesting in their
> own right and they deserve to exist in their own right. So it was nice. I
> wouldn't have interacted with them for any other reason … I enjoyed it. I
> did enjoy it. This coming from elitist Chor Pharn, yes?

Despite its patronizing tone (note the reference to a certain infamously callous
French queen), Chor Pharn's reply shows that NS creates an organic bond
through which male citizens can relate to each other across various social
boundaries. More than any artificial nationalistic campaigns the State could
have implemented, this bond provides a common base of lived experiences
through which recruits challenge their pre-conceived notions about other
people of different backgrounds. They forge their own national identity this
way. As Ah Ren pointed out:

> You go into the army, it doesn't mean that your Chinese racism about
> Indians is going to disappear, or your Indian racism about Malays is going
> to disappear, but at least you get to know them when they're there. In some
> cases, you might find that, 'Hey, they're not too bad.'

To gay men, full-time service in the military's highly heteronormative
spaces can be a trying two years. During my basic military training, a very
feminine and supposedly gay man worked in the quartermaster's office as a
clerk. When I went to the storeroom to fetch equipment, I often witnessed him
getting teased not only by his peers and superiors, but also by recruits whom
he technically outranked. Facing such teasing and bullying, gay soldiers can
remain closeted throughout NS—I came out only shortly after my active tour
of duty—or they can officially declare their sexuality. The rarity of coming out
cases and their highly confidential nature mean that most people know what
happens thereafter more through rumours than actual facts. Driven by a need
to clear the mysteries, a brave enlistee called Lim Chi-Sharn outed himself
in the army and published his experiences online (Lim, 2002a, 2002b). Lim's
account coheres with the stories that I heard, so I take it as representative of the
military's coming out procedures. I summarize his story below.

Lim enlisted in 1998, but he disrupted his training in the Officer Cadet School shortly after to dedicate time for his overseas university education. During his re-enlistment medical examination, he was asked if he had "any social problems (e.g. homosexuality)". He ticked "yes", but scribbled "I don't think it's a problem!" next to the question. He reminded the doctor who saw him later of the tick. Caught flat-footed, the doctor pulled out a thick, dog-eared manual, flipped to the page entitled "Homosexuality and Trans-sexuality", and started reading earnestly. After questioning Lim whether he had sex with men and whether he cross-dressed—Lim affirmed both queries—he rated Lim as temporarily unfit for duty. In a follow-up review, a doctor named Tan asked him more questions from a printed list: "How do you feel about NS?", "Are you a homosexual?", "Do you have a boyfriend?" and, most pertinently, "Are you the man or the woman?" Upon Lim's protest about the last question's phrasing, Tan clarified by asking about Lim's sex role.

Tan said that the review gauged the degree of Lim's homosexuality using a scale that placed heterosexual men on one end and women on the other. Purportedly, it ascertained the impact of Lim's sexuality on his military deployability and his ability to fit into communal military life. Tan surmised that Lim could not serve in "sensitive" areas, but he did not clarify what he meant by that. Tan assured Lim that the military laws protect his rights to privacy. Only Lim's human resource and commanding officers would know the real reason behind his physical fitness rating. In reality, the military cannot keep such information as confidential as it should. Administrative clerks who otherwise should not be privy to this data may stumble upon it by accident when they file someone's personnel documents. Lim also claims that his gay friends had their civil service careers outside of the military hampered because of alleged information leaks. This claim echoes persistent rumours that those who come out to the military will receive a black mark in their files that prevents them from working in the government ever again.

After the review, Lim received a physical fitness rating that excused him from up to two stations in the annual physical fitness test, even though he was not physically disabled in any way. He ceased his officer cadet training, as he could now only be deployed for operational (read "administrative") duties in military bases. Indeed, he was posted to the Ministry of Defence headquarters. At the new unit, Lim's new manpower officer remarked with a little surprise that he did not look gay. He also said that because he already had an officially 'out' recruit in the human resources office, he would post Lim to another branch. Military policies specify that gay recruits must be kept apart. Lim was assured that no one would harass him as long as he observed sexual proprieties on military premises. "There is no bias towards you, you know," the officer said. Lim countered insightfully, "I know that people are probably not biased, but the system is."

Lim's story shows that military personnel still comprehend gender and sexuality in antiquated terms. They confuse differences in biological sex with sex and gender roles, such that military medical handbooks equate homosexuality with trans-sexualism. Policies configure gay men correspondingly as feminine in behaviour and receptive during sex. Officers do not know that not all gay men cross-dress, or that actual cross-dressers may in fact self-identify as straight (Wheeler and Schaefer, 1988). Neither do they see the possibilities of masculine gay men taking penetrated sexual roles or feminine gay men taking penetrating ones.

Lim also explains *302*, the military medical designation for officially gay recruits. Lim (2002b) traces the number to the *International Statistical Classification of Diseases and Related Health Problems* (usually abbreviated as "ICD"), a list of known human diseases and medical disorders that the World Health Organization publishes. In it, the WHO codes each condition to facilitate medical administration. As a WHO member, Singapore uses the ICD. The WHO published its latest revision of the ICD, the ICD-10, in 1992. However, military policy-makers used an earlier revision, the ICD-9 published in 1977, to formulate policies towards gay recruits. The ICD-10 does not list homosexuality as a disorder. Strictly speaking, as I found out subsequently, neither does ICD-9. Under the code "302", ICD-9 lists transsexualism, pedophilia and other "sexual deviations" often fallaciously attributed to homosexuality—but *not* homosexuality itself. The fact that the military doctors designate gay men as "302" attests not only to their limited comprehension of gender and sexuality, but also to the tardiness with which military bureaucracy adopts the ICD-10's new medical classifications.

The military adopted its policies towards gay recruits to shield the other enlistees from their alleged negative influences. Citing Lily Wong-Ip's article, 'Understanding Homosexual Servicemen' in *Council Link* (a publication of the military's Counseling Centre), Lim (2002b) explains the rationale behind these policies. These policies assume that gay soldiers threaten discipline and morale, hinder male bonding, and are subject to blackmail. Lim refutes all three reasons. Firstly, since gay men are not exempted from NS, generations of them must have served without disclosing their sexuality or causing disciplinary incidents. Lim insists that his openly gay presence did not affect his unit's work efficiency. Secondly, a person's sexuality has no causal links to his capabilities for self-discipline, professionalism and teamwork. If gay men disrupt group cohesion through their alleged eroticism, then all women should be banned in an organization dominated by heterosexual men (including Lily Wong-Ip herself). Lastly, Lim acknowledges that while people with secrets to hide may be more easily turned into security liabilities, gay men who openly disclose their sexuality should logically become less susceptible to blackmail. Why then does the Military Security Department explicitly forbid openly gay personnel access to classified information and, with that denial, to promotion up the ranks? In effect, ignorance of gender and sexuality creates a glass ceiling that contradicts organizational goals to remove the red tape that chokes the military bureaucracy.

The anti-gay glass ceiling appears impenetrable, but gay men have breached it. The ceiling bars the advancement of officially 'out' personnel, but no laws demand that gay men must officially declare their sexuality. A gay man may come out to all the people he works with, but as long as he does not declare "302", the MSD cannot "read" his homosexuality and act accordingly (Scott, 1998). I met a number of men during fieldwork who had breached the glass ceiling with some success. For instance, Bryan attained the rank of staff sergeant (a mid-ranking non-commissioned officer) as a career soldier with considerable access to classified information, before he was discharged honourably in 2004. He outed himself willingly to those colleagues and superiors who asked. He also claimed that he was neither harassed nor did he encounter problems commanding respect from his subordinates. Yet, he never officially declared his sexuality. He never felt the need to. Bryan's case clearly does not indicate a gay-friendly environment in the military. Rather, he must have worked sufficiently well with his colleagues that his sexuality became a non-work issue.

Furthermore, military policies take a pragmatic, result-oriented approach towards gay soldiers. Even a loud and effeminate recruit may find much room to manoeuvre in, *provided* that he produces expected test results. Nick, a gay informant, illustrates this point perfectly. When I interviewed him, he had just been discharged from active duty in the navy. Nick spoke in a slightly high-pitched but reverberating voice, and he punctuated his replies with emphatic gesturing. He never bothered to suppress this demeanour, perhaps because he realized the futility of any such attempts. He disabused his detractors of the stereotype of the weak, feminine gay man by attaining the gold standard in his last physical fitness test. This meant that he ran 2.4 km under 9 minutes 45 seconds, an astonishing feat that only the fittest soldiers could achieve. This led his commanding officer to choose him to address his ship's crew. In a speech that incensed his staff sergeant, Nick spoke on the need for more tolerance for sexual minorities in the military. Yet, he received no punishment for his audacity. I attribute this lack of retribution to Nick's excellent test results and their contributions to his unit's overall competitiveness in the annual Best Unit Competition. Nick did not say whether his unit won the contest that year, but his physical fitness test scores definitely added to his unit's edge. Had he failed his test, I doubt his commanding officer would have honoured him with the speech in the first place.

The fact that both Bryan and Nick flourished in the military despite being openly gay suggests that ignorance about homosexuality afflicts the organization more than informed homophobia. Like other soldiers, gay ones must also measure up to existing high standards for results. Openly gay recruits who satisfy these demands can in fact remain as they are, even though effeminate ones must undoubtedly work harder than their more masculine counterparts to break the conceptual links between effeminacy, homosexuality and physical frailty. As I argued elsewhere (Tan, 2009), homosexuality by itself does not provide sufficient cause for dismissal from one's government job. It may hinder an individual's career if he has a homophobic boss, but it must combine with corruption, incompetence or some other more pressing problem before he can be reasonably dismissed. More critically, openly gay soldiers can change the inaccurate opinions their colleagues have about them, and perhaps even alter the military's attitudes towards homosexuality in the long run. Nick recognizes the enormous potential to affect positive changes in people's mindsets just by coming out:

> That's why I always say that change in Singapore is all about the grassroots … It's all about the grassroots. Change in Singapore will only happen when we, as gay Singaporeans, are able to affect a critical mass of people. That's the only way we can hope for change … The government in Singapore is hierarchical. There are people in power … who have a fundamentalist Christian background, and it's people like these who are stopping change … instead of using this battering ram and try to ram things in, we ought to adopt a more outreach mode … to wear down resistance like water does stone. I believe we shouldn't start at the top. We should start the bottom, you know, where the majority of Singaporeans are … Singaporeans will say, "Ah, I'm just one person. What difference do I make?" But like I said, you as an individual, being openly out as a gay person, project a normalized image of what gay people should be and in that sense, break stereotypes because that shifts the image [of homosexuality] from that [portrayed in the] media.

Nick's enthusiasm about NS and his citizenship illustrate my last point: NS occupies such a central position in the conception of Singaporeanness that a (dis)like of NS often parallels a (lack of a) sense of national belonging. David finds NS abusive and, not surprisingly, said he feels alienated. His partner, Chor Pharn, professed otherwise. He enjoyed his NS and, working now as a civil servant in the international trade ministry, he witnesses and appreciates the hard work the government puts in to attract critical foreign investments:

> When I went to Shanghai, and I came back … Then I could actually understand how hard it is to run a small city, a small country, given such incredible challenges around it … And I started respecting what they were doing here … because jobs are really hard to come by.

Unlike David, Chor Pharn feels he belongs. Likewise, Nick feels the same.

Conclusion

In this chapter, the notion of cultural citizenship was invoked to analyze gay men's experiences in the Singaporean military. Firstly, these experiences illustrated the idea of illiberal pragmatism discussed in this volume's Introduction. A conscripted military such as Singapore's is already always illiberal, and its strongly heteronormative environment only accentuates the sense of oppression. Yet, actual performance often trumps ideologies. Even flamboyantly 'gay' soldiers can thrive in the military by satisfying the high standards expected of them. In turn, this primacy of actual performance substantiates my second observation: the State determines the contours of Singaporean cultural citizenship and Singaporeans react only to those strictures that work against their interests. Gay men cannot refuse the State's demands for NS. By performing well, however, these men can manipulate military pragmatism to challenge the misconceptions of homosexuality held by ignorant colleagues. Subsequently, these colleagues may abandon their prejudices to make the military gay-friendlier and more conducive for feelings of national belonging to develop.

5

Transnational Lesbian Identities

Lessons from Singapore?

Shawna Tang

Introduction

Lesbians in Asia have come under scholarly attention within the study of non-normative sexualities. This is due to the theoretical insistence on including accounts of non-Western sexualities and sexual identities that disrupt hegemonic Western practices and meanings as embodied by the globalised lesbian and gay subject. Understandings of sexuality, as this claim goes, have been dominated by Anglo-American images of the 'out' gay person with a fixed and unitary identity who has access to particular sexual rights and freedoms. This conception casts sexuality as an autonomous and anterior aspect of identity, and at the same time, elides the different meanings and expectations placed on sexuality in other contexts. As and where alternative conceptions of what it means to be lesbian and gay emerge, these are indexed against a Western developmental teleology that renders these sexual variations as 'premodern', 'inauthentic', 'not legitimate' or simply 'not lesbian and gay enough', much to the chagrin of Western and non-Western scholars studying sexualities outside the West.[1]

Ethnographic studies of female same-sex relations have appeared across Asia, complicating and contributing to this core debate in sexuality studies. These include monographs on female non-normative sexual identities and practices in Japan, India, Indonesia, Hong Kong, Thailand and Taiwan.[2] Further exemplary research focusing on lesbians in Asian contexts can be found in Wieringa, Blackwood and Bhaiya's (2007) collection, as well as Khor and Kamano's (2006) edited volume. These works attest to the burgeoning intellectual interest in Asian women's non-normative sexualities.

Lesbians in Singapore?

The case of Singapore, however, is strangely missing within these accounts. This anomaly was particularly evident in *AsiaPacifiQueer* which sought to reclaim academic province from "western-trained experts" and resist "drawing on imported theory to account for local sexual and gender cultures" in the Asia Pacific (Martin et al., 2008: 1). Inside this collection, Singapore was featured briefly in the introductory chapter as an emerging site of queer intellectualism and singled out as the 'queer Mecca of Asia' (Martin et al., 2008: 13). Yet, the case of Singapore was left out subsequently, even though Japan, Thailand and Taiwan, the other three Asian contexts featured alongside Singapore in the introduction, made interesting research contributions to the collection. Several of these studies paid critical attention to the experiences of lesbians in Taiwan (Silvio, 2008), the *toms and dees* in Thailand (Sinnott, 2004) and the tomboys in Hong Kong (Kam, 2008; Tong, 2008). If these works exemplify scholarly interventions into the Western-dominated universe of lesbian and gay studies from the geographically-defined discursive spaces of Asian queer sexualities, then Singapore's absence from these academic arsenals is significant. Might the 'modern' Singaporean lesbian and her immaculate mimicry of Westernised ways be seen as poor counter evidence to global gay colonisation?

This chapter is an anthropological analysis of this question. It argues the case that Singapore warrants attention precisely because of its 'cultural location' as one of, if not the most, globalised Asian city. Yet, the context of Singapore caught between postcoloniality and neoliberal globalisation is different from Western societies. Correspondingly, there is little evidence of the desire for Western affiliations among local lesbians, even as they seem to mimic Anglo-US forms of sexual identity. Instead, their seemingly globalised sexual subjectivities are shot through with local meanings and practices conditioned by the postcolonial state. Even as lesbians in Singapore tap onto the global circulation of discourse on gay rights, desires and freedoms in forming their sexual subjectivities, these delocalised conceptions are reconfigured in a specific national context, producing distinct sexual identities and practices.

The question thus arises: if women's same-sex experiences in Singapore do not offer a 'natural' site of resistance or opposition to the globalising identity politics of sexuality, nor display any affiliations to a global gay discourse, how might one account for local lesbian subjectivities within this discourse? In what follows, this chapter situates the theorisation of lesbian subjectivities in Singapore within the 'transnational turn' in feminist sexuality scholarship, and then turns to the empirical reality of lesbian lives in the postcolonial context to illustrate how Singaporean lesbians embody a more complicated model of transnational sexuality that neither assumes a position of local resistance nor global gay embodiment, but a contradictory, complicit and contingent negotiation of the local and global. The emergence of such 'transnational' lesbian identities, argued in the concluding analysis, problematises the postcolonial elites' naturalisation of non-normative sexualities in Singapore as Western afflictions.

Transnationality, Materiality and the Postcolonial State

The term 'transnational' has gained contemporary currency within feminist cultural studies of sexual identities that attend to the inequities of globalisa-tion through the focus on female sexual specificities in non-Western contexts. Theoretically, this work aligns itself with that "transnational turn" (Povinelli and Chauncey, 1999: 439) within the scholarship, particularly that shift in the usage of terms from 'global' to 'transnational' to assuage the asymmetric flow of sexual meanings presumed in the globalisation process (Grewal and Kaplan, 1994). The transnational, as opposed to the global, disrupts uni-linear flows in such a way that "the 'global' and the 'local' thoroughly infiltrate each other"(Blackwood, 2005: 221). Such a formulation crosscuts the problematic binaries of West and non-West, modernity and tradition, liberation and oppres-sion that persistently mark the global-local divide (Kim-Puri, 2005). When such movements are traced in conjunction with historical processes and power relations, the 'transnational' could signal "cultural and national difference" (Grewal and Kaplan, 2001: 666), not just as forms of resistance, but as sites from which new sexual subjects and sites of power are produced.

This chapter makes the case that lesbian subjectivities in Singapore provide a rich field site for the illustration and elaboration of transnational sexuali-ties, and the scholarship has been remiss in omitting the case of Singapore. Through an ethnographic inquiry into the lives of working and middle class Singaporean lesbians, this chapter highlights how the women strategically access and appropriate local and global cultural resources that render their bodies as sites of transnational flows of sexual meanings. The complexity of these transnational circuits is comprehended through the empirical narratives of lesbians in Singapore. This work therefore relies on a critical empiricism that restores the subject within transnational studies that tend to "read social life off external social forms—flows, circuits, circulations of people, capital, and culture—without any model of subjective mediation", when, as Povinelli and Chauncey remind, it is the "travail of the subject, fashioned far afield of herself, that globalization has yet to track" (1999: 445).

Implicit in this transnational analysis of sexualities is therefore the material-ity of lesbian lives, shaped as they are by class location, the political economy and power structures. Theorising these differences adds a material dimension to the transnational frame, addressing one of its most persistent criticism: that the cultural is often privileged over the material in transnational cultural studies (Kim-Puri, 2005: 143) as if social life is produced through cultural representations and discourses without regard for how material conditions shape the reception of these cultural meanings. This is to say, comprehending local sexualities in a globalising era entails examining how these sexualities articulate with both discursive and material productions of that particular locale. By turning to the empirical realities of lesbians in Singapore, this chapter reveals how subjects make sense of their sexual practices and identities through both cultural logics as well as social and economic structures that mediate their sexual subjectivities. The intersections of the cultural and material dimensions produce contingent forms of a 'reverse discourse' evident in the women's reconfiguration of the everyday, which this ethnographic inquiry addresses.

In order to understand the production of local lesbian subjectivities, the historical specificity of Singapore and the postcolonial state is embedded as both a material and ideological structure in the creation of lesbian subjectivities. The postcolonial state, as a number of scholars note (Blackwood, 2002; Boellstorff, 2007; Grewal and Kaplan, 2001), has been overlooked within a simplifying transnational equation that links the formation of non-normative sexual identities to global and cultural flows. However, Grewal and Kaplan remind "what we are really grappling with here is not just representation; it is also the emergence of new forms of governmentality with an entire repertoire of strategies, regulatory practices, and instrumentalities linking the State to bodies" (2001: 672). Cultural contexts for sexual subjects, as Boellstorff also points out, are 'often national in character', and such a conception gives way to an "understanding of how most nation-states make underwriting normative heterosexuality central to their practices of governance and ideologies of belonging, and how in the process they inadvertently help people conjure 'alternative' sexualities and desires" (2007: 22). In analysing "sexual tensions" in contemporary Singapore, Oswin called for a shift in analytic attention away from the coloniser-colonised binary to the "postcolony" wherein postcolonial governors are "key actors in the regulation of sexuality in the era of independence" (2010: 130). This paper builds on Oswin's argument that the postcolonial elites have been complicit in extending the colonial regulation of sexuality to "civilize the rest of the colonised community" (2010: 131), rendering Singapore a case for a "more complicated model of transnational relations in which power structures, asymmetries and inequalities become the conditions of possibility of new subjects" (Grewal and Kaplan, 2001: 671). Bringing the postcolony and a critical empiricism to bear on transnational sexualities enables a re-imagination of a historicised, contextualised transversality in which the material and cultural dimensions are conjoined to shape unique sexual subjectivities.

Singapore Lesbian Population: Terms and Methods

As much as lesbian lives are the focus of this study, the interest is not in lesbians per se but in how they come to their sexual subjectivities in a locale intersected by postcoloniality and globalisation. This chapter looks at the formation of lesbian subjectivities in postcolonial Singapore starting from the mid-1990s, when the Internet made visible and crystallised same-sex identities in the same way the development of information technology gave rise to queer cultures around East Asia (Berry et al., 2003). As one informant earnestly reminded, "You must remember, nothing happened before the Internet!" The birth of non-normative female identities and forms of selfhood in Singapore could therefore be viewed as one delivered through the city-state's umbilical connection to the global system. The State's rapid postcolonial modernisation programme and the 'plugging in' of Singapore into global cultural flows mean that local lesbian subjectivities are shaped by global forms. At the same time, local lesbian sexual subjectivities, typical of Singaporean subject positions formed within the particular postcolonial condition of Singapore, are heavily inflected by the logics and rhetoric of postcolonial governance based on what Audrey Yue in her introduction to this volume identifies as the "illiberal pragmatics of survival". On the one hand, the State continues with the illiberal practice of preserving the British colonial statute, Section 377A,[3] a law widely interpreted to make homosexuality illegal in Singapore. On the other hand, 'pragmatism' and 'survival' requires the state to support an unrelenting project of neoliberal economic growth, which, as Yue notes has created variegated space for LGBT expression. Thus, Singapore holds the distinction of being one of the last few ex-British colonies in the region maintaining the colonial law, which criminal-ises homosexuality. Yet, it is also regarded as "one of Asia's gayest city" (quote taken from Chan, 2008: 305). It is from within this ambivalent socio-cultural milieu that local lesbian sexual subjectivities have emerged. What happens then when such localised subject positions meet dominant global understand-ings of what it means to be lesbian?

The answer to this question can be gleaned from the ethnographic data col-lected from in-depth interviews with twenty individuals during 2009–10. In addition, I spent time with some of these informants, observing and participat-ing in their informal social circles. The participants come from two main socio-economic backgrounds: Chinese, mainly middle-class lesbians involved in local activism, most of whom are tertiary-educated; and the everyday middle and working class lesbian, including a minority number of Indian, Malay and Eurasian women, who have received at least secondary-level education and have little or no affiliation to activist organisations. The socio-economic makeup of this group, though unrepresentative, roughly reflects the composition of the lesbian community at large. I listened to the life stories of these women and asked questions about their sense of identity as queer women living in Singapore. Apart from the activists whose names are real, all other names in this chapter are pseudonyms and details of my interactions with individual informants have been altered for confidentiality.

I use the terms 'lesbian' and 'queer' to refer to my participants generally. Applying these English terms to women who desire women in Singapore avoids the sort of issues that researchers run into when comprehending non-Western contexts.[4] In Singapore, where English is the *lingua franca*, all the participants of this study identify with these terms. I also use 'gay' as a shorthand form of referring to the local homosexual community as a whole, consistent with how 'gay' is popularly used in the Singapore context.

Originating from activists' networks in the US, the global signifier 'queer' appears on the mission statements of local activist organisations, on their websites and events outreach collaterals. The appropriation of 'queer' seems unremarkable given that Singaporeans speak English and could easily borrow terms and definitions already developed in the global gay ecumene. However, in making sense of how global terms circulate within local knowledge, I was struck by how little 'queer' means to the individual lesbian. Most participants in this study seem to assume 'lesbian' as an identity more easily, given it means women loving women in plain English terms, but found it harder to connect to the term 'queer'. As one participant remarked, "Queer? No way! I am not weird. Why do I have to be the abnormal one compared to heterosexual society? I think people in the English-speaking world should know that 'queer' holds negative connotations. All this negativity is self-imposed!" Ironically, the meaning this participant attached to the term was completely at odds with globalised understandings of 'queer' as an inclusive identity category. She nonetheless provides the first clue as to how local queer activists and individual lesbians selectively respond to and identify with the global gay discourse, shaped as they are by their social locations. Already crucially connected to the global discourse through language access, the usage of these linguistic terms does not signify for them global or Western identifications. The women, both activists and individual lesbians, sought instead to reinterpret or redefine Western categories according to what made sense for them, as the following two sections will show.

Transnational Local Activists

Lesbian activist organisations started to emerge from the late 1990s onwards amid transitions in the socio-political sphere. The handover of Prime Ministership from Lee Kuan Yew to Goh Chok Tong in 1990 held hopes for greater acceptance of lesbian and gay subjects, as Goh himself had promised a 'more compassionate, kinder, gentler' society (1990). For the first time in 2003, homosexuality was broached officially when Goh spoke about the appointment of gay Singaporeans to "sensitive positions" in the civil service (Elegant, 2003:

4). Indeed, under Goh's tenure as Prime Minister, the social scene for lesbian and gay Singaporeans was observed to be "fairly open" (Au, 2009: 407).

By the early 2000s, gay and lesbian establishments such as bars, bathhouses and karaoke lounges drew local crowds and foreigners; annual gay parties organised by the largest, Singapore-owned gay Internet portal in Asia, attracted thousands of foreign visitors to the country and was nominated for a national tourism award; State-subsidised film and theatre frequently portrayed queer themes; and on the Internet, lesbian women and gay men developed networks with both local and global queer communities.

At the same time, however, a conservative socio-political climate clamps heavily on the community. Following religious and conservative backlash, the Prime Minister jettisoned his statements on gay civil servants, clarifying that his comments "do not signal any change in policy that would erode the moral standards of Singapore, or our family values" (Goh, 2003). The gay parties were banned in 2005 after four years, following the Health Minister's suggestion that foreign gay visitors at these parties were 'seeding' HIV in the local community (Balaji, 2005). Meanwhile, Section 377A stands as the legal encoding of the postcolonial state's anxiety towards homosexuality. At the National Day Rally speech, Goh (2003) directly addressed, "Let me stress, I do not encourage or endorse a gay lifestyle. Singapore is still a traditional and conservative Asian society". The juridico-discursive deployment of sexuality, as Foucault (1980) showed, is of course one that operates through a multiplicity of mechanisms, serving to consolidate State power in the end. By yoking the gay community to the discourse of 'conservative', 'Asian' values, Goh reinvoked the PAP's unwitting reverse-Orientalist discourse that deemed Westernisation as undesirable in Singapore. Within the postcolonial State's moral discourse of 'good' Asian culture versus 'bad' Western culture, homosexual bodies were naturalised as symbolic bearers of moral degeneracy in the West. Despite the explicit legal and social censures of lesbian and gay subjects in Singapore, they have not been as much banished out of the postcolonial state's imagined nation, in Anderson's sense (1983), as they have been subalternised at the sidelines of society. The subaltern class, as Spivak (1988) has argued elsewhere, is imperative to both colonial rule and postcolonial nation-building. In the case of Singapore, State ideology re-functions lesbian and gay subjects as subaltern structures to bulwark against the tide of global disjunctive flows, thereby ratifying the postcolonial elite's monopoly of cultural capital.[5]

Nevertheless, lesbian activism emerged within this shifting socio-political context, borrowing elements from the global gay discourse to articulate their transnational visions for the local community. Although their early involvement was with AIDS activism or the pioneer gay advocacy group, People Like Us, which were largely dominated by men, the women went on to establish organisations that addressed the specific needs of queer women. Eileena Lee is one; she founded RedQuEEn! in 1998, a mailing list to engage lesbians in Singapore. Apart from online discussions, RedQuEEn! also provides counselling, discussion groups, and social networking channels. Another leading activist, Jean Chong, founded Sayoni, an advocacy group with a mission to "empower queer women towards greater involvement in the community" (quote taken from Sayoni's website). Articulate and outspoken, the women activists are educated and well-travelled. They participate in humanitarian activism or attend international queer conferences, and are closely aligned to global queer circuits. Yet, the women's individual subjectivities seem to be constituted through localised forms of knowledge production rather than through any global gay discourse.

In the first place, the lesbian leaders I spoke to did not see themselves as 'activists' despite their contributions and involvement. The women's self-effacement did not stem from fears of political reprisal: the activists I spoke to were either insistent that I use their real names in my research or were indifferent to my use of pseudonyms. "The government are aware we are around", one informant said to me, "it doesn't matter." Indeed, for a nation with nearly ubiquitous Internet access, information on lesbian activists and their organisations are easily accessible online.

Lesbian activists explained to me that their involvement with the local community was the outcome of their personal struggles and search for clarifications on what it means to be gay in Singapore. A few lamented the lack of local role models. "We only had Western role models back then", said one informant, "I had to take things in my own hands." Western understandings were sought through the Internet and books because local resources were scarce, if not non-existent. "Where else to find literature?" asked Eileena rhetorically. For Jean, it was a matter of:

> going through difficult times, not having role models, not having supportive resources. I also saw a lot of conflicted gay people. I can't sit around and wait for people. I got sick of waiting.

Lesbian activist subjectivities were in this sense crystallised around addressing specific local needs rather than by notions of a global discourse. Unlike diasporic, Western-educated, Indian lesbian feminists who develop activist networks in India by drawing on their transnational experiences, ideas and connections (Bhaskaran, 2004), the lesbian activists in this study are mostly born and bred in Singapore. Apart from short-term holidays, student overseas exchange stints or work-related travel, most of the women received education in Singapore and had spent the majority of their lives in the city-state.

Even as local lesbian activists look to the queer movements and literatures of Europe and the US for role models and resources, these global knowledge productions of homosexuality are translated locally. One clear evidence rests with, ironically, their understanding of the Western tropes 'coming out' and 'gaining visibility'. During an interview with an international women's advocacy group, Eileena, was quoted as saying:

> If all of us gay people can just come out to our parents or work, that's half the problem solved! I can't make people do anything. I can, as myself, give visibility to something that has been rendered invisible. I can provide positive visibility to oppose the negatives and, hopefully, normalise homosexuality (as cited in Marte, 2006).

However, in my conversation with Eileena, I found her politicised views laced with a certain pragmatism about coming out in Singapore. I had suggested to her that individual lesbian women in Singapore generally avoided coming out to their families not out of fear, but out of a sense of duty and protectiveness towards their elderly parents. "They don't need to know", individual lesbian respondents had told me. Then Eileena asked with concern, "Until when? Until when, you know? It's very hard to live like that." Being closeted within the family was not judged by this activist as an act of political capitulation but posed as a genuine question of how one might pragmatically live with one's family.

Out in the City-State: Individual Lesbian Subjectivities

It is indeed impractical to lead closeted gay lives in Singapore. In a tightly populated country where land is scarce and property-ownership is expensive, lesbian and gay Singaporeans often share close quarters with their families and have limited opportunities for expressing their sexualities. Up to eighty percent of Singapore's resident population live in, what is called, HDB flats (Housing and Development Board, 2008), a State-subsidised provision materially and ideologically tied to the aims of population management and its heteronormative logic, which privileges the nuclear, heterosexual family and marginalises the individual gay Singaporean. For example, one requirement to qualify for newly built HDB apartments is a "family nucleus" (taken from HDB's website) configured fundamentally around heterosexual marriage. Single citizens are not allowed to purchase new State-subsidised flats, but are eligible to buy market-determined resold units on the condition that they are at least thirty-five years of age or living with their parents, among other requirements. As a consequence of the State's national housing policy, the majority of the queer women I spoke to live in public housing apartments with their parents and mitigate their lives within the structures of the family.

Without the Western historical trajectory of leaving familial homes to establish new lives and new sexual identities, these women find their own ways to assert and experience their gay identity. Several women reported that they live with their partners in family homes, either bringing their partners back home or moving into the partner's family home. None reported any particular difficulties with this living arrangement, although most harbour the ambition of moving out in order to lead their lives "more fully". As Das who identifies as masculine, said to me:

> My parents don't mind me bringing my girlfriend back. To them, she is my friend and we share my room. Sometimes my mother looks unhappy but she doesn't say anything. Of course they know we share one single bed, but sometimes I go out and sleep on the couch so they don't get suspicious. When she's around, I also make sure that we spend more time in the living room. After a few months, they got used to her. Now when we have family gatherings, even with my uncles and aunties, it is *normal* for us to go together. It is quite obvious to my entire family that I am not straight, but nobody wants to talk about it.

Intrigued by this respondent's complex performance of heterosexuality within the home—in a contradictory re-enactment of a 'straight' person by avoiding intimate displays at home as well as being a part of a normative 'heterosexual' couple by their involvement in the extended family—I asked what if it all came out? "Maybe they will chase me out?" Das replied. "I don't know. If housing becomes easier in Singapore, I guess a lot more gay people would come out," Das ruminated. Midway through our conversation, Das stood up as her girlfriend, Lysa, approached our table. As Lysa, immaculately dressed in feminine clothes, took her seat next to Das, it struck me that Das' parents could not have possibly averted their eyes from the observable, even stereotypical, fact of their couple-hood.

Conditioned by the material reality of living in Singapore, the Singaporean lesbian treads in and out of the closet of the family, one that is also constructed around State ideology linking family values to national piety. Characteristic of postcolonial societies, the family in Singapore is fundamentally constituted as a metonym of the nation and the basis of national development. Unsurprisingly then, the domestic unit has been a central object of social regulation (Salaff, 1988) and the continual subject of state rhetoric, as Tan (2007) analysed of National Day Rally speeches. Within the moral economy of the State's national development programme and its ideological construction of the Singapore family, a particular heteronormative model of the family is valorised as homosexuality is demonised. In the words of a government minister, "If more Singaporeans end up embracing this sexual orientation openly, the foundation of the strong family, which is the core building block of Singapore ... would be weakened" (Lim, 2000).

Insightful research has shown how the heteronormative family is for the Asian queer subject an 'impossible hideout' (Davies, 2010), a site where queer Asian women work safely within the structures of patriarchy (Dasgupta, 2009) and operate undetected within familial circles (Gopinath, 2005). The Singaporean lesbian, even as she pragmatically navigates within the heteronormative family, is not like her Indonesian female counterpart who sometimes marry heterosexually to appease her family, pursue same-sex relationships clandestinely or put on hold her same-sex desires indefinitely (Blackwood, 2008; Davies, 2010). Neither is she like the individualised Western gay subject, bound as she is by familial obligation, material conditions and social mechanisms, to live within the family. Yet, the so-called closet she is locked in is not quite the same as that of her Western counterpart. In it, she operates not quite so invisibly, and acceptance within the family, though tacit, appears largely to be taken for granted.

Queer women in Singapore generally desire coming out, which is a reflection of their Westernised subjectivities. But this desire is expressed in terms of a particular cultural logic, not according to the formularised Western model of coming out in widening "concentric spheres of decreasing familiarity" (Boellstorff, 2005: 34)—first to oneself, then to family, friends, colleagues and so on until one is completely 'out' in all spheres of life and achieves a unified sense of self. Applying this Western logic to Singaporean lesbian subject positions is to forever estrange the women from their sense of selfhood. But the sense of self-confidence and self-control run through all of the women's narratives. The women I spoke to were out in discrete spheres—to specific people, in certain places, at special times. But quite consistently, the women were not 'out' within the closer sphere of the family where they bring their partners home. I was struck by their complex and contradictory, yet clear and logical, assertion of their sexual identities. Yuen, who has been in a long-term lesbian relationship, illustrates this:

> Being surrounded by people who accept you and who accept your relationship, like my partner's parents and her friends, makes a lot of difference. It begins to give me courage that it is okay to be in this relationship, to enjoy it now and not be ashamed about it.

Having said that, Yuen then expressed very little affiliation with the global gay discourse on sexual identity and rights, which was surprising of someone who had lived three years overseas in a foreign country:

> To me it's really something that is very personal and very private. I don't need to assert my sexual identity to the whole word. I don't want people to know as well. I think that it is irrelevant. *I think that who I am and how I contribute to society is sufficient. I still can contribute to the economy of the society and to the community. I can still be a functional person. I don't want to fight for*

gay rights or participate in certain demonstrations to force everyone to accept it.
It's none of their business to tell me what is right and what is wrong in my
private life. I can do what I want! (Author's italics)

Although insisting on the rights of her private life, the reasons behind Yuen's logic and her particular language fall in line with the postcolonial State's rhetoric of 'national survival'. If Singapore were to survive, as the political rhetoric goes, every citizen must pull in the same direction of public spiritedness, discipline and self-motivation to make a living (Chua, 1995). These were the very qualities that Yuen speaks of in defining her sexual subjectivity. She carried on to say:

> I feel that my rights are not deprived. I am not deprived of the education I want to pursue. I am not deprived of the resources I want to have. If I want a car, a big house, a certain status, I go out and get it, and I get it! I am not being deprived of that because I am gay.

Yuen's comments are also illustrative of how the State's meritocratic ideology is deeply ingrained, keeping alive the "Singapore Dream of social improvement for oneself, one's family, and the society as whole" (Brown et al., 2001: 257). Indeed, for Yuen and the women I spoke to, their sexual subjectivities seem powerfully infused with State rhetoric, including, ironically, its valorisation of the heterosexual nuclear family and its construction of homosexuality as a social ill. "For this relationship, it's good to just protect my parents from it", one informant told me. She explained further:

> It's not that I think being gay is shameful. It is deviant, out of the social norms. I don't think they can take this deviant act. I just want to protect them. All they need to know is that this daughter is taking care of herself, who is striving, who is doing well professionally and in all aspects of her life. That is all they need to know.

Western concepts of homosexuality, particularly that of coming out, are in these instances, clearly reconfigured through State discourse and cultural interpretations of what it means to be lesbian, and it is these intersections that produce the transnational Singaporean lesbian.

A Queer Turn

As I reflected on my informants' sexual subjectivities, wondering how much they spoke for queer women in Singapore, my attention was drawn to a particular Facebook furore. An activist had posted the comments of a Singaporean actress, well known in the local lesbian circle but known to the general public as the heterosexual wife of *Phua Chu Kang*, a Singaporean caricature in a popular family sitcom. Sharing her views on the gay community's public rally called 'Pink Dot',[6] the actress was quoted as saying, "My take on Pink Dot will probably offend a lot of people. I feel that it's just for the young gay boys and girls to have fun. They don't even know the message behind the unity" (Koh, 2010). Her politicised message on unity reproduced the global gay discourse, but then she went on to say how being gay is contingent. "As a gay person, you have to earn respect. You must be of use to your society first, before being gay" (Koh, 2010). Her latter views were considered by many lesbians and gay men as an affront to the local gay community, evident in the number of outraged online comments the activist's post elicited. "I really don't agree that anyone need to earn their right to be gay", read one comment (quote taken from Facebook discussion, 12 August 2010). The actress' views and the reverberations it caused, nonetheless, demonstrates that queer knowledge circulates unevenly on transnational lesbian bodies despite the seemingly totalising global subject positions they represent or are made to represent by the postcolonial State.

The ethnographic data supports the conclusion that lesbian subjectivities, rather than being thoroughly Westernised, are also forged through the ideological discourses of the postcolonial state, which produces complex, contingent and contradictory negotiations of what it means to be lesbian in Singapore. This reliability of this conclusion finds support in Yue's concurrent work, which demonstrates how lesbian consumption practices in Singapore's global media hub create "a local lesbian identity without assimilating into the liberal Western discourse of sexual rights and emancipation" (2011: 250). Any easy naturalisation of gay subject positions as 'global' or 'Western' as opposed to 'conservative' or 'Asian' are, on these bases, invalid.

Characteristic of the political culture and social practices of Singaporeans, queer women in Singapore appear, above all, pragmatic about their sexual subjectivities. In their negotiation of the everyday, they take in stride the challenges of their same-sex desires and work out how they might lead their lives as lesbian women even within the most heterosexual of domains, the Singapore family. However, such pragmatism, as Yue (2007) argued elsewhere, cannot be reduced to a 'whatever works' attitude or be merely understood as a response to social crisis and problems. Instead, as the women go about 'doing gay' (Yue, 2007), visibly within the family and out in society, they consciously and creatively destablize asymmetrical knowledge productions of what it means to be lesbian. Drawing pragmatically from both global and local cultural resources, queer women in Singapore embody a particular transnational sexual subjectivity that enables them to re-fashion their sexual selfhoods as a form of 'reverse discourse' against the powers that define them. Singaporean lesbian practices may very well be the realistic undercurrent of queer liberalism in non-Western contexts. As Yue (2007) argues similarly, therein lies the potential of pragmatism as a form of creative democracy.[7] The women's everyday experiences and experiments of 'doing gay' is the invisible and not so invisible constitution of democratic social action. Therefore in Singapore, we have this peculiar phenomenon of globally conscious lesbian and gay citizens who appear politically apathetic and quite content to lead their individual lives. Yet, it is they, and not the parties, parades and politics of the out, global gay subject, who make Singapore the queer Mecca it really is.

6

Both Contagion and Cure

Queer Politics in the Global City-State

Simon Obendorf

Introduction

Alex Au has described the regulation of queer rights and cultural expression in Singapore as being unpredictable, even arcane, in nature. He writes of "reading the tea leaves" (Au, 2007b): of attempting to extrapolate from official pronouncements the range of queer identities, spaces and behaviours that will be tolerated by Singaporean state managers. Au is just one of many commentators to identify the opaque nature of the Singaporean authorities' response to queers' claims for social space, legal reform and cultural visibility within the Singaporean polity. Scholarship on queer Singapore has identified how the regulatory and policing powers of the Singapore government give it a unique capacity to coerce, surveil and intervene in varied aspects of queer life (Lim, 2004; Ng KK, 2008; Ng and Wee, 2006; Tan and Lee, 2007; Leong, 1995, 1997). Yet, as the voices assembled in this volume clearly attest, queer Singaporean lives, cultures, politics and passions *have* been able to find spaces and opportunities for expression. In most cases, they have done so with the knowledge and tacit consent of the authorities. As a result, Au has described government policies towards homosexuality as "full of absurdities", pointing to the contradictions inherent in condoning certain aspects of gay and lesbian life and culture while continuing to implement laws and regulations that criminalise male homosex, censor queer cultural visibility and close off opportunities for political reform (Au, as cited in Youngblood, 2007).

This chapter offers one explanation for the ambiguities Au identifies. I argue that official Singaporean approaches to queer politics, cultural expression and civic participation cannot be adequately evaluated unless we understand that they are shaped by Singapore's unique position within the realms of international affairs: it is a sovereign state entity whose compact territory is simultaneously—and practically exclusively—occupied by a singular urban environment designed to function and be consumed (by both citizen and foreigner) as a global city. To analyse the nature and future possibilities of queer politics in contemporary Singapore, we must remain critically aware that in today's world order, Singapore stands alone in its status as a "global city-state" (Murray and Perera, 1996; Hack, Margolin and Delaye, 2010; Olds and Yeung, 2004).[1]

In managing the demands of this distinctive status, the Singapore government has positioned the country as an assertive postcolonial nation-state, engaged in the quest for national and regional security and international stature. At the same time, governmental policy has been to develop urban infrastructure, economic facilities and social spaces designed to facilitate global flows of capital, trade and commerce and to provide an idealised playground for a transnationally mobile cosmopolitan elite. In the sections that follow, I examine how the implementation of these two (sometimes complementary, often divergent) visions of Singapore's role and nature has impacted upon queer Singaporeans. I firstly explore how queer politics and lifestyles figure in the narratives of global city development before moving on to analyse how narratives that link homosexuality to compromised citizenship and threats to national security have limited queer politics and empowerment in Singapore. I identify the tension between Singapore's status as both global city and nation-state as giving rise to the government's illiberal and seemingly paradoxical regulation of Singaporean queer lives. Here I extend Yue's (2007a) analysis of the illiberal yet pragmatic way in which socio-legal regulation of homosexuality has developed in Singapore, by placing it within the frame of Singapore's preoccupations with international security, global competitiveness and the management of transcultural influences. In doing so, I also provide a broader context for many of the other contributions to this volume, by signposting the importance Singaporean government and society accord to particular understandings of Singapore's role and position within the arenas of international affairs and global economics. My contention is that analysis of the socio-political affairs of a small, outward-looking and trade-reliant state such as Singapore must give due heed to issues deriving from the state's foreign policy, international relations and enmeshment with the flows of globalization. The chapter concludes by looking at future possibilities for political reform, arguing that while some positive changes may well be foreseen due to Singapore's project of self-transformation into a global-city, the particular nature and spatial organisation of queer practices and politics that the Singaporean state is prepared to tolerate in the name of global competitiveness could also act to divide the Singapore queer community and perpetuate its disempowerment.

Queer Politics and the Global City Narrative

Since the earliest days of its colonial settlement, Singapore has been progressively developed into a key hub for flows of transnational trade and commerce

(Chua, 1998: 982). Singapore's post-independence leadership has vigorously pursued this project. Following Singapore's exit from the Malaysian federation in 1965, Foreign Minister S. Rajaratnam stated that "[i]f we view Singapore's future not as a regional city but as a Global City, then the smallness of Singapore, the absence of a hinterland or raw materials and a large domestic market are not fatal or insurmountable handicaps" (Rajaratnam, as cited in Acharya, 2008: 130). He went on to lay out Singapore's claim to membership within an elite global network of cities linked by the technologies of globalization and acting as key hubs in the transnational circulation of people, products, capital and ideas (Rajaratnam, as cited in Acharya, 2008: 128–30).

Rajaratnam's comments are echoed in the extensive literature that has since emerged on the emergence, functioning and role of global cities in contemporary forms of worldwide economic and cultural exchange (Friedmann, 1986; Sassen, 2001; Gross and Hambleton, 2007; Kotkin, 2006; Taylor, 2004; Clark, 2003; Scott, 2001; Isin, 2000). Summarising this thinking, *Foreign Policy* magazine wrote in 2010 that a global city is defined by "how much sway a city has over what happens beyond its borders—its influence on and integration with global markets, cultures, and innovation … everything from a city's business activity, human capital and information exchange to its cultural experience and political engagement" (Foreign Policy 2010: 124). The recent history of Singapore has been marked by continual processes of elite-led urban and social refashioning designed to ensure that the city remains among the leading such cities worldwide (Low, 1998, 2002; Murray and Perera, 1996; Olds and Yeung, 2004; Sim et al., 2003; Yeoh and Chang, 2001). Earlier stages of this process largely involved physical development, with major infrastructural investments designed to support the movement of goods, capital and people and an *entrepôt* economy. Tremewan (1994) has also suggested that many of the Singapore government's domestic policies in areas such as housing, public transit, conscription and vocational education contribute to the global city aspirations of the state, being at least partially motivated by a desire to provide local and multinational corporations with an easily-accessible, healthy, disciplined, productive and well-trained pool of labour from which to recruit.

In recent years, however, Singaporean policy-makers' understanding of the global city narrative appears to have experienced a marked shift. Singapore now seems to see its global city aspirations as requiring interventions into the realm of culture. A series of governmental reports and programmes have argued that Singapore needs to assume roles as a "Renaissance City" and a "Global City for the Arts" (T. C. Chang, 2000; Ministry of Information and the Arts, 2000). Senior Minister Goh Chok Tong outlined these aspirations in a 2010 speech, explicitly linking Singapore's status as a successful hub for global finance and investment to its ability to provide a vibrant, lively and exciting lifestyle for Singaporean citizens, expatriates and tourists. He went on to laud the government's large investments in artistic and sporting infrastructure in attracting investment in the recreational, leisure and tourist sectors, and its success in drawing in high profile international sporting events and high-profile foreign artistic performers to Singapore (Goh, 2010).

The connections between attractive lifestyle and leisure opportunities, the smooth functioning of service-and knowledge-based economies and notions of international economic competitiveness have become a common basis for policies of urban planning and economic development in global cities around the world (Chiu, Ho and Lui, 1998; Huang, 2006; Kong, 2007; Ku and Tsui, 2009; Wu, 2004). In Singapore they have informed high levels of investment in arts and educational institutions, and creative and recreational infrastructure. Significantly, such investments (and the urban spaces that they bring in their train) are directed both domestically, to foster a sense of civic-national pride and particular lifestyle consumption practices within Singaporeans, and externally, to attract tourist visitors and highly skilled and globally mobile expatriate talent—especially in the financial, research and development sectors. They have also been understood as requiring a relaxation—if not a liberalization—of certain governmental and social codes of regulation in order to maximise the economic benefits such changes in the urban environment are designed to facilitate (da Cunha, 2010; Chang and Lee, 2003; Wee, 2002; Kong, 2000; Kwok and Low, 2002; Wong, Chong, and Millar, 2006; Chang and Yeoh, 1999).

Two key values—"cosmopolitanism" and "creativity"——now appear to provide the guiding logic for many of the policies underpinning Singapore's project of urban redevelopment and strategic global economic positioning. It is believed that the inculcation of these values within the Singapore populace will foster economic growth, attract investment and investors and promote cultures of risk-taking, entrepreneurship and innovation of benefit to the country's economic bottom-line. Government reports identify creative and artistic expression, improved educational opportunities aimed at creating a skilled, knowledge-based and entrepreneurial workforce, and a vibrant living environment designed to attract and retain a globally mobile pool of local and expatriate talent, as central to ensuring Singapore becomes globally renowned for its "high-skilled people, innovative economy, [and] distinctive global city" environment (Economic Strategies Committee, 2010). Cosmopolitanism and creativity are not just the desired *outcomes* of Singapore's urban and social redevelopment, they are also presented as the *means* of achieving Singapore's economic aspirations: an appropriate guide to behaviour and self-improvement for Singaporean subjects. For Singaporean policy makers, a competitive, creative and cosmopolitan global city must be populated by people who are "world ready, able to plug-and-play with confidence in the global economy" (Singapore 21 Committee, 1999: 45).

Sandercock (2006) characterises urban cosmopolitanism as being built around the encounter with difference that takes place within the city-space and the management of the competing, often conflicting, demands this places on space and resources. Discourses of cosmopolitanism (as they are understood in Singapore) have been seen as a way to provide locals with the skills needed to engage profitably with the external and the foreign, whether encountered at home or abroad.[2] As a government report puts it, the cosmopolitan Singaporean "is familiar with global trends and lifestyles and feels comfortable working and living in Singapore as well as overseas … [and with] social norms from around the world" (Singapore 21 Committee, 1999: 45).

For queer Singaporeans, there is much that is significant in Singapore's deployment of these twin tropes of cosmopolitanism and creativity. Urban economies have been identified as both the location and catalyst for queer politics, activism and social life (Aldrich, 2004; Bech, 1997; Betsky, 1997; D'Emilio, 1983). Tolerance for diversity, expressed as government policy and promoted as a desired ingredient of Singaporean subjectivity, would seem to hold out many possibilities for queer Singaporeans to articulate a place for themselves within the new urban environments of the global city and to participate fully within Singaporean economic and civic life. It would also seem to provide legitimate reasons for Singaporean authorities to justify a less punitively regulatory approach to queer individuals and groups within Singapore. Exploring such possibilities, Chris Tan has identified how economic and pragmatic understandings of cosmopolitanism lie behind the Singapore government's 2003 announcement of its willingness to hire openly gay civil servants, arguing that this represents a discursive conscription of queers into the state's cosmopolitanising processes (Tan, 2009). Such thinking is also detectable in the much-heralded decision to relax restrictions on bar-top dancing in Singaporean nightspots and to allow a French cabaret featuring nude female dancers to open in Singapore (Au, 2004; Hing, 2008). In each of these cases, the liberalisation of regulations to do with sexuality was justified to Singaporean publics in rationalist terms of how it would contribute to national economic objectives and fulfil governmental policy aspirations.

More importantly, the linking of notions of *creativity* with tolerance towards sexual minorities has brought Singapore officialdom increasingly into engagement with issues relating to homosexuality. The impetus for this can be traced to the work of urban theorists such as Richard Florida and economists such as Marcus Noland. Florida argues that high levels of tolerance for diversity and the ability to attract a "creative class" of residents and workers make it more likely that a city will succeed economically within the frameworks of global capitalism (Florida, 2002, 2005a, 2005b). Developing this point, he asserts that the presence of visible homosexual subcultures and the socio-political tolerance of sexual diversity within a city-space functions as a predictor of both the city's creative potential and its likelihood of economic success. Gays, he asserts, "are the canaries of the creative economy. Where gays are will be a community—a city or a region—that has the underlying preconditions that attract the creative class of people" (Florida, cited in Dreher, 2002: unpaginated). Under this logic, a city that is prepared to welcome and find civic space for sexual minorities will also have the requisite attributes to attract creative professionals in science, technology, research, design, finance, and the arts who will in turn contribute to economic growth. Similarly, Noland argues that social and political tolerance of homosexuality can be linked statistically to increased levels of foreign investment and higher sovereign bond ratings (Noland, 2004a, 2004b). The growing perception is that a successful global city will not merely structure and create many of the preconditions for the emergence of queer politics and cultures; it may actually *require* them.

Singaporean opinion leaders and political elites have been quick to embrace such logic. Terrell Carver writes that Singapore has

> embarked on a massive attempt to fulfil the hypothesis, articulated in the literature of business and management, that there is an important and imperative productive connection between regimes of sexual tolerance and the in-migration, development and retention of the 'creative class' in 'the city' (Carver, 2007).

Writing in *The Straits Times* in 2003, commentator Chua Mui Hoong unambiguously echoed such thinking: "If Singapore is serious about attracting smart, talented people, whether gay or not, many more bigger steps towards greater tolerance—and not just towards gays—must be made. Remember, this is not about gay rights. This is about economic competitiveness" (Chua, 2003). The *Far Eastern Economic Review* went so far as to proclaim on the cover of a 2004 issue that "gay rights make economic sense", flagging a lead story whose headline "Gay Asia: Tolerance Pays" was superimposed on a photograph of a government-sanctioned gay and lesbian dance party in Singapore (Fairclough, 2004a). Elsewhere, the *Wall Street Journal* reported approvingly on the economic reasons why Singapore was "getting rather gay friendly" (Fairclough, 2004b). The connections between culture, creativity and queer visibility are also apparent in the huge increase in the number of theatrical performances addressing queer themes being staged in Singapore by government funded troupes and with the consent of local censorship authorities (Lek and Obendorf, 2004).

By the time Lee Hsien Loong assumed the Singapore premiership in 2004, Singaporean queers appeared to have carved out a niche within (and to no small extent because of) the structures and processes of the global-city. A sophisticated and self-confident community of queer consumers inhabited the streets and shopping malls of Singapore's urban space. Gay and lesbian festivals and dance parties were regular occurrences, discotheques, bars and nightclubs provided social spaces for queers, lesbian and gay characters and issues were commonplace on the stages of Singapore's new creative arts venues, a gay street press was in its infancy and a range of sex-on-premises venues designed to facilitate male homosexual encounters were dotted about the island. Even the government-linked press had been prepared to concede the economic benefits of queer tourism and local patterns of queer cosmopolitan consumption (Chasing the pink dollar, 2003). From abroad, the commentators' consensus seemed to be that as Singapore enmeshed itself with the processes of economic and cultural globalization, and as its urban environment evermore-closely resembled other leading global cities worldwide, queer rights and cultural visibility would become increasingly assured (Levett, 2004; McGirk, 2004). The global city narrative, powered by the twin engines of creativity and cosmopolitanism, seemed to offer the potential of political reform, social visibility and belonging for Singaporean queers.

Keeping Things Straight

Of course, matters are not so clear-cut. Despite its courting of creative, cosmopolitan and even queer citizens and expatriates, and its assiduous project of urban self-reformation to those ends, Singapore's embrace of queer lives and politics remains at best strategic in nature and partial in extent. This is most apparent in the fact that Singapore retains its legal criminalisation of male homosex. This seems a paradoxical, even contrarian, stance for Singaporean legislators to adopt, running as it does in the face of the thinking that queers can and should be encouraged to play a key role in fostering national competitiveness within a world economy. Indeed, of 41 cities recently identified as "Alpha World Cities" (Globalization and World Cities Research Network, 2008), Singapore is conspicuous for being one of only two[3] whose authorities criminalise consensual male homosexual relations. Yet it continues to do so, even after a protracted debate over the issue in Singapore's parliament and media in 2007 (Sanders, 2009). It does so even in the face of evidence that its anti-queer policies and laws negatively impact perceptions of the country abroad and government attempts to attract and retain creative workers in line with policy goals (Panthera, 2008). The actor Sir Ian McKellen spoke out against Singapore's anti-sodomy legislation when in the country to perform in a production of *King Lear*. What should have been a major vindication of the government's policy of attracting high profile arts events and world-famous performers to demonstrate Singapore's cosmopolitanism, instead became a demonstration of how the warm welcome extended to an openly gay performer such as McKellen was contradicted by the existence of Singapore's legal restrictions on homosexuality. Addressing comments from Lee Kuan Yew that it would be difficult to repeal the anti-sodomy laws due to the conservative nature of the Singapore polity, McKellen opined that Lee

> must expect gay people not to come here, he must expect gay people to emigrate, he must expect no company to have their gay employees work here. Under that pressure he will change the law, I guarantee you. I'll take a bet (McKellen, cited in Tong, 2007: unpaginated).

It remains to be seen whether the pressures McKellen identified will lead to a legal change, just as it is arguable whether the connections between sexual politics and corporate and personal migration choices will play out in the way he posited. What is clear is that there has been a remarkable reluctance for the Singaporean authorities to allow increased legal or political rights or recognition for queer individuals, relationships and communities. Homosexuality remains a subject that is censored or invisible within local broadcast and mass media, and within school curricula; queer civil society groups continue to be refused registration (a prerequisite for legally raising funds) by the Singaporean authorities; homosexual servicemen are still punitively regulated within the domain of compulsory military service; and access to state-owned housing (in which over 80 per cent of the population resides) is still largely predicated upon married heterosexual relationship status. Even the large-scale queer dance parties that were previously *fêted* by foreign observers as evidence of Singapore's liberalisation and cosmopolitanism have been banned by the authorities.

It is my contention that this apparently paradoxical stance becomes explicable once we take into account those consequences that the PAP government sees as flowing from Singapore's status not as a global city, but as a sovereign state. The successful embrace of the global city narrative holds out particular assurances of worldwide relevance and the tools required to excel within a world dominated flows of global capitalism. Yet the world appears a different and far more hostile place when viewed through the eyes of those responsible for the security and order of a geographically tiny, ethnically diverse city-state. And just as creativity and cosmopolitanism have been adopted as the quintessence of Singapore's attempts to become a global city, so security and order have come to be regarded by Singaporean policy makers as essential prerequisites for the country's survival as a sovereign political entity. To a significant extent, the tension between these two policy objectives explains the ongoing hostility towards queer politics within Singapore and the ambiguous nature of Singaporean policies towards queer subjects, politics and lifestyles.

Former Singaporean diplomat, Kishore Mahbubani, has described how Singaporean policy makers see Singapore's city-state form as contributing to the country's existential vulnerability. He states:

> City-states don't survive that long. They have flashes of brilliance–fifty years, a hundred years—then they go. The eternal challenge for Singapore is how do you ensure what we have had in these 40 years [since independence] is not just a brilliant flash ... [that] just goes away (Mahbubani, cited in Lion Television, 2005).

Similarly, Linda Low has pointed to the failure of former city-states that functioned as transnational commercial hubs, and how these serve as a warning to Singaporean policy makers about the potential for loss of sovereignty and influence in a world shaped by power politics (Low, 2002). Such threats to state survival are part of the accepted wisdom of Singapore's international relations and inform mainstream academic and policy understandings of the security challenges confronting the island nation: its tiny geographical size (Lee, 1993; Singh, 1988); its vulnerability to external threats resulting from its small population and geopolitical location (Ganesan, 1992; Leifer, 2000) and its need for strong regimes of internal order and external security to secure sovereignty and survival (Huxley, 2000; Singh, 2007). Accordingly, the political management of vulnerability and implementing policies aimed at ensuring Singapore's survival as a sovereign political entity—above all those policies aimed at fostering internal order and external security—take central priority.

These concerns have profound consequences for Singaporean queers. They inform a raft of elite views on what forms of citizenship, subjectivity and behaviour are desirable within and (crucially) *for* the Singaporean state. The state clearly defines what it regards as appropriate forms of gendered identity and sexual behaviour. These authorised and essentialised visions in turn construct a narrative of what makes a good Singaporean citizen: one who complies with the norms of appropriate, state-sanctioned heterosexual subjectivity and who fulfils their duties to the state through procreation and the founding of a family unit (Heng and Devan, 1992: 344). A whole range of policy interventions into Singaporean sexual life worlds can be read as encouraging and rewarding conformity to these understandings: from the bonuses paid to couples who reproduce, to policies regulating access to public housing. For Lyons, the intervention of the Singaporean state into the sexual lives of its citizens to reward certain forms of sexual subjectivity and to marginalise, even criminalise, what it regards as deviant or aberrant sexualities demonstrates the seriousness with which the state approaches the protection of its particular conceptions of appropriate gender and sexual relations and the pervasively gendered and heterosexist understandings it holds regarding citizenship, social order, and nationalism (Lyons, 2004).

But in a small city-state like Singapore the need to privilege reproductive and normative heterosexual subjectivities is understood by elites as having a more significant rationale than simply privileging traditional social understandings of gender and sexuality. M. Jacqui Alexander writes powerfully of the ways in which those subjectivities—above all queer subjectivities—that refuse to comply with state-sanctioned versions of heterosexual identity or behaviour are marked as posing "a profound threat to the very survival of the nation" (Alexander, 1994: 6). Following Alexander, we can see how concerns over Singapore's international security and internal order act to flavour debates over queer citizenship and national belonging.

Scholars have noted how citizen support for both authoritarian governance and social control in Singapore is constructed through the regular deployment of "crisis narratives" by the PAP government (Ortmann, 2003; Ang and Stratton, 1995: 182; Heng and Devan, 1992: 343–44). These crises usually turn on a perceived threat to Singapore's international standing in areas such as military security, economic performance or cultural competitiveness (Ortmann, 2003: 34–84; National Security Coordination Centre, 2004). Yet such "crises" of international legitimacy and state security also resonate within the Singaporean state's regulation of sexuality: most obviously in the area of ensuring population growth and biological reproduction of the nation. Population decline—specifically the decline in the number of babies born to Singaporean families—is regularly presented to the public as a threat to national survival (see, for instance Goh, 2000). Government-led debate on this issue invokes the spectre of declining birth rates as compromising the quality and size of Singapore's national community and its labour pool (and hence its international economic competitiveness) and negatively impacting the availability of conscripts and soldiers for the Singapore Armed Forces (and hence national security itself) (Boey, 2003; Goh, 2000). Queer rights and the visibility of queer communities within Singapore are presented as one of the causes of the decline in birth rates and as contributing to the threats these supposedly represent. As Leong explains, "homosexuality constitutes a threat and an aberration to the paternalistic state because same-gender unions usually do not result in procreation" (Leong, 1995: 18). Reflecting such thinking, the Anglican Archbishop of Singapore was reported in national media in 2009, criticising what he saw as the "erosion of mainstream culture by homosexuality" and warning that (supposedly consequent) low birth rates would ensure "that the mainstream population, its sociocultural norms and ethos, will dwindle and diminish down the generations" (Yen Feng, 2009). Elsewhere, discussion of homosexuality in Singaporean news outlets continues to pose queer politics and lifestyles as threatening to national security and order and as a threat to the communitarian stability upon which the nation's success is supposedly based (Tan, 2003: 409–10; Goh, 2008).

Singapore's international diplomatic assertion of state sovereignty and domestic political control also acts to colour domestic Singaporean debates over queer rights and visibility. There have been comprehensive attempts on the part of the government to reject aspects of international liberal politics—most notably certain discourses of human rights (including queer rights)—and to differentiate Singapore from the institutional, cultural and social politics of the Western world (Thio, 2006). This, many scholars have argued, has led to the emergence of binary understandings of a communitarian, economically successful and cohesive postcolonial Singaporean nation defined against the supposedly individualistic, economically stagnant, conflictual and immoral West (See, for instance, 1999; Tan, 2003; Berry, 1994). Queer politics and lifestyles are frequently referenced in such debates. Home Affairs minister Wong Kan Seng recently warned queer Singaporeans not to "assert themselves stridently as gay groups do in the West" or "import into Singapore the culture wars between the extreme liberals and conservatives that are going on in the United States" (Wong, 2009). It is but a short step from such linkages of queer rights claims as intrinsically Western to the depiction of queer identities as foreign in essence—a depiction Wong himself helped reinforce by stating at a global human rights conference that homosexual rights were a purely Western concern (Wong, cited in Berry, 1994). This has helped ensure that in popular understanding, homosexuals are thought of—precisely *because* of their homosexuality—as always and already alien: of compromised national belonging, threatening to the order of the polity and jeopardising their fellow citizens' continued enjoyment of the economic wealth and sovereign security that are presented as fruits of the Singapore developmental model's success (see more broadly: Obendorf, 2006: 190; Goldberg, 1992: xvi).

Both Contagion and Cure

In light of the story I have told thus far, Singaporean queers would be forgiven for feeling confused and resentful given the Janus-faced nature of their treatment by the Singapore state. On the one hand, they are told that they are valuable (and valued) participants in Singapore's processes of urban remaking, idealised global-city citizens and consumers whose presence serves to boost levels of global competitiveness, cosmopolitanism and creativity. Simultaneously—and with no trace of irony—queers are told that they represent a blight on the nature, if not a threat to the very survival, of the Singaporean nation, and that their ongoing marginalisation, criminalisation and regulation within national life is therefore both necessary and justifiable.

This paradox has become paradigmatic of contemporary queer Singaporean life. The possibility of self-expression has become predicated upon local queers' skills in negotiating repressive socio-legal codes and their ability to maximise the benefits deriving from certain government attempts to position the country as a creative, knowledge-based economy and as a city-space marked by sophisticated patterns of cosmopolitan consumption. Yue (2006, 2007a: 24) has described this as a process of "illiberal pragmatism": a bargain whose terms are perpetually in the process of (re)negotiation, struck between the government (in pursuit of national economic goals) and queer Singaporean subjects (in search of visibility and cultural self-expression). But this illiberal pragmatism takes its shape not merely within discourses of domestic social control or economic planning but in dialogue with broader understandings of Singapore's international security and its role as a world city within the structures of global capitalism. In the latter part of this chapter I sketch out some possible futures and consequences of this interaction between the discourses of global governance and Singaporean illiberal pragmatics.

The first of these concerns to what extent the Singaporean authorities will maintain or even extend their tolerance of certain aspects of queer life being expressed within Singapore. Most obviously this impacts on the question of decriminalisation of male homosex, but could potentially extend into areas such as employment non-discrimination legislation, relationships recognition and civil rights protections. At present these appear a remote possibility. The recent reaffirmation by the government of Singapore's anti-sodomy statutes was justified on the basis of those laws' contribution to protecting social stability and promoting the heterosexual, reproductive family unit (Lee, 2007). At the same time the government signalled a continuation of its pragmatic approach to the regulation of queer lives and bodies. While seemingly offering a promise that the criminal law would not be enforced to punish consenting private sexual acts between adults, or to close off existing spaces of queer expression, the government was also quick to signal its powers of policing and surveillance. In Parliament, Prime Minister Lee stated:

> De facto, gays have a lot of space in Singapore. Gay groups hold public discussions. They publish websites. … There are films and plays on gay themes. … There are gay bars and clubs. They exist. We know where they are. … We do not harass gays … and we do not proactively enforce section 377A on them (Lee, 2007).

The extent to which this apparent compromise is informed by internationally imbued understandings is easily demonstrated. In his 30-minute Parliamentary speech on these issues, Lee spent much of his time addressing the provision of queer rights in Europe and America, which he argued had led to a moral decline within Western societies. For Lee, queer politics and visibility in the West had caused social cohesion to weaken and spurred socio-political conflict. Singapore, he suggested, was right to have chosen a different developmental path. Yet he went on to praise queer Singaporeans who were "contributing" to Singaporean society and expressed a wish that queer Singaporeans not leave the country in search of "more congenial places to live" (Lee, 2007).

Lee's words offer a classic example of an illiberal and pragmatic solution to the perceived dilemma of ensuring national stability and survival while still promoting Singapore's global openness and economic growth in a global knowledge-based economy. In this scenario, the status quo is protected, social norms are assured and queer Singaporeans continue to be denied legal recognition or protections in return for a limited range of spaces and opportunities for social and cultural expression and with the expectation of both their political quiescence and their ongoing contribution to national economic objectives. Yet perhaps it is this latter point that may hold out some promise for the expansion of queer rights in Singapore. If queer lifestyles, cultures and individuals are perceived as proxies for economic growth potential, and queers as desirable participants within new forms of global neoliberal knowledge production and consumption, might not the need to attract and retain queer individuals and groups spur political change (as Ian McKellen has argued)?

There is some evidence to support this line of thinking. In the 2007 debates on the criminalisation of male homosex, elder statesman Lee Kuan Yew offered the following as justification for his opinion that it is inevitable that the Singapore government will at some point be forced to change its stance:

> [I]f this is the way the world is going and Singapore is part of that intercon-
> nected world and I think it is, then I see no option for Singapore but to be
> part of it. They tell me and anyway it is probably half-true that homosexu-
> als are creative writers, dancers, et cetera. If we want creative people, then
> we [have] got to put up with their idiosyncrasies so long as they don't infect
> the heartland (Lee, 2007). [4]

These comments demonstrate the seriousness with which the management of queer issues is taken at the highest levels of the Singaporean government—and how regulations governing queer lives are framed in terms of Singapore's self-positioning within the arenas of global economics. Lee depicts homosexuals as blessed with innate creativity, ideal contributors to Singapore's ongoing project of transforming itself into a creative, cosmopolitan city and a key player in transnational knowledge-based economies. Yet at the same time, he uses the metaphor of contagion to present the homosexual as a figure to be feared and quarantined, capable of infecting Singapore's national heartland. Lee explicitly presents Singapore's active role within contemporary flows of social, cultural and economic globalization as the likely instigator for any potential liberalisation of Singaporean law and society. Critically, he also points to the fact that any such changes will be managed by the government in *spatial* and *economically pragmatic* terms: maximising the supposed benefits of queer participation in the arenas of economic and cultural activity while minimising any influence this might have on and within zones of nationalist self-imagining. By linking homosexuality to the idea of an infectious agent compromising the health of the body politic, Lee also revivifies understandings of queer individuals, cultures and politics as threatening to the survival and stability of the nation-state. Finally, while conceding that legalisation of male homosex may "eventually" take place (cited in Au, 2007a), Lee's comments also present homosexuality as an "idiosyncrasy" to be tolerated only inasmuch as it can be made to serve governmentally defined goals and be kept corralled within certain spatial and political limitations. Two key factors underpin Lee's thinking: the structure of urban divisions within the global city, and economically rationalist approaches to the extension of civic and political rights. Each signposts possible future developments for queer politics within Singapore.

Many scholars have written of how the transformation of particular urban environments in line with the logic of the global city narrative has created certain social and spatial divisions. Sassen writes that global cities invest heavily to create neighbourhoods comprised of "airports, top level business districts, top of the line hotels and restaurants", describing these as "a sort of urban glamour zone" (Sassen, 1996: 220). Taking this analysis further, Tsung-yi Huang has identified how Asian global cities with their hyper-dense urban environments construct strict divisions between these "glamour zones"—inhabited by those with a certain level of cosmopolitan awareness, skill in global languages, afflu- ence, professional status and education—and the everyday life worlds inhab- ited by the majority of local residents of the city. Certain parts of the city are built to enable the pursuit of cosmopolitan patterns of consumption, leisure and lifestyle, to facilitate transnational commerce, trade and investment and to undergird a city's aspirations to global relevance (Huang, 2006, 2004, 2000). But as Huang writes, "the picture-perfect global space lies outside of the everyday reality of those lower-middle class" inhabitants of the city (Huang, 2000: 395). While geographic compactness, increasing wealth and higher education levels blur such distinctions in the Singapore case they are definitely apparent in national discourses that paint suburban family life in Singapore's so-called "heartland"—the city's numerous satellite towns and public housing estates— as the location and source of authentic Singaporean identity (Ng, 2008; Yue, 2007b). Robbie Goh has described the Singapore "heartland" as thought of in nationalist discourse and public policy as a "bastion of a non-cosmopolitan, contentedly 'local' identity" (Goh, 2003: 70). These spaces are understood as distinct from Singapore's own global-city glamour zones—the central business district; Orchard Road with its gleaming malls full of international luxury- brand shops; the integrated resort and casino developments of Marina Bay and Sentosa; the various arts, research and development clusters; expatriate and diplomatic neighbourhoods; Changi International Airport—which have been designed to be inhabited and consumed primarily by a globally mobile cosmopolitan elite.

It is the nationalistically-imbued and "authentic" heartland identity that Lee Kuan Yew sees as being vulnerable to "infection" should it come into contact with recognisable queer bodies or cultures. And it seems further apparent that Westernisation, political turmoil and social decline are understood to be the inevitable symptoms of this contagion. The Singapore leadership has convinced itself that visible aspects of queer culture should be permitted only within the transnationally-configured and cosmopolitan zones of Singapore-as-global city while the heartlands remain protected as a quarantined zone of heteropatriarchal family life, cultural specificity and nationalistic purity. This plays out in a whole range of Singaporean public policy interventions. Even those films judged to contain adult themes (including homosexual characters) that are passed by the censor as appropriate for viewing by adult Singaporeans are forbidden in heartland estate cinemas and can only be screened in central city locations. Despite the overwhelming majority of Singaporeans being resident in the public housing heartlands, it seems that the visible expression of queer culture and spaces of queer social interaction are to be tolerated only in those urban spaces where Singapore is at its most global and outward looking. For most queer Singaporeans, the search for visible queer social or commercial space, artistic representation or even sexual opportunity requires a journey into the cosmopolitan spaces of the Singapore cityscape. It is in these zones that one is able to find and access the gay and lesbian bars, the gay saunas, queer commercial outlets and queer literature, films and theatre.

Such spatial divisions have several key consequences. First of all they code homosexuality—and queer Singaporeans—as belonging not to the imagined community of the nation but as cosmopolitan, if not foreign, in nature. They structure a distinction between heterosexual/heartlander/local (on the one hand) and queer/cosmopolitan/global (on the other). They ensure that queers are denied visibility in the very social and spatial locations in which national identity is forged, and thus in the imaginings of the nation itself. And even when queer cultures and social groups are allowed space within the glamour zones of the global city it is clear that this is permitted primarily due to the contribution it makes towards meeting national objectives and only to the extent that it does not threaten to change the sexual and cultural self-imaginings of Singaporean nationhood. Indeed queers' very visibility in such locations can be a boon to the pragmatic Singaporean state administrator. A thriving gay and lesbian consumer culture and both domestic and international arts projects referencing homosexual themes act as markers of Singapore's cosmopolitanism, sophistication and global city urban chic—especially to those expatriates, business people and tourists who are unaware of (or who have the skills, knowledge and income to evade) the broader legal and social frameworks that restrict the possibilities of queer cultural life in Singapore.

But the limiting of queer space to those particular parts of the city that are understood as cosmopolitan and transnational in nature has other consequences. Alex Au has stated that gay culture in Singapore is "largely inspired by the progress achieved in the West" (Au, cited in Offord, 1999: 309) and certainly the sorts of queer identities, cultures, politics and rights claims that have emerged within Singapore seem reflective to a large degree of Western gay and lesbian identity politics and consumerism. This is understandable given both their urban location and the openness of Singaporean society to flows of students, expatriate workers and tourists. We must resist assuming that the identities and politics that emerge in these settings are merely reflective of European or American urban gay and lesbian life (Aldrich, 2004; Connors, 1997; Hawley, 2001a, 2001b). Yet on another level the very fact that queer identities and politics are conceived of—by both queer Singaporeans and their ruling authorities—as being shaped by Western cultural influences is of significance (Adam, Duyvendak and Krouwel, 1999; Altman, 1995, 2001). Offord (1999: 310) identifies the Westernised nature of Singaporean queer politics as giving rise to many of the government's fears over the changes that a more liberal approach to homosexuality could wreak within Singaporean society—despite (or perhaps because of) the fact that it is the government itself that has ensured Singaporean queer life remains largely contained within the most globalised parts of the Singaporean cityscape.

More significantly, the very Western, cosmopolitan and outward looking quality of much of Singaporean queer life and politics acts to divide local queer communities along linguistic, cultural and class lines—most obviously between those with the educational, cultural and financial wherewithal to participate in the cosmopolitan envisioning of queer sexuality that takes place within Singapore's global city spaces and those Singaporean queers less able to access or participate in queer life as it is practised in such spaces. As Altman has provocatively argued, Westernised gay and lesbian life in contemporary urban Asia "seems highly correlated with class, ability in English ... exposure to Western media and involvement in AIDS activities" (1997: 41). While consumer culture is a significant aspect of self-definition for most Singaporeans (Chua, 2000, 2003), the financial cost of pursuing an urban gay consumerist lifestyle within Singapore can be high (Chasing the pink dollar, 2003). The fact that the vast majority of permitted queer space in Singapore is *commercial* space can mean that those who do not have the confidence or income to enter into the high-cost and cosmopolitan glamour zones of Singapore's urban environment face significant barriers to forming queer identities, participating in queer social life or engaging with queer politics. This serves to divide the Singaporean queer community and ensures solidarity over political claims is less likely to emerge.

Similarly the very nature of the illiberal yet pragmatic regulation of queer visibility, rights and social existence in Singapore serves to divide queer communities and diminish the potential for political organisation. The reasons for this turn on the perceived fragility of the compromise that exists between governmental authority and queer Singaporeans and the sheer inequality of power that subsists between these two groups. The government has warned queer groups that they must "accept the informal limits which reflect the point of balance that our society can accept" (Wong, 2009). Accordingly, some within Singaporean queer communities have come to view attempts at gaining greater legal or civil rights and recognition as risking governmental ire and the potential removal or reduction of existing spaces and opportunities for queer cultural expression. A culture of contentment, in combination with what Cherian George has identified as the government's finely calibrated strategies of coercion and reward, works as a powerful disincentive to political risk-taking for many Singaporean queers (George, 2005; Lek and Obendorf, 2004).

The changes that have flowed from the remodelling of Singapore into a 21st century global city—politically, socially, culturally and spatially—have provided queer Singaporeans with certain avenues through which to make claims for greater levels of self-expression and cultural visibility. Indeed, in some respects, queer lives and lifestyles have come to be understood by political and business elites as a necessary part of the country's project of urban self-fashioning and as contributing to national economic goals and global economic competitiveness. Yet this awareness has not translated into widespread legal or social change in today's Singapore. While some concrete gains have been made, and others may be foreseen, the global city narrative as it has unfolded in Singapore has not given rise to either legal protections for sexual minorities or levels of social acceptance comparable to those extant in other global cities around the world. My analysis suggests that while change to benefit sexual minorities in Singapore has been (in some limited respects at least) enabled by Singapore's global city ambitions and transformations, the extent and nature of such change continues to be constrained by governmental prioritisation of those policies perceived as critical for maintaining Singapore's sovereignty, security and national reputation, and widespread understandings of homosexuality as threatening such ambitions. More significantly, where tensions do arise between the competing narratives of state security and competitive enmeshment with a network of global cities—and especially where these impact queer lives—they are invariably resolved in favour of those policies that prioritise traditional understandings of the composition, viability and security of the state. Significant work remains to be done to foster social acceptance and accommodate queer Singaporeans within the imaginings of Singaporean nationalism and citizenship rather than relegating them to the status of anomalies to be tolerated due to the desirability of their contributions to state economic objectives. Only then will the limitations and closures I have identified here begin to lose their potency.

Part 2

Queer Media Cultures

7
Photo Essay

A Brief History of Early Gay Venues in Singapore

Roy Tan

Where could a young gay adult go to meet like-minded people in Singapore in the 1970s? This was the predicament the author of this chapter found himself in, in an era when there was no ready information available on the subject. The situation may have been vastly different for his street-savvy counterpart who lived in the vicinity of an area where homosexual men would congregate nocturnally for social, as well as sexual, intercourse; or another gay person who had already built up a nexus of friends who could clue him in on the hotspots where such activities took place.

But the social isolation and heart-wrenching loneliness that a typical English or Chinese-educated school graduate experienced with respect to his homosexual orientation was a major life issue at that time. One could read up about the topic of homosexuality in popular psychology treatises such as the acclaimed bestseller, *The Hite Report on Male Sexuality* (Hite, 1981). Books like these were available at the larger book stores, the best known of which was the MPH (Malaysian Publishing House) located on Stamford Road. However, these tomes dealt with studies on homosexuality in the West, specifically in America, and gave a local person no inkling as to where he could meet gay people in Singapore.

In addition, more often than not, when the word 'gay' was mentioned in the press, it conjured up the image of a man dressed in women's clothing. In the consciousness of mainstream Singaporeans, 'gay' still retained its traditional meaning of 'happy', as evidenced by the name of one of the most popular entertainment centres, Gay World (where no homosexual activities were to be found) and the captions of photographs in the media. One prominent example is a framed collage of photographs on display at the National Museum entitled, 'Singapore goes gay for Malaysia Day'. There were, no doubt, sporadic reports in the press that attempted to tackle the local gay subculture, the most widely read of which was the four-part series by tabloid newspaper *The New Nation* called 'They are different' published in July 1972.

It should be noted that in the 1970s, the definition of 'gay' as a socially constructed identity of the self was not widely know. Therefore, the terms 'gay' and
'homosexual' are used interchangeably in this chapter. Through the form of a
photo essay, this chapter provides a cultural history of early gay venues based
on the author's personal experiences and oral histories provided by members
of the gay community, including his ex-partner and friends.

Figure 7.1

A transvestite, dressed to the nines, sashaying down Bugis Street, enjoying the attention
from gawking tourists and locals alike in the 1970s (see Tangawizi, 2009).

Figure 7.2

Cross-dressing male street walkers posing at the seedier Malabar Street, a short distance
away from Bugis Street in the 1960s (see Tangawizi, 2009).

In view of the mainstream public's misconceptions of gay men being trans-gender women, a gay person with absolutely no information about where to meet other homosexuals would have ventured into Bugis Street to try his luck. He probably would have found a few gay men with the same purpose there. However, if he were to wander around the vicinity, he may have chanced upon the seedier lanes around Bugis Street, such as Malabar Street, Malay Street and Hailam Street, where the less glamorous and aged transwomen plied their trade or offered free sex to the men they fancy. The chances of meeting other gay men looking for sex along these lanes were higher. Some would spill into the Sungei Road area as well.

Figure 7.3
The Muslim cemetery at Jalan Kubor as it exists today.

Other men would go to the disused Muslim cemetery at Jalan Kubor. It became known as one of the more popular cruising grounds. People would walk around the periphery of the cemetery next to the main road and retreat further into the area shielded by trees with luscious foliage for sexual activity. In the 1970s, the area was patronised mainly by local Chinese but as Singapore's South Indian foreign worker population swelled, the racial character of the patrons of the Jalan Kubor cemetery changed. In 2010, after a lapse of almost two decades, a police entrapment operation was carried out there and an unfor-tunate Malaysian Indian foreign worker was arrested after he chatted with and touched the chest and groin of a police decoy.

Frequented mainly at night by a stigmatised minority who are in fear of running afoul of the law every time they congregate for social or sexual intercourse, these outdoor gay hangouts have remained largely unknown to the mainstream public. It was only in the mid-1990s that police harassment of homosexuals at these venues declined, although sporadic complaints by members of the public may still lead to investigations. The following list includes several cruising areas that some conservative gay people may feel unrepresentative of the Singaporean homosexual image, but for the sake of academic comprehensiveness and as a record of the collective local gay memory, has been drawn up accordingly.

Parks and Beaches

The first gay meeting place to be listed in the premier international gay tourist reference, the *Spartacus International Gay Guide*, was Hong Lim Park. Officially known as Hong Lim Green, it probably gained its reputation as a cruising ground for gay men, most of whom were Chinese of the lower socio-economic strata, since the 1950s. The layout of the park was instrumental and conducive for meeting and fondling other men. There were large rectangular flower pots which contained dense shrubbery. Men could sit on the perimeter of these flower pots to chat, and if they show mutual interest, some would fondle each other there and then. The presence of shady trees with overhanging foliage would also conceal their activities from passers-by.

In the early years, Hong Lim Park (now current venue for the groundbreaking Pink Pot LGBT annual gathering as discussed on this volume's introduction and other chapters) was also affectionately code-named 'Honolulu' or 'Hollywood' by some English-educated gay men. Relatively 'cruisy' during the night-time for more than half a century, its dim lighting and tall shrubbery provided ideal conditions for quickies between gay men, especially elderly Chinese-educated ones, until the bushes were pruned and bright lights installed in the early 1990s to deter such activities. Nightly cruising and sex also took place in a small two-storey shopping centre that was demolished and replaced by the present car park. The setting-up of the Kreta Ayer Neighbourhood Police Post in an old building which was an erstwhile post office located next to the car park was also considered a measure to curb late-night cruising. However, these activities were largely allowed to take place if they did not draw too much adverse attention as the authorities were aware of the impossibility of eradicating them completely. As with so many of the other cruising grounds, this situation could be construed as an example of illiberal pragmatics. Straight patrons were shocked at some young boys holding hands and wrote letters to the newspapers in the 1980s to complain. In spite of several police patrols in which these boys were questioned, no one was charged as nobody was caught in *flagrante delicto*.

From the early part of the century to the 1970s, there used to be a public toilet situated in the middle of Circular Road and close to Hong Lim Park that was known to be somewhat 'cruisy' and probably one of the first in Singapore where toilet sex took place. A public bus service with a two-digit number had its terminus right next to it. Gay passengers would alight from the bus and pretend to use the toilet. Whilst at it, they would look surreptitiously around and at the other men who were at the urinals. A few would have sex in the cubicles if they met someone to their liking, while others would proceed to Hong Lim Park. During the same period, homosexual taxi drivers, mostly married, who would station their taxis along the periphery of the park after their shift was over and go cruising around the vicinity.

Among the interesting anecdotes connected with Hong Lim Park at that time was one concerning a famous businessman known as the 'Abalone King', who had monopolised the local abalone market. His shop was located along a road near the park. Although he was a married family man, he used to go cruising at Hong Lim Park where he frequently picked up younger men for sex. His inclinations were an open secret amongst his employees. On occasion, one of the 'boys' would venture into his shop to look for him, whereupon he would instruct his employees to give the boy a drink or some pocket money. It is rumoured that he had since migrated to Taiwan.

Figure 7.4

Postcard of The Esplanade in the 1970s showing the plant receptacles where men would sit and wait on the outside or indulge in petting on the inside, shielded from the gaze of passers-by (see *The Lycan Times*, 2011).

The Esplanade, more accurately Queen Elizabeth Walk (and not the current arts establishment which inherited its name), was also a popular area for gay men to meet each other from the 1970s to around 2000, when the Theatres on the Bay were being built. Today, it is known as Esplanade Park and comprises the whole area between Queen Elizabeth Walk and Connaught Drive. Flower pots, painted white and with a more complex shape than those found at Hong Lim Park, were also found there. One difference from those at Hong Lim Park was that they contained a hollow interior, which allowed men to sit inside the pots and indulge in petting or have oral sex whilst being shaded from external view by the shrubbery. The erstwhile Esplanade was frequented especially by young gay men who acted more girlishly than usual to attract straight pick-ups for the night. Others came looking for South Asian men, of which there were many.

A tunnel underpass located at The Esplanade also saw raunchy cruising activity during the same period. Especially on Saturday nights, crowds of 'straight' couples could be discerned in the dark just across the road on the Padang (Malay for 'field') making out on mats, which they had brought with them to lie on. Other parks relatively 'cruisy' but less well known in the 1970s were Central Park, accessible via the long flight of steps up from River Valley Swimming Pool, Fort Canning Park, Labrador Park, accessible only by car or motorbike, Mount Faber, the Botanic Gardens and MacRitchie Reservoir.

In the 1980s, a new experience in open-air cruising afforded itself when a huge stretch of the East Coast was reclaimed by land filling. The minimum period for the earth to settle before the new land could be developed or have structures built upon it was ten years. Therefore, during this time gays would venture there, despite having to brave a long trek through secondary forest, to be able to cruise along the beach in splendid seclusion. This cruising ground became popularly known as Fort Road Beach by the cognoscenti although there existed no official name for this stretch of beach. There were two main stretches. The moiety on the left, facing the sea, became closed off to the public in the mid-1990s and thus could no longer be used for cruising. This area became overgrown with undergrowth in due course. Gay cruisers had to be contented with the right half that had a slightly different character because of different geographical features.

Fort Road Beach also became so popular with gay men who used it for skinny dipping and sex, either in the more interior forested area or, the more daring ones right on the beach or in the sea, that it attracted several tabloid articles with headlines such as 'Homosexuals pollute East Coast'. *The New Paper* and the Chinese-language evening tabloids often carried blurred pictures of men apparently having sex or walking naked along the beach. The right half of the beach was eventually closed to the public in early 2010 as development of the area was ramped up.

Figure 7.5
Fort Road beach during low tide in 2008.

From the above examples, we can discern the factors which made an area popular for nocturnal gay cruising: (1) it must be a relatively large, open-air space that people could walk around and 'go shopping' as it were; (2) there must preferably be a place where they could sit and chat up each other before indulging in petting or oral sex; and, (3) the areas in which these activities happen must be shielded from the gaze of passers-by by foliage, man-made structures and the relative absence of lighting.

Urbanised Open Spaces

One important principle governing the peculiar locations of contemporary outdoor cruising areas is gentrification. Older areas which had been patronised in the past had to be abandoned as urban redevelopment destroyed conditions conducive to cruising such as poor lighting, sparse human traffic and the presence of dark, derelict buildings or environs. Thus, the present situation of cruising areas in the Ann Siang area may be explained by the gradual shift of activity from Boat Quay to the vicinity around China Square, and finally to Ann Siang Hill as these areas were successively gentrified. To some extent, the redevelopment of a shopping centre or public building would also see cruising spots relocated, such as from Plaza Singapura Shopping Centre, to the former National Library at Stamford Road, and finally, to Raffles City Shopping Centre.

Figure 7.6

One of the back alleys at Boat Quay where nocturnal cruising was rife in the 1980s and early 1990s, before the area was redeveloped.

Figure 7.7

The stair landing behind OCBC building where newspapers were laid for men to lie on at night and a piece of plywood to block them from the view of passers-by in the 1980s.

In the early 1990s, Boat Quay and the adjoining back alleys parallel to the Singapore River's west bank used to be very 'cruisy' at night with the younger crowd before the area was rejuvenated with the present row of restaurants. However, Hong Lim Park remained popular with the older generation, possibly for nostalgic reasons. Police patrol cars would occasionally drive up and record the Identity Card (IC) numbers of gay men who were doing nothing other than chatting with each other as a form of intentional harassment. Surreptitious sex also took place nearby at the foot and back alley of the OCBC Centre, before bright lighting was installed which served no real purpose other than to deter nocturnal cruising. Areas surrounding the OCBC Centre such as the Raffles Place train station and the construction sites of buildings on the other side of Philip Street were also popular and gave rise to the novel phenomenon of car-cruising. Unattractive cruisers could increase their chances of picking up handsome gay pedestrians if they drove big flashy cars, for instance.

Figure 7.8
The courtyard at Ann Siang Hill was a hotbed of nocturnal cruising activity in the 1990s.

Figure 7.9
The most cruisy back alley in the Ann Siang area in the 1990s.

In the 1980s, the streets traversing China Square, namely Hokkien Street, Nankin Street and Chin Chew Street, were especially overrun on weekend nights by gay men and car-cruisers when the whole area was lined with abandoned, dark, derelict buildings. Many would stand or sit along the corridors of these dilapidated buildings and people-watch, chat, fondle each other or step into passing cars. Owing to the decrepit environment from a bygone era, this area was affectionately known as 'Jurassic Park' after the movie became a hit in the 1990s. The entire area around Ann Siang Hill, especially its back alleys, was also very cruisy in the early 1990s. It only became much less active after a landscaped sanctuary named Ann Siang Hill Park was built in 2004 installing more lighting resulting in clandestine activities to be less convenient than before.

Figure 7.10

The area just beyond the entrance gate at River Valley swimming pool.

Figure 7.11

The ubiquitous, long, wooden benches found in all public swimming pools and changing rooms in the 1980s and 1990s that facilitated loitering and cruising. They have since been removed to deter such activities.

Other public places where gay men meet include the Odeon Theatre and River Valley Swimming Pool. Of the latter, which was one of the few public pools built in the city area with the imposing backdrop of the Fort Canning Park, it was the most notorious and perhaps why it is no longer extant. In one incident, two men were caught by the lifeguard for underwater fellatio and were jailed. It was also one of the few swimming pools where outdoor photography was banned. Some other less well-known cruising grounds were the Yan Kit, Jurong and Bukit Merah swimming pools. The now-demolished Odeon Theatre which used to stand along North Bridge Road was known to be a meeting point for gay men. Some young boys also sold sex services there. In a typical example, an elderly man would bring a younger person he had gotten to know to watch a movie there. They would fondle each other in the darkened cinema. If more serious activity was desired, they would adjourn to a cubicle in the toilet, which was located conveniently to one side of the theatre's vestibule.

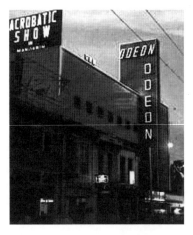

Figure 7.12
The Odeon Theatre along North Bridge Road in the 1970s (see Melnick, 2001).

Saunas and Bathhouses

Before the 1990s, local homosexuals had to journey all the way to Bangkok, Thailand to experience the pleasures that gay saunas offered. It became more convenient in the early 1990s when an establishment called **Ryu**, meaning 'dragon' in Japanese, opened in Taman Pelangi near the Pelangi Complex in

Johor Bahru, Malaysia. Hot on the heels of its overwhelming success in attracting huge crowds of both Singaporeans and Malaysians, another gay sauna called **New Blue Boys** opened at 104 A-B, Jalan Serampang, Taman Pelangi, 80400 Johor Bahru about a year later. Some Singaporean gays would charter taxis in groups to traverse the one kilometre causeway and experience what was sorely lacking at home.

Figure 7.13
The row of shophouses along South Bridge Road where Spartacus was located.

Savvy entrepreneurs like the pioneering Max Lim realised the strong demand for such a facility locally. In 1997, he opened Singapore's first gay sauna and named it **Spartacus**, after the Roman gladiator. It was located, amusingly but unintentionally, at 69 South Bridge Road. It aimed to be a scaled-down version of the mega-sauna complex Babylon in Bangkok and had three storeys of hedonism with a daily gay disco on the ground floor fringed by an overhead observation deck, showers, a gym and sauna above it. It was strict about sex at first to avoid complaints and police harassment. Signs such as 'No obscene acts allowed' were prominently displayed. But the rule gradually relaxed and the signs removed after everyone realised that the police did not intrude. The sauna could be recognised immediately from its external façade because of its colossal signage and the painted sketches of nude gladiators on its external wall facing South Bridge Road, near its junction with North Canal Road.

Figure 7.14
Spartacus membership card.

The entrance fee to Spartacus and the majority of subsequent gay saunas was made affordable so that men from all socio-economic strata could use the facilities. Lim experimented with the novel concept of giving its customers the option of buying shares in the business. It also pioneered services like offering upmarket buffet meals on its premises. Unfortunately, demand for the meals and disco was poor, even though the spa facilities were a resounding success. To expand its clientele, it even held lesbian nights on the ground floor disco on Thursdays. This juxtaposition of lesbians and gay men in common spaces occasionally took on comical overtones. People on the second level were visible to patrons on the dance floor as there was no ceiling to completely separate the first from the second level—only a peripheral encircling narrow corridor. So, lesbians dancing on the ground floor could see men clad only in towels walking around on the second level and many thought it a strange sight that most had probably never encountered before. Despite its initial popularity, Spartacus' patronage gradually declined. It closed in late July 1999 due to high rental costs among other factors.

Figure 7.15
Internet advertisement for Stroke sauna, Courtesy of Max Lim.

Figure 7.16
The row of shophouses along Ann Siang Road where Stroke was located.

Stroke was the successor to Spartacus under the same management and was located at 22 Ann Siang Road. It had a spell of success from 2000 to 2002 when it was the only gay sauna in Singapore and also the first to open 24 hours a day, all year round. The opening of other gay saunas broke its monopoly and forced its owner to move into newer premises to refocus its strategy two years later.

Figure 7.17
The external facade of the building that housed Rairua, along Neil Road.

Figure 7.18
Rairua membership card.

Rairua, which opened in 2002, is a multi-level sauna along Neil Road. The brainchild of activist Alex Au, it positioned itself as Singapore's first luxury gay sauna with prices to match. It pioneered Singapore's first 'skin nights' touted as 'all nude, all floors, all night', a concept that unexpectedly proved so popular amongst supposedly 'conservative' Singaporean gays that such nude nights had spread to all saunas within the span of one year and continue to be a major draw. It also organised special events like cultural talks, naturist art sessions, and erotic dancing by shower-boys. Unfortunately, due to the expiry of its lease and disagreements with its landlord over maintenance, it closed in April 2005.

Figure 7.19
The building that housed RAW sauna, at the end of Ann Siang Road in 2006.

RAW was the third sauna Max Lim managed from 2003 to 2010 and was located next to Ann Siang Hill, which is already a popular cruising ground. Its competitive advantages are its budget entry fees, 24-hour opening times and a 'barracks' containing individual rooms for those desiring to stay for pro-longed periods. It pioneered the concept of theme nights, which later spread to all saunas. This introduced variety and catered to segments of the gay crowd such as chubs, foam party lovers, minority races, foreigners and sun worship-pers. It also experimented for a short period with an à la carte restaurant on the ground floor, a transvestite cabaret and male undergarment or swimming trunk fashion shows. It was the only sauna to proudly hang a rainbow flag outside its main entrance.

Figure 7.20
The external facade of Shogun sauna's first location at Telok Ayer Street.

Located on Telok Ayer Street, **The Box** was Singapore's first cruise club, where one could cruise for sex fully clothed. This was a concept that proved less popular locally and resulted in its lacklustre business. It was later converted into a sauna called **Shogun** and was one of the last saunas to introduce nude nights. No membership was required. It has now moved to another location in the same vicinity, closer to the Chinatown precinct.

Figure 7.21
The entrance of Diamond Health Centre at Jalan Sultan Plaza in 2005.

The **Diamond Health Centre** was located on the fifth floor of the Sultan Plaza on 100 Jalan Sultan at the junction of Beach Road. It was unique amongst gay saunas in that it charged a standardised entry fee of $19 and closed relatively early at 11pm even on weekends.

It started as a straight sauna offering massage by women masseuses, but gradually gained a predominantly gay, elderly Chinese-educated clientele. This phenomenon of homosexuals eventually forming the majority of patrons in a previously straight establishment is affectionately known as 'colonization'. It was the first sauna to have a coin-operated karaoke machine on its premises, free buffets and Hollywood/Hong Kong movie screenings, all of which proved to be very popular. It relocated in 2009 to Jalan Klapa and assumed a new name, **Hercules Club**.

Bars and Clubs

The English educated homosexuals, who did not want to potentially sully their image by being seen at nocturnal open-air cruising grounds, which were deemed seedy and low-class, had the option of going to nightspots where well-dressed homosexuals would congregate. The first of these, according to Russell Heng's (2005) seminal article, 'Where Queens Ruled!: A History of Gay Venues in Singapore', was a seafood-restaurant-turned-gay-disco at Punggol. However, few contemporaries have any recollection of this venue or its name.

Instead, more widely known and acknowledged as Singapore's first gay bar was **Le Bistro**, which opened in the 1960s. It was located at the basement of a landmark building called Tropicana along Scotts Road. The latter was a four-storey entertainment complex renowned for its topless dancing girl revues and occupied the exact spot where Pacific Plaza now stands. Le Bistro was a well-known chill-out bar, especially amongst English-educated gays and was a reputed pick-up haunt for white tourists and local, deeply-closeted homosexuals. Gay gatherings began on Sundays, a tradition which grew out of earlier attempts by Singapore food and beverage outlets to copy an American practice current during that era of Sunday afternoon tea dances. During that time slot, bars and discos were officially closed but Le Bistro's owner would admit his "friends" for a private party. As numbers grew and confidence increased, the afternoon tea parties eventually took over the Sunday nights.

One retired New Zealand serviceman, in a chance encounter with Alex Au, claimed that in the early 1960s when he was stationed in Singapore, there was a **Golden Venus bar** in the Orchard Hotel along Orchard Road. This claim has not been corroborated by Singaporeans. The old Orchard Hotel has since been reconstructed beyond recognition. Le Bistro and Golden Venus are today no longer extant.

Figure 7.22
Postcard of the Hotel Singapura Intercontinental along Orchard Road in the 1970s. Pebbles Bar was located on the ground floor (see Bugge, 2009).

In the 1970s, a local band called Tania started performing at **Pebbles Bar**, located to the left of the ground floor lobby of the Hotel Singapura Intercontinental along Orchard Road. Its lead singer was Alban de Souza, a flamboyant, energetic and very camp performer who donned outrageous make-up á la David Bowie or Kiss. He attracted a loyal following of English-educated, gay men from the upper economic strata of society and they formed a nexus that enticed other gays to congregate there. Gay European expatriates and visitors also frequented the nightspot and many a local-Caucasian pairing was spawned. The clientele could watch Tania's performance, socialise and get to meet new friends. Although it was the only one of Singapore's first three gay bars to have a dance floor, dancing between men was strictly prohibited. It was a common sight, however, to see men embracing and giving each other air kisses, a phenomenon rarely witnessed elsewhere in Singapore.

Figure 7.23

Alban de Souza, lead singer of Tania, the resident band at Pebbles Bar in the 1980s (see Tania, 2006).

Outside of the bustling city area, a bar-cum-disco called **The Hangar** also gained a reputation for being a gay venue in the 1970s. It was not easy to locate as there were no prominent surrounding landmarks. It was situated within The Summit Hotel along Upper East Coast Road, where The Summit condo-minium now stands. The Summit Hotel was a linear, angular series of single-storey whitewashed buildings, which one could only access by trudging along a length of unpaved road, up a slope leading up to the top of a gentle hill. It was possibly converted from a military barracks used by British servicemen. The area on the opposite side of Upper East Coast road was an empty patch of grass, so Singaporeans who drove could easily park on the grass, cross the road and reach The Hangar.

The Hangar gradually attracted a clientele of gay men, especially on Sunday nights starting from the early 1980s. Here, they could dance with each other and were not prevented from doing so by the bouncers. Sundays were relatively quiet nights when heterosexuals, who had to work the following Monday, were not so inclined to spend late nights, so this was a lacuna which the management of these establishments and the gay community were eager to fill. Looking back, some patrons presently in their late fifties could not imagine how they could have grooved to the now seemingly 'uncool' hits of that era like 'Beautiful Sunday' by Daniel Boone (1972).

Following the popularity of Pebbles Bar as a gay nightspot, gays gradually started to 'colonise' **Treetops Bar** along nearby Scotts Road. It was located to the right side of the lobby of The Holiday Inn, as the hotel was known in the 1970s. This morphed into the Royal Holiday Inn for several years before assuming its current name of Plaza on Scotts. Treetops Bar also hosted a live band that was popular with its clientele.

More wealthy gay socialites would occasionally patronise the more expensive and exclusive nightclub, **Chinoiserie**, situated on the second level of Hyatt Hotel, also along Scott's Road. However, gay men formed only a small minority of the clientele at Chinoiserie. After being entertained and socialising till the wee hours of the morning at Pebbles and Treetops Bars, gay men were eager to assuage their hunger pangs. Fortunately, The Holiday Inn also housed **Café Vienna** that was conveniently located just opposite Treetops Bar, on the left side of the hotel lobby.

Figure 7.24
Café Vienna still exists today, to the left of the lobby of Plaza at Scotts.

Russel Heng recalls:

While Treetops Bar is no longer around, Café Vienna still is and some of the stained glass décor to simulate a Viennese café remains part of its look today. The café also had live music. A small orchestra played light classical music, mainly Viennese waltzes. So the whole set-up was rather elegant or pretentious depending on how you look at it. What is undisputed is the gay crowd loved going there because if you got tired of sitting in the bar, you hopped across the lobby to have a cup of coffee, a piece of pastry or part of the café's breakfast menu.

Unfortunately, after several years, the proprietor of Treetops Bar felt that having a sizeable gay clientele was bad for its image and discouraged their patronage. The hotel management decided it did not want Treetops to be a gay venue and started refusing to serve people whom they thought were gay. It was not a pleasant experience to be turned down and some gay people protested. I had a friend who did just that and the hotel's Public Relations department backed down. But not enough gay people stood their ground and so Treetops lost its gay reputation quickly. If this were to happen nowadays, I think the bar would run into greater resistance from the gay community.

I want to emphasise a difference between then and now. Way back then, the ambience of a gay bar was never as comfortable as what they are today, beginning with the act of ordering your drink from the bartender. In most gay bars today, customers take for granted that the bartenders know they are working in a gay venue probably owned by gay people and have to serve gay people with a welcoming friendly attitude. In the old days, you got a feeling that you were in the bar at somebody's sufferance. There was always a touch of tension or suspicion when you ordered your drink, very unlike the easy casual relationship that you could have with waiters and bartenders in gay bars today. There was no sense of ownership of a gay venue that today's gay community enjoy.

People often asked me how a bar became gay. I have never investigated this deeply. I suspect it was mostly serendipity; for example, a group of gay people going to a place, then liking the music or the ambience and went back frequently. They then told other gay people and the word got around that the place was attracting a gay clientele and this trend would grow unless the bar owner put a stop to it, as was the case with Treetops Bar. This is very different from today's bars where the proprietor set up a venue deliberately for a gay clientele. The practice of 'colonisation' also occurred at straight saunas in later years.

Another significant difference across the decades was the prevalence of the 'rice queen' in the 1970s and 1980s. A vast majority of gays in the Orchard Road bar scene were also unmitigated potato queens. 'Potato queens', gay Asian men attracted to Caucasian men, are stereotyped as those who had found it beyond their imagination to have sex with another Asian person, while rice queens are also stereotyped as gay Caucasians who are only into Asian men. Looking back, it was rather restrictive dreary scene and I am glad the gay scene has moved on since.

Figure 7.25
The location of Marmota disco, on the second level of Kallang Leisuredrome.

One of the first discotheques to be widely known and to enjoy massive patronage by the gay community was **Marmota**. It underwent renovations and several name changes over the years—from **Shadows** to **Legend**. It was located on the second level of Kallang Leisuredrome above the bowling alley and operated from the early to the mid-1980s. It catered to the mainstream community on every night except for Sundays, which were gay nights. Many a homosexual man who was unaware that there was a sizeable gay community in Singapore, on being brought there for the first time by a friend, would be emotionally overcome by the sight of the dance floor packed with attractive young men dancing with each other. For some, it was almost a spiritual epiphany as a lifetime of anticipated isolation and loneliness dissipated before their very eyes.

However, the dance floor was crowded only during the fast numbers. When the slow songs came on, it cleared faster than as if a tsunami threatened and only the daring ones irresistibly smitten with their partners were left in tight embrace to be ogled at by those on the sidelines. Marmota was the first disco to organise unofficial masculine *Mr. Gay Singapore* contests long before Manhunt began. Ironically, the first winner of the contest was a straight boy named Oliver. He was dressed in a bright red outfit with a black dragon emblazoned on it. The manager of the establishment was a balding, moustachioed, middle-aged man whom patrons affectionately called 'Ah Lau'.

Figure 7.26
The entrance of Vincenz at Duxton Road.

After the closure of Pebbles Bar, there existed no venue where the European rice queens could meet potato queens. A talented entrepreneur, Vincent Thnay, who was also a good amateur writer and poet, met this demand by opening a pub on 18th May 1989 named after himself—Vincent's. It was located at #06–05, Lucky Plaza, 304 Orchard Road and was the first dedicated 'East-meets-West' pub where Caucasian gay men could hook up with Asian Singaporeans, a large proportion of whom were Malay. Vincent's offered karaoke as well as booze. It relocated many years later, shortly after its 14th anniversary in May 2003, to a street-level shophouse at 15 Duxton Road in Tanjong Pagar, renaming itself **Vincenz**. The pub contained a handsomely elegant wooden bar, which offered a large selection of beers on tap. The establishment was called 'Venerable Vincent's' and 'The Grand Dame of Singapore' for good reasons. The newer outlet closed down on 26th March 2005 after 16 years of promoting East-West relations.

Originally catering to a gay customer base only once a week, usually on Sundays, newer small establishments have managed to survive on the burgeoning pink market by going full-time, on every night of the week. One such locale was **Niche** at Far East Plaza on Scotts Road. It opened in April 1983 to cash in on the popularity of **Marmota**. It was more popular with the English-educated crowd and spawned a popular latter-day namesake at Pagoda Street in Chinatown. This second incarnation had its liquor license withdrawn in 1989 and was given only a week to close down. No reason was provided for the police action but a person, personally involved in the running of the disco, believed it was a reaction to the first reported case of an AIDS death in Singapore.

Figure 7.27
The row of shophouses along Tanjong Pagar Road where Babylon and Inner Circle were located.

Figure 7.28
The second location of Inner Circle, at Duxton Hill.

During that era, one could not practically go on an outing to the disco with more than a handful of gay friends. The reason was that mobile phones had not yet been invented and if you were to lose sight of one of your friends in the crowd, it was not easy to regroup and arrange to go elsewhere that night for further entertainment. When the karaoke craze hit Singapore in the early 1990s, an enterprising pair of twin brothers opened a pub that catered exclusively to the gay community. It was called **Babylon** and was a narrow, miniature version of the legendary mega-sauna complex in Bangkok and the original Sumerian city. Unsurprisingly, it was a big hit as many gay men could sing well and liked to impress their friends with their crooning. Along with the now-defunct Babylon, **Inner Circle** is a pub considered to be the grand daddy of all gay karaoke joints. It provided 'divas' with an outlet to show off their vocal skills for almost 10 years before drawing its shutters on 24th July 2004. It was later resurrected at 3 Duxton Hill, a stone's throw away from its former location.

Figure 7.29
The external façade of the former Taboo, Happy and Play discos, along Tanjong Pagar Road.

Figure 7.30
The entrance of Happy in 2005.

At the turn of the century, Tanjong Pagar became developed as a locale for the preservation of heritage and culture in Singapore. The building on 21 Tanjong Pagar Road, under the management of Guan Seng Kee Pte. Ltd, used to house several gay establishments. **Taboo,** a pub-cum-disco, was one of the most popular with the trendy young crowd for seven years since 1997 and attained quasi-iconic status. It closed in August 2004, only to be reincarnated the year after on Neil Road, almost directly opposite **Tantric Bar**. Taking over when Taboo vacated, a gay disco co-owned by impresario Alan Seah expanded the floor space with the incorporation of the next-door unit, which gave it a sizeable dance floor. It was named 'Singapore's hottest nightspot' by *Wallpaper Magazine* in 2005, breaking new ground by hosting international DJs, which can be considered a first for a local gay club. It was also Singapore's pioneering socially responsible gay entertainment venue. Its SWEAT parties raked in more than S$25,000 for Action for AIDS. The bartenders concocted their signature vanilla, vodka and lime cocktails called 'happysexuals', which were gleefully sipped by celebrities and wannabes alike. It closed its doors for good after a grand finale on New Year's Eve 2006.

Figure 7.31
The interior deçor of Mox Bar in 2005.

Figure 7.32
Another view of the interior of Mox Bar.

Figure 7.33

The Attic, which later changed its name to Bianco, was above Mox Bar, 2005.

MOX Bar and Café is a versatile venue on the fourth storey. It also functioned as a bar-cum-event space equipped with lights, sound and platforms
to hold events like product launches, birthday bashes and cabaret shows. On
the other hand, The **Attic** (now **Bianco**) on the topmost floor is a vault-like loft
under the same management as MOX Bar & Café. It has a seating capacity of
up to 150 people and is suitable for exhibitions, fashion shows and performances. It was the former location of the Sunday services of the Free Community
Church and Toy Factory Theatre Ensemble.

Utterly Art @ Space 21 provided exhibition space and management services
to a diverse and vibrant range of local and Asian artists, and internationally-
renowned photographers. The most active gallery on the Singapore art scene,
it is a leading showcase of works by established painters like Martin Loh and
Chng Seok Tin, as well as popular young artists like Aiman Hakim. It was the
venue for the very first event of *IndigNation*, Singapore's historic, inaugural,
government-approved gay pride month celebration in August 2005. This was
an exhibition of paintings by artist Martin Loh entitled 'Cerita Budak-Budak',
meaning 'children's stories' in Peranakan Malay. The event was followed up
with *ContraDiction: A Night with Gay Poets* held on 4 August 2005, Singapore's
first public gay poetry reading session which was attended by over 70 people,
with standing room only.

Conclusion

Gay venues in Singapore have evolved over half a century from the seedy nocturnal venues known only by a street-smart, well-connected minority to the varied genres of almost-mainstreamed businesses and non-profit spaces we find today. Even though the cruising grounds of earlier years have declined in prominence in the panorama of local gay culture, they continue to be patronised by a subsection of the MSM (men-who-have-sex-with-men) community, the latter being a catchphrase which gained currency in the late 1990s. With the increased visibility of the gay community and interaction with mainstream society facilitated by the Internet and with social media such as Facebook, it is likely that in another few decades, places where homosexual men and women socialise will not be vastly different from those frequented by any other segment of Singapore society.

8

The Negative Dialectics of Homonationalism, or Singapore English Newspapers and Queer World-Making

Jun Zubillaga-Pow

> I believe I am capable of loving a woman. I am getting very restless. Being gay and a pervert is a very painful thing. I am willing to live my whole life with a woman if she loves me. I am waiting for her.
>
> —'Anna' (Khoo, 1972)

> [I]t's not the President alone who decides such [protectionist] matters. The Congress, the unions and the mass media have a lot to do in formulating policies.
>
> —Lee Kuan Yew (1977)

When one reads the story of Anna forty years after it has been published, one wonders what has become of her today. One very much hopes that she has found and remained with the woman who loves her. Uncannily, if the word 'nation' is substituted for 'woman' in the same statement, national love for homosexuals becomes equally a kind of waiting, waiting to be loved by the nation. Alluding to such an appropriation, queer theorist Sara Ahmed believes that inter-personal "love may be especially crucial in the event of the failure of the nation to deliver its promise for the good life" (Ahmed, 2004: 130–31). In this chapter, I argue that this 'failure' in receiving national love is a result of the incongruence between a homophobic print media and the nationalist politics, both of which have been enforced upon homosexuals by the postcolonial government. If this diktat of compulsory nationalism is offered as a contingent philosophy of queer praxis, my present literary reading of homosexual-related news reports in Singapore's English newspapers aims to subvert the nationalist discourse via an utilitarian counteraction of, what Lauren Berlant and Michael Warner (1998) advocate for, a *queer world-making* methodology, or "the historical embedded production of practical and critical knowledges" (Floyd, 2009: 198). That is, the invention of knowledge about queer lives and practices should be positioned amidst the existing resources of historical news archives and other public information within and without the boundaries of a foreclosed heteronormative world.

This latter approach can largely be possible with the recent introduction of the National Library Board's digital archive of Singapore newspapers published between 1831 and 2006—that is almost two centuries of information![1] A keyword search of 'homosexual' and 'lesbian' would indicate the number of articles and advertisements which contains the word, and categorizes the items according to the year, the source of the news and which paper it is in. The system makes tracing an editorial dialogue or a criminal case more convenient, and allows a researcher to compare and contrast the socio-historical context and implication of the article, such as the frequency and relevance to other news reports in the same paper. Alongside the comprehensive results, there are other benefits with the advent of technological empiricism: the accompanying illustrations are shown vividly, while the positioning of the article with respect to the other news reports, which could be crucial to how a reader perceives the news, is also indicated. Given the sole reliance on this particular literary medium, the caveat remains that there would be inevitable misrepresentations of the historical queer world due to the facts that not all Singaporeans are literate in English, have daily access to the papers, or pay similar attention to world news in comparison to local news. Thereby, the queer narratives as interpreted within this chapter could only belong to a smaller percentile of upper class, English-speaking Singaporeans from the 1960s to the 2000s.

Historical and Theoretical Foundations

The period after the Second World War has been a time of turbulence and restructuring for many new nations as well as other bigger organisations such as the United Nations. Like other states across Africa and the Caribbean, Singapore is one of the first few countries to gain independence from the colonial forces at the turn of the 1950s. To placate the anti-colonial sentiments hovering over the new world, Singapore's erstwhile retention of the British constitution and military bases in the 1960s had to be clarified diplomatically to her African and Asian counterparts by the then Deputy Prime and Foreign Ministers no less via personal visits to countries from Kenya to Cambodia, and meeting up with revolutionaries like President Jomo Kenyatta and King Norodom Sihanouk (Turnbull, 2009: 329).

If it seems disparate comparing the development of these countries with that of Singapore's, it should be apparent that numerous political manoeuvres on the part of the then Singapore government are accountable for these dissimilarities. To be sure, the governance of this country by the postcolonial office has been categorised in negative light as illiberal (Mutalib, 2000), authoritarian (Rodan, 2004) and even tyrannical (McCarthy, 2006), but justification for the policies from the Lee governance are often rebutted as grounding on the utilitarian rules of pragmatism (Chua, 1985), Asian-values (Barr, 2002) and, most significantly, neoliberal (Sim, 2005). That is, the polar connotations of the 'docile' East and the 'wild' West have continued to thaw any socio-political alignments within the everyday governmentality of Singapore since independence. Albeit with a quasi-Asian self-identity, it is uncanny, as much as the Freudian term allows for, that Singapore remains one of the few countries after British Victorian rule to derive her political orientation within, what Homi Bhabha connotes as, a postcolonial hybridity. Larbi Sadiki, a Middle Eastern specialist, has suggested that most postcolonial countries had to 'construct' a political discourse by assimilating a "post-colonial identity [which] owes its existence to force" and one not more democratic than its colonised version (Sadiki, 2004: 122). This theory could serve as an analogous explanation for the authoritarian and dictatorial nature of many postcolonial States after independence and the Singaporean political regime could not veer too far from this critical diagnosis.

If this grand narrative contains certain factuality, albeit being antagonistic to a total decolonialisation, then the mass media, being one of the many bureaucratic apparatuses of State propaganda, would weld itself acutely upon this socio-political clockwork and replicate itself automatically as the surveyor and controller of the population. For media commentator Cherian George (2007), the Singaporean newspapers have been absolved of guilt for working alongside the 'calibrated coercion' of the government and deny being more or less propagandistic when toeing the political lines of the standing party. To be sure, this consequence is derived not without the illiberal antecedent of newspaper closures, personnel detentions and legal alterations in the 1970s.[2] It should be pointed out that the number and outlook of Singaporean newspapers before and after the 1970s have been drastically different.[3] When one surveys the content production of newspapers before and after the 1970s, a marked contrast, political or otherwise, can be discerned. According to the authoritative edition of Singapore's history by Mary Constance Turnbull, one of the four English newspapers in 1971 had "attracted quite a following, with its lively, entertaining, refreshing irreverent approach" (Turnbull, 1995: 291) despite also having "shown some spirited criticism of government policies" (Turnbull, 2009: 323). The popularity of the publication would have immediately annoyed the then single-party government given efforts in nation-building and quietening dissidence. It then became obvious to the cabinet that the content generation of the country's mass media has to be regulated bureaucratically for the greater good of the young nation.

For an effective governance of a postcolonial nation, it could be instigated that the then Singapore government may have been misguided by the modus operandi of nation-building so much so that their essential world view could have been constrained within geopolitical borders. The wish to create a 'Malaysian Malaysia' in 1963 was already a political faux pas at least with respect to international relations, but to restrict the flow of information among the meagre population of less than 2.5 million people in the 1970s could be deemed as protectionist on the part of the then government. Despite the inherent intention to ensure equality, racial or otherwise, within the country, the nationalist idea reveals its flaws with the management of the populace, whose developing world view has been speculated by some critics, such as Singapore's veteran novelist Catherine Lim (2005), as being a centripetal plunge towards a state of dystopia. Thereby, the fervent of nationalism can be considered to be a double-edged sword with respect to a government's protectionist policies. Since the nineteenth-century, nationalism as a political instrument has been accused of being the illogical rejoinder to the capitalist empire so much so that the anarchist Fredy Perlman can claim nationalism as "so perfectly suited to its double task, the domestication of workers and the despoliation of aliens, that it appealed to everyone—everyone, that is, who wielded or aspired to wield a portion of capital" (Perlman, 1984: 26). It is not surprising to see the recent reprisal of nationalistic policies, such as the 'Singapore Heartbeat' and 'YourSingapore' projects, instilling a juxtaposed sense of docility and belonging.

How then do homosexuals in Singapore fit into this political regime? After Perlman, who believes that nationalism "holds out the prospect of eliminating parasites from human society" (Perlman, 2002: 48), gay men and lesbians are posited correspondingly as anti-national aliens and parasites. This can be accounted for by two among many other everyday phenomena: on the one hand, homosexuals are unable to contribute more significantly to economic and demographic regenerations than the heterosexuals;[4] on the other hand, homosexuals are perceived to disrupt the stability of numerous heteronormative social structures, such as healthcare services and the law.[5] Why should a purposeful government want such deviating aliens and parasites in his or her country? The counterargument comes appropriately from the portmanteau concept of homonationalism.

Homonationalism, as formulated by Jasbir Puar, is the buttress of nationalism upon the foundation of homonormativity among its other propagators. To be clear, homonormativity is not the reactionary equaliser of heteronormativity as used commonly in Queer scholarship. It is, contingently, a neoliberal form of sexual politics. Accordingly to Lisa Duggan, homonormativity is "a politics that *does not* contest dominant heteronormative assumptions and institutions but upholds and sustains them while promising the possibility of a *demobilized* gay constituency and a privatised, depoliticized gay culture anchored in *domesticity* and *consumption*" (Duggan, 2002: 179). That is, gay men and women are integrated, with or without force, into the normative everyday mechanism of the capitalist laissez faire system, and are governed to partake in the socio-political formulae of quiet lives and personal exchanges. Accordingly to Puar, this "politics of privatisation" has its fundamental agenda rooted in "the separation of economic justice from identity politics" (Puar, 2007: 29), and vice versa. As much as the neoliberal system results in the disregard for an 'intimate citizenship' (Plummer, 2003) and an alienating 'society of strangers' (Tan, 2009), a compromise to one's personal rights and homosexual desires is reached in the name of the necessities of the national economy.[6]

This social and societal balance may appear to be a win-win situation for the cosmopolitan queer subject and the capitalist government, but the latter is aware of the catch behind this economic apparatus. That is, *homonormativity begets state regulation.* Geographer David Harvey delineates that:

> if 'there is no such thing as society but only individuals', as Thatcher initially put it, then the chaos of individual interests can easily end up prevailing over order. The anarchy of the market, of competition, and of unbridled individualism (individual hopes, desires, anxieties, and fears; choices of lifestyle and of sexual habits and orientation; modes of self-expression and behaviours towards others) generates a situation that becomes increasingly ungovernable …. In the face of this, some degree of coercion appears necessary to restore order (Harvey, 2007: 82).

The intervention on the part of the government would then be perceived as an act of benevolence for the greater good of the economy and its people, although it is actually a pre-empted policing of her citizenry. For Puar to attempt a juxtaposition of homonormativity as a queer political tactic and the postcolonial government's interest in invoking a national identity among the populace would be a masochistic subscription to the manoeuvres of the 'neo-colonial' master. After Schopenhauer (1974), *nationalism is inherently anti-personal* and thus stands in total opposition to neoliberalism;[7] after Hegel, it can be deduced that the neologised concept of homonationalism then becomes a dialectical snowballing of the connotations and implications of both nationalism and homonormativity as understood in their separated guises. As has been exposed by Puar in her justifications against such unethical American politics, the homonationalist government can inevitably exercise her power in manipulating the electoral loyalty of the citizenry to their advantage at the expense of the anti-national minorities, be they queer or otherwise. Hereby, I want to suggest, albeit being anachronistic and depreciatory, that the portrayal of homosexuality by Singapore's postcolonial news media as an epitome of this neoliberal phenomenon.

Queer News-Making as Homonationalism

Having understood the historical and theoretical contexts in which the mass media in general and the newspapers in particular are situated, I shall now differentiate my methodology in doing a news analysis from the prevailing sociological or textual hermeneutics. While sociologist Laurence Leong (2005) has discussed the topics of criminality, molestations and arts and culture by segmenting fifteen years of news reports from 1989, the political scientist Kenneth Paul Tan (2008) and media scholar Debbie Goh (2008) have examined the religious and socio-medical revelations in recent news media via the language and logic of the writers. Comparing their analyses of Singapore's only authorised English newspaper *The Straits Times*, it becomes obvious how these academic researchers merely reproduce the lines of argument inherent to their resources. While Tan has remarked without being sceptical of the Singapore media that: "... responded to [the Prime Minister's] remarks [on hiring openly gay people into the public service] with what seemed like *surprisingly* gay-positive messages" (Tan, 2008: 417), Goh's rhetoric perpetuates her conclusion of how "the newspaper *unfailingly* supported [the minister's] claim that the gays were to be blamed" (Goh, 2008: 389) for the rise in new HIV/AIDS infections in Singapore.

Given the close associations between the news editors and the government, if one were to understand the modus operandi of the press in their coverage of homosexual-related news, he or she would be disillusioned not only by the political or social orientation of the newspaper, but also by the sexual politics of the Singapore government. Apparently, this institutional alliance would turn out to become more controversial in the subsequent years as witnessed from reviews of the paper's treatment of the 377A penal code debate in 2007, the 'AWARE saga' in 2009 and the anti-censorship campaign in 2010.[8] To be sure, there are other contentious issues, such as the death penalty and migratory discontent, of which *The Straits Times* has failed to provide balanced reportage. In contrast, rather than brood over the nitty-gritty of, what some call the tabloid style of reporting, the 'mosquito press', my literary analysis is neither to categorise nor frame the articles into subjective post-structural tropes. Although it has been the trend, at least within recent academic work, to stockpile the specifics and argue for a general theory, this objectifying essentialism of numerous social practices, queer or otherwise, is unhelpful in the emancipation of homosexuality regardless of the field of research. In the end, what is produced in recent queer scholarship becomes a reified affirmation of social phenomena: commodification (Hennessy, 2000), promiscuity (Klesse, 2007), shame (Munt, 2008) and unhappiness (Ahmed, 2010), all of which are readily present in news articles since 1960s.

To extend these discursive practices with the portmanteau concept of homonationalism would lead eventually into a negative cul-de-sac, because a survey of the reports, which deal with or touch upon homosexual-related news from 1960 to 2010, has largely replicated the position of the government with respect to sexual identity and politics. The Hegelian synthesis of homonormativity and postcolonial nationalism, as I have discussed earlier, would show its dialectical predicament coherently from the news coverage. From the juridical rule on gay marriages to the cultural values of pride parades and queer film festivals, whatever homosexual-related news is being reported on, reading the news media with homonationalism as a critical politico-economic discourse would result in negative dialectics for the homosexual subject who attempts a synthesis of his or her queer and national identities.

According to Adorno's (1990) philosophical theory, negative dialectics create a position of non-identity for the subject. In this case, the reader or analyst of homosexual-related news is unable to fulfil the political demands of nationalism and a privatised market economy for the very reason that he or she is disassociated from the 'truth content' of being a nationalist and a capitalist or neoliberalist. Positing this situation within that which Harvey (2007) has proposed as the inevitability of state intervention, if each homosexual individual is only interested in homosexual-related goods, an unregulated neoliberalism would result in an overtly ostentatious production; an appropriate example could be extrapolated from Puar's analysis of the gay and lesbian tourism industry (Puar, 2006: 62–67). While homonormativity may be highly effective for the American economy, the negative portrayal of homosexuality in the news has adverse implications for the already meagre presence of a Singaporean gay market. As exposed by Leong (2005), the national press's adherence to a homophobic agenda in their partial reporting of homosexual-related news is part of the ideological state apparatus in the regulation of homonormativity. Coupled with the deliberate exclusion of queer representatives in nation-building campaigns as a form of 'calibrated coercion', the government's nationalist discourse posits homosexuals as *a priori* anti-national.

For Singaporean readers, queer or otherwise, the negative dialectics of homonationalism is the Adornian moment when the homosexual subject could neither identify themselves with the homosexual lifestyle, be it real or imaginary, nor be persuaded by a compulsory nationalism to change their personal consumption patterns. This model of homonationalism is dependent on a homonormative contingency, which results in a compromise between the reification of the homosexual lifestyle and the alienation of being nationalist. The readers of such anti-personalised news reports as founded upon the homonationalist ideology will develop a homosexual world view that is always negative and illiberal. As an alternative approach to circumvent the negative dialectics of homonationalism, I suggest the critical methodology of queer world-making. For Kevin Floyd (2009), queer world-making appropriates "to the production of historically and socially situated, bounded totalities of queer praxis inherently critical of the ultimately global horizon of neoliberalized capital itself" (Floyd, 2009: 199). Instead of enforcing a 'politics of privatization', the queer world-making project endeavours to reveal the complete 'constellations' of stories of love and hatred, to make public all positive and negative perceptions of homosexuality, and to empower the suppressed and liberated to receive empathy and support. It is this integrative methodology of queer world-making that would allow people to understand the lives of homosexuals in the past and the present.

Newspapers for Critical Queer World-Making

In this final section, I will analyse several news excerpts from the late 1960s to the early 1990s. As mentioned earlier, this is the period after Singapore has been liberated from colonial governance and was experiencing a surge of industrial and political reforms. Reflective of the socio-historical milieu, the news extracts will serve as illustrations to justify my arguments for the queer world-making methodology and against the homonationalist discourse as corresponding to the representations of positive and negative dialectics within a Singaporean homosexual genealogy. The first case study is extracted from a 1972 feature report where several men, who have identified themselves as gay, homosexuals or bisexuals, revealed their personal stories. To begin, this is what a married 31-year-old business executive recalled when asked to elaborate on his situation:

> I felt this strong urge to kiss him. He was like a baby to me, almost like a girl. I kissed him on the lips. I was shocked at myself. I drove home, bewildered, and revolted at myself, and lived in misery for the next few weeks … Would I lose interest in women, in my wife? These doubts raged in me … (Yeo, Khoo and Lee, 1972).

An interpretation using the queer world-making method would encompass a literal reading of the interviewee's homosexual desire as a part of his greater world view. The other nuances of displaying a sense of guilt and shame with himself, his spouse, and the society at large can also be evoked. The verbal expression of his 'urge' would be labelled as an irrational gesture, and it is as if he is possessed with a pathological disorder not being able to differentiate between a 'boy', a 'girl' and a 'baby'. The emotional extremity and self-hatred could be read against the contemporaneous discourse of abnormality, such as a weak masculinity, a social deviance or a sustained unhappiness. While a staunch moralist would continue to interrogate him on his spousal fidelity and perverted promiscuity, the liberal ethicist would welcome the progressive sexual practice without restraint. On the other hand, the homonationalist would be solely concerned with how a homosexual, like the subject in question, affects the gross consumption patterns and other national economic affiliations. That is, the homonationalist approach would situate the protagonist as a capitalist subject, identifying him as the main arbiter of the economy, due to the facts that he comes from the upper class, owns a car and has business dealings in early developing Singapore. A homonationalist reading is oblivious to the social and emotional well-being of the individual and other implicated persons, but focuses essentially on the national gains this particular homosexual can obtain for the state. With all else being equal, his homosexuality is *a priori* foreclosed within a homonational ideology.

This method of reading media history is unfortunately myopic. Historians and politicians should instead be more critical by asserting world-making viewpoints of the homosexual subject; they need to ascertain the state of affairs from the social, psychological, economic, religious, educational and legal-political perspectives in order to build a substantive queer world using as much of the given information as possible. Another instance of applying the critical queer world-making method against the homonationalist one can be observed from the famous 1968 Gene Koh murder trial where the accused was later deemed to be a homosexual:

> On the thirtieth day of the trial, the judge added that the new diagnosis of the accused, who is married and unemployed, is 'very important as homosexuality is one of the planks in the platform of the defence on which the contention that the accused is a psychopath is based' (*The Straits Times*, 1968).

Given the numerous medico-legal developments concerning the treatment of homosexuality over the past half a century, it would be injudicious to frame this news report within any singular discourse without total knowledge of postcolonial, medical and legal history. The catch-22 situation for the queer world-making theorist would be to make any verifiable generalities about the jurisprudence towards homosexuality during the 1960s. Whether the queer subject is charged with murder or manslaughter, the dogmatic reliance on the two standing policies from Britain (section 377A) and the United States (DSM-I) would in actual fact presume a queer world-making project under the imperial guises of moralist and psychoanalytic inventions.[9] Contrastingly, if a homonationalist discourse is applied in the process of settling this legal suit, it would be predicated primarily on the negative dialectics between the homosexual accused and a wider national good. In this case, because the criminal subject is unemployed and the probability of him being diagnosed as a psychopath could diminish his prospects of achieving an outstanding career, the subject in question would deem to deviate from the profit-making and nation-building aspirations as structured by the homonationalist framing. That is, the positioning of homosexual subjects within a homonationalist ideology is always and already dialectically negative for both the subject and the nation.

On the one hand, the queer world-making methodology could also be applied to news that share a similar theme but occur at different moments within the nation's history. On the other hand, a homonationalist perspective would be less able to discern these periodic and gradually more liberating attitudes towards homosexuality because it has an *a priori* capitalist trajectory defined. As empirical support, excerpts from three news reports dating from 1970, 1980 and 1992 will be analysed with respect to the changing social attitudes towards homosexuality.

> An editor of a publishing house which markets children books with homosexual, shotgun, and abortion topics believes that 'parents who censor what their children want to read are hiding their heads in the sand, underestimating how adult they are' (*The Straits Times*, 1970).

A homonationalist interpreter would posit the publisher firstly as a capitalist who directs all his comments as a marketing ploy for the want of higher sales figures. He or she would want homosexual, shotgun, and abortion topics to become nationalised and mainstreamed by the money-minded government. Notwithstanding the mindset of its people, which include the parents who are protective of their children, the import and sales of these books would be perceived by a homonationalist government as potential contributions to the nation's gross domestic product from additional duty charges, and so on. If such an ideology prevails, the homonationalist reading could imminently be charged for endorsing homosexuality and other mentioned topics collectively for their attached exchange value. The reification of homosexuality and an economic nationalism is implicated through the negative dialectics of amalgamating one with the other.

> Dr Ow Chin Hock, the permanent secretary of the Ministry of Culture, clarifies that his office 'banned [*Saint Jack*] not because [the director] represented Singapore as a haven for prostitutes and gangsters, but for other reasons. There are certain very explicit homosexual scenes not consistent with [the] censorship criteria' (*The Straits Times*, 1980).[10]

As opposed to prostitutes and gangsters, a homonationalist framing would categorise homosexuals or, in this case, its filmic representations for being not only socially, but also economically deviant of the nationalist discourse. Contingently, homonormativity is now embraced by the national vanguard as *outside* the domain of financial profiteering and is selectively barred from entering its domestic market. As an indication of prevailing homosexual attitudes, homonationalism, in this particular case of bureaucracy, wield its power in the total rejection of homosexual subjects and behaviour.

> The Censorship Review Committee survey found that 'Singaporeans strongly disapprove of homosexuality and lesbianism as a way of life, but they may be more tolerant of books or songs which accept or encourage such behaviour' (*The Straits Times*, 1992).

As a thematic synthesis of the first and second news reports, the cultural representations of homosexuality are now tolerated by 'Singaporeans' as collectively approved national artefacts. As compared to the market intervention of 1970 or the authoritarian diktats of 1980, sociological data is now used to buttress public opinion resulting in the production and consumption of cultural material to take on nationalist connotations. This is homonationalism *par excellence*: the sanction or disavowal of homonormativity both within and without the cultural industry is measured through qualitative national consensus. Homonormativity, along with homosexual-related issues, is being determined through the lenses of nationalist arbitrators. In part, a homonationalist treatment could be deemed as democratic, but it casts unjust imperatives for the homosexual subjects, who remain a minority group among the Singaporean *doxa*.

After Foucault (1990), the subjectification of the homosexual as a cause for nation-building would be considered as politically unethical, but time and time again, it is being raised as the yardstick for the aspirations of national cohesiveness. Such is the homonationalist ideology as espoused by the erstwhile government: 'In every society, there are gay people. We should accept those in our midst as fellow human beings, and as fellow Singaporeans' (*The Straits Times*, 2003). From comparative readings of the above news excerpts, it can be affirmed that the homonationalist world view is in the first instance antagonistic to the accurate and progressive queer world-making ideals towards homosexual emancipation. As I have mentioned at the start of the chapter, the National Library Board's digital newspaper archive has enabled a comprehensive survey of queer life in Singapore. It is crucial that historians and social theorists who make use of these resources to thwart any political infestation of homonationalism and utilise the critical methodology of queer world-making for an integral genealogy of homosexuality in postcolonial Singapore. The negative dialectics of homonationalism must eventually be circumvented in the course of political history.

9

Impossible Presence

Toward a Queer Singapore Cinema, 1990s–2000s

Kenneth Chan

To map the film history of queer sexualities in contemporary Singapore cinema is to articulate the artistic struggles, negotiations, compromises, and persistence of filmmakers and producers in a conservative cultural and political environment that often resists or actively works against queer representational presence. A quick scan of the historical, political, and cultural factors will help crystallize how difficult the conditions have been and continue to be for this cultural phenomenon. Firstly, the contemporary Singapore film industry is a comparatively young one. For, according to film historians Jan Uhde and Yvonne Ng Uhde, "Singapore's film revival began in 1991" (Uhde and Uhde, 2010: 73). A new film industry struggling against the ideological tide of the State's illiberal pragmatism, which is grounded in a survivalist logic of putting economic progress first,[1] can hardly be the ideal condition for instituting an expansive artistic policy that sufficiently accommodates alternative voices such as queer sexualities, particularly when funding and resources for the arts are scarce and competition for them extremely keen. Even today, with MediaCorp Raintree Pictures spearheading Singapore's mainstream film production and the Singapore Film Commission providing much needed seed funding for budding filmmakers, the deep and inextricable ties these organizations have to the political establishment ultimately restrain and constrain the cultural spaces that allow queer representation to breathe and survive.[2]

Secondly, sodomy remains criminalized under Section 377A of Singapore's Penal Code. Sodomy's illegality translates, by extension, into homosexuality's discursive liminality in the public and media sphere, thus forcing representations of queer sexualities into the margins of Singapore's pop cultural consciousness. This point leads me to the third and most crucial factor for the anti-gay conditions faced by filmmakers: the State's draconian censorship laws function as the ideological state apparatus through which Penal Code Section 377A and the government's reification of the Asian value system's supposed rejection of queerness can be further articulated, hence asserting a strong material impact on cinematic cultures. While the Board of Film Censors (BFC) have positively and necessarily moved from "a single-tier" to a "classification ratings" system on 1 July 1991 (Media Development Authority, 2011), queer filmic representation can still be classified as "obscene" under the Films Act (Chapter 107). Because the Films Act does not specify in detail, rather strategically I might add, what constitutes obscenity, one could turn to, for example, the Media Development Authority's stricter "Free-to-Air Television Programme Code" to get a sense of the moral semantics at work: according to the section on "Sex", "portrayals of sexual behaviour [sic] should be non-explicit" and "programmes on sex education ... should not be presented in a sensational or exploitative manner, nor should they encourage or promote sexual permissiveness, promiscuity or *unnatural sex acts*" (Media Development Authority, 2004: 5–6; emphasis mine). Queer sexualities can conveniently fall into the category of "unnatural sex acts". Because evidence of the BFC's, at times, arbitrary application of its censorship guidelines is legion, one need only look at the recent withdrawal of Boo Junfeng's *Tanjong Rhu* (2009; re-titled *The Casuarina Cove* for international release) and Loo Zihan's *Threshold* (2009) from the 6th Singapore Short Cuts film festival (Tan, 2009), and the trials and tribulations experienced by the organizers of the 2010 *IndigNation* Film Festival (Zubillaga-Pow, 2010), to realize the dire need for drastic changes to the country's censorship practices.

In delineating briefly these extremely difficult conditions, I am also offering a cultural political context in which to posit the notion of cinematic queerness in Singapore as a minor miracle of sorts, despite its political imperfections. As I track, in this chapter, the filmic occurrences of queer sexualities over the past two decades, and later analyze Kan Lume and Loo Zihan's *Solos* (2007) as Singapore's most recent feature-length film that brazenly tackles the question of gay male sexuality, I celebrate the very possibility of queerness in this cinema, while simultaneously lament its inadequacies and complicities. This ambivalent reception I attribute to what one could call the "impossible presence" of queer representation—or, liminal presence, or half-presence, depending on the specific theoretical valence one wishes to emphasize—in Singapore film. This cinema's "impossible presence" marks a contradictory and contingent materiality that shifts according to the political winds and whims on the ground. Directors, producers, and distributors adopt an uneasy flexibility in order to negotiate the shifting cultural and political boundaries of sexual acceptability, while finding tactically opportune moments to push back and/or to resist the legal and political structures of heteronormative disciplining. Some would even choose to ride the waves of global cinema's capitalist distribution network to situate their films outside the boundaries of the nation, as *Solos* has done, in order to reach local audiences from the outside in, thus underscoring how cinema as a transnational commodity puts into question the very idea of a *Singapore* cinema in a traditionally nationalist sense (Uhde and Uhde, 2010:

4–5). While one must be critical of the oppressive impact that transnational capital has on global living conditions, and rightly so in that critique, I want to suggest Singapore's queer cinematic culture as one of the contrary instances where riding the flows of capitalist commodification has enabled filmmakers to enlist the transnational in the circumscription of the confines of the national as a mode of critical intervention (keeping in mind, of course, there will always be problematic compromises and complicities involved in terms of queer cinema as transnational commodity). The uneasy interface between the national and transnational opens up a tentative space for queer cinematic existence, one of the possible reasons why queer sexualities in Singapore cinema are currently in emergence. This possibility also illustrates the tactical negotiations queer cultural productions engage in as part of what Audrey Yue, in the introduction of this book, calls "the illiberal pragmatics of survival". One can only hope that the State's uneasy shuttling between a conservative national identity and a need to move toward a cultural liberalization (that is in sync with the nation's desire to be a global city as part of a transnational capitalist network) will generate enough political momentum in the future to enable the repeal of the sodomy laws of the Singapore Penal Code, which can then create a cascading effect of liberalization in the culture and arts industries. The strengthening currency of the pink dollar might one day, ironically, help tip the scales to this effect.[3]

Before I begin mapping the contours of this "impossible presence" by selectively and strategically identifying and close reading queer moments in contemporary Singapore films, it is critically and politically necessary to reflect on not just a definition but also the possibility of a "queer Singapore cinema". What exactly constitutes such a cinema and what categorizing valence of the term "queer" should one fall back on? Does and should such a cinema exist from a critical and institutional standpoint? For practical purposes, one could define an instance of queer cinema as a cinematic text where LGBT sexualities find their way front and centre in the film's narrative—I disavow the essentialist quality of such a definition for two key reasons. Firstly, my usage of "queer" abides by the fluidity and openness of non-heteronormative sexualities first articulated by key queer theorists of the likes of Judith Butler, Eve Kosofsky Sedgwick, and Michael Warner, to name a few; in contrast to more essentialist claims to the term for the purposes of shoring up a gay identity politics. This fluidity could be represented, for instance, in cinematic imagery that occupies the spectrum of Sedgwick's "male homosocial desire" (Sedgwick, 1985: 4), thereby allowing filmmakers to insinuate queerness into their "mainstream" work as a means of circumventing censorship's bureaucratic rigidities. Secondly, to cement too quickly the definitional terms of "queer cinema" is to not only go against the spirit of queer politics but to also invert the oppressive limitations of heteronormativity onto Singapore cinematic practices, reinforcing the very legal and cultural restrictions that have been imposed upon queer cinematic representations in the first place. Any conception of a queer Singapore cinema should, therefore, allow it to transgress boundaries, embed itself secretively in the mainstream, or out itself flamboyantly, in order to negotiate and engage the political contingencies faced by filmmakers in the alternately (and cyclically) expanding and contracting spaces of Singapore's film and arts scenes.

The definitional problematics I have registered above do lead one to the same critical quandary Song Hwee Lim finds himself confronting in his resistance to naming a "queer Chinese cinema" (Lim, 2006: 185) in his book *Celluloid Comrades*:

> There is no question that "queer" remains the most flexible term in use ... However, the term has also been mobilized, in both the English-and Chinese-speaking contexts, as an identity category. In this regard, I would caution the assumption that the category of queer is necessarily more progressive ... Similarly, in reference to its cinematic representation, "queer cinema," "lesbian and gay films," and "homosexual films" are not concentric circles with the former occupying the outermost space; rather, they overlap and shore up each other's deficiencies and efficacies (Lim, 2006: 184).

Lim's nuanced approach in culturally contextualizing terminology deserves emulation here. Does the term "queer" resonate in Singapore the same way it does in the United States since the emergence of queer activism and queer theory?[4] Should we resist the premature labeling of a "queer Singapore cinema" precisely on the complex anti-essentialist grounds that Lim has articulated, and the fact that representations of queer sexualities are only struggling to surface in Singapore cinema? What are the quantitative and qualitative parameters for such a definition of this cinema? Yet, on the other hand, there is a certain discursive power in naming, calling into existence a category as an enunciative act of intervention. To name a "queer Singapore cinema" is to legitimize and empower a cultural entity that has long been delegitimized and erased in Singapore. Hence, in suturing together a filmic textual history of queer sexualities, I see myself participating politically in a call to existence a queer Singapore cinema, with the hope that these effective and/or flawed cinematic moments of "impossible presence" I identify will serve as the growing foundation of a robust anti-essentialist queer cinema to come.

Finally, I want to invoke the theoretical work of Linda Williams in her book *Screening Sex* as a way of negotiating both the possibilities and the pitfalls, in other words the political contradictions, of this "impossible presence". This theoretical intersection will hopefully produce a framework for my interpretive cinematic history of queerness and for my reading of *Solos*, a framework that resists the reductive politics of labeling all queer cinematic representations as critically interventional and eliding any complicities and contradictions potentially inherent in queer cinema. Williams begins her discussion of depicting sex in cinema by punning "on the double meaning of the verb *to screen* as both revelation and concealment", explaining that "to screen is to reveal on a screen"; while to screen, citing a dictionary, can also mean "to shelter or protect with or as a screen" (Williams, 2008: 2). Though much of her book deals with American cinema and, thus, engages the question of American censorship practices, Williams' semantic play allows her to deploy a Foucauldian argument that sex on screen should be read "not as liberating transgressions, but as the two-edged swords of liberation and further disciplinary control" (Williams, 2008: 13). My notion of "impossible presence" owes much to Williams' critical manoeuvre here, both in terms of the cinematic visuality of sex (not only the depiction of queer sex on screen but also screening "sex" as the mediating condition for human relations) and the double-edged inflections of queer Singapore cinema's interpellation into the State's defining boundaries of cultural political production. Queerness registers its presence as a mode of liberation, and yet it cannot help but must subscribe to the very terms of official discourse in order to be able to have a presence in the first place, even in the negative. For queer sex and sexualities to be embodied in varying degrees of visual presence on Singapore screens is to see Williams' ironic pun at work, but with a specifically Singapore valence, especially when we understand the circumnavigation filmmakers deploy to work with and around the unpredictable censorship climate. Of particular significance to the ludic quality of screening is Williams' discussion of film theorist Miriam Hansen's analysis of Walter Benjamin's term "innervation". Drawing from a "lesser-known second version" (Williams, 2008: 18)[5] of Benjamin's famous essay *The Work of Art in the Age of Mechanical Reproduction*, Hansen argues that, "Benjamin [may have] borrowed the term from Freud or from the neurophysiological and psychological discourse of the period." "To imagine ... an enabling reception of technology" such as cinema, "it is essential that Benjamin, unlike Freud, understood innervation as a *two-way* process, that is, not only a conversion of mental, affective energy into somatic, motoric form, but also the possibility of reconverting, and recovering, split-off psychic energy through motoric stimulation" (Hansen, 1999: 317). Williams describes this two-way process as a method where "our bodies both take in sensation and then reverse the energy of that reception to move back out to the outside world" (Williams, 2008: 18). This conception of motor sensory relay Williams applies to watching sex on screen where "a variety of responses are possible: shock, embarrassment, arousal, but also, and most important, imaginative play" (Williams, 2008: 19). Such dynamic play as a form of reception theory infuses the difficulties of "impossible presence" with political potentialities, as filmmakers tease us with glimpses (truncated glimpses often being the only legalized possibility available) of bodies, queer sexed bodies, queer sexed bodies in motion; "a way of habituating our bodies to a newly sexualized world in which vicarious forms of sexual pleasure are now on/scene" (Williams, 2008: 18). Toying with queer visual corporeality is to electrify and politically energize queer audiences into imagining an idealized queer cinema that such cinematic beginnings can only begin to hint at.

Screening the Queer Body in Singapore Cinema

I want to start this brief thematic history of Singapore's queer cinematic representation with an unlikely instance of obscure American cinema of the 1970s, auteur Peter Bogdanovich's *Saint Jack* (1979). Shot entirely in Singapore under the guise of a different script title, *Jack of Hearts*, in order to circumscribe the Singapore censors disapproval of Bogdanovich adapting Paul Theroux's novel (Millet, 2006: 76), *Saint Jack* chronicles the adventures of an American (Ben Gazzara) living in Singapore as a pimp facing off the intrusions of both Singapore's moral policing and gangster violence, in order to cater to the sexual needs of the local British colonial remnants and newly arriving American GIs en route to Vietnam. First "banned by the local censors in 1980 for 'misrepresenting' the city", the film eventually received its limited Singapore premiere at the 1997 Singapore International Film Festival with only "a single screening", and was finally granted an M18 rating for general release and distribution as late as 2006 (Uhde and Uhde, 2010: 53).[6] Both Raphaël Millet and the Uhdes confirm *Saint Jack*'s "documentary" significance, with the former observing how the film "gives an unusually gritty portrayal of the city, showing what some would call its dark side" (Millet, 2006: 76), and the latter corroborating this observation with the argument that the film "has become an invaluable historical record of the country's past, a veritable treasure of images long lost" (Uhde and Uhde, 2010: 53).

One of the reasons I begin my discussion of queer Singapore cinema 1990s–2000s with this 1970s film is that my analysis relies on this notion of narrative cinema's "documenting" tendencies as articulated by historians like the Uhdes, thus pointing to the fraught queer visuality of "impossible presence" in Singapore cinema. While clearly not a queer film in any critical sense of the term, *Saint Jack*'s fictitious capturing of the seedy "dark side" of Singapore, the red light districts and its prostitution culture,[7] opens up a fissure in official Singapore discourses on taboo subjects that the government would prefer not to discuss publicly in order to reify the nation's squeaky clean image propagated by the Singapore Tourist Promotion Board. And despite its Orientalist and racially myopic underpinnings, the film's (probably unwitting) intervention establishes thematic trends and a cinematic visuality that queer cinematic representations in the 1990s and 2000s would continue to build upon.[8] The theme of queer prostitution, despite its politically problematic valence, finds its way into Hong Kong director Yonfan's Singapore production *Bugis Street* (1995) and Loo Zihan's short film *Untitled* (2005); while heterosexual prostitution in Singapore's Geylang red-light district takes center stage in Ekachai Uekrongtham's significantly gay film *Pleasure Factory* (2007).

Another visually obvious reason is the narrative inclusion of a gay sub-plot element in *Saint Jack* that plays a crucial role in the moral and ethical transformation within Ben Gazzara's "Jack Flowers" character. Enticed by an American government operative to spy on a US Senator (George Lazenby) so as to capture pictorial evidence of the politician's gay activities, Flowers tracks the latter to the northern section of Orchard Road, Singapore's key shopping district, where the senator solicits sex from presumably a gay prostitute. Bribing the young man into cooperation, Flowers follows them into the Singapore Hilton Hotel and positions his camera in the partially cracked hotel room door ready to capture the scandalous evidence. What is intriguing in this *mise-en-scène* is, of course, an early, if not the earliest, representation of gay sexuality in Singapore's filmic culture; but even more important is the fact that it is framed by a visual mode of voyeurism, the cinematic gaze coinciding with Flower's camera gaze. The voyeuristic image also deploys strategic masking through a partially closed hotel room door, a peek-a-boo image tantalizing audiences with gay sex that is about to transpire behind closed doors. Approaching the Senator seated on the couch is the call boy, who immediately drops his towel to reveal his frontal offerings to the Senator and present his tight naked rear to the audience. The fully dressed Senator then stands up towering over the boy and gripping his shoulders. The sight of a gay sexed Singaporean body and the visual synesthesia of touch must reverberate through queer Singapore audiences fortunate enough to see the film when it was first released. Not only does this image offer erotic titillation, it also engenders "innervation" the way Williams has discussed the concept. As problematic as the image is in terms of its racial politics, its impossible presence seeds in queer audiences a desire for new modes of cinematic representation of the queer self in all its sexual and corporeal glory.

While it is disingenuous to accord this sexualized moment in *Saint Jack* total political efficacy, I think it is fair to mark the visual contiguities between this initially banned film and other key queer Singapore film texts. For instance, Yonfan's *Bugis Street*, produced by Singaporean outfit Jaytex Productions, offers a sensational reconstruction of an actual street in Singapore in "the mid-1960s" which "was a colourful haunt of sailors, transvestites, and transsexuals" (Uhde and Uhde, 2010: 77). With the State's urban development policies completely erasing and "cleansing" this space, Yonfan's representation turns a cinematic fabulation out of Bugis Street's contemporary absence, thereby mediating its historicity through the film's impossible presence of forbidden sexual and gendered bodies.[9] Particularly incredible are the opening sex scenes between a transsexual Lola (Ernest Seah) and a drunken American sailor, who in his inebriated stupor mistakes Lola for a biological woman; and the sequences featuring Lola's boyfriend Meng (Michael Lam), whose almost naked muscular body Yonfan's camera lovingly and obsessively captures (a fetishistic practice we also see in the Hong Kong director's other films like *Bishonen* and *Color Blossoms*). But while just the very presence of naked queer sexed bodies in a strict censorship context may catalyze a visual politics of resistance, young upcoming Singapore filmmakers are also conscious of not allowing this visuality to slip into a complacent representational mode of superficial presence. To transcend the sexual objectification of the Singaporean gay body in its hollowed-out representation of the male prostitute in *Saint Jack*, Loo Zihan's short film *Untitled* infuses the gay prostitute protagonist with a complex subjectivity, as signaled by his final emotional breakdown after having sex for money. In Uekrongtham's *Pleasure Factory*, the explicit masturbation segment as Jonathan (Loo Zihan) nervously prepares to have sex with a young female Chinese prostitute and the fantasy sequence of gay sex between Jonathan and Kiat (Katashi Chen) where Kiat imagines their naked bodies passionately entwined infuse explicit sexual representation with the complex formation of sexual identities in Singapore. Against the backdrop of heteronormative socialization that straight male participation in prostitution supposedly offers, Kiat's gay tendencies, and his desire for Jonathan, emerge cinematically as part of a liminal dream world, a return-of-the-repressed fantasy Kiat harbours for his buddy.

Contributing to the multi-dimensional facets of this impossible presence are not only the diegetic aspects discussed above, but also the distribution circumstances of these films. Full-length features such as *Bugis Street*, *Pleasure Factory*, Lim May Ling's documentary *Women Who Love Women* (2006), the omnibus film *Lucky 7* (2008), and *Solos*; or queer short films such as Loo's *Untitled*, Boo Junfeng's *Tanjong Rhu*, and Loo Zihan's *Threshold*, all have to work around the difficult constrains of Singapore's censorship rules pertaining to both theatrical and DVD releases. If not suffering censorship cuts that would compromise filmic integrity and thus denying a presence in Singapore (ironic considering the fact that Singaporeans will not get to see queer Singapore films), films rated as R21 are allowed theatrical screenings only in the city centre and not in the so-called "heartland" housing districts. Many of these films are also not granted DVD release permits in Singapore because of the R21 rating. In illustrating how ridiculously outdated these censorship practices are in the context of globalization, Singaporeans often gleefully relish the anecdotal accounts of how they have successfully acquired both legal and bootleg copies of these films in their travels overseas, or have easily accessed these films online or through personal network exchanges. While the yearly Singapore International Film Festival further functions as a significant venue where certain films are given special permission for limited screenings, the paucity of theatrical spaces have motivated many to invent creative ways of working around censorship legalities, such as the 2006 *Short Circuit* (Au, 2006). The outside-in method has also become a production-related tactic. One example is where Singapore actors are willing to appear in gay films made outside the country. Television, stage, and/or screen actors such as Adrian Pang, Gerald Chew, Ivan Heng and Steven Lim have appeared in the UK-based work of Ray Yeung, such as the short film *Yellow Fever* (1998) and Yeung's first feature *Cut Sleeve Boys* (2006).

But, for now, with the glacial momentum of legal and cultural change in Singapore, filmmakers who are eager to take on queer subject matter or adopt a queer aesthetic will have to choose between the outside-in approach, or creatively incorporate narrative and aesthetic choices that allow queerness to occupy an impossible presence in *mainstream* Singapore cinema. Past examples of these choices—and I am also including here mainstream representations of homosexuality that are not motivated by queer activist concerns and that reinforce gay stereotypes—include the banal deployment of cross-dressing in Teng Bee Lian's *Liang Po Po The Movie* (1999); the popular deployment of transgenderism as social resistance in films like Glen Goei's *Forever Fever* (1998; re-titled *That's the Way I Like It* for its US release) and Ekachai Uekrongtham's *Beautiful Boxer* (2004); the typology of effeminacy as a negative foil to nationalist masculinity in Ong Keng Sen's *Army Daze* (1996); the alignment of "effeminacy and homosexuality" with the "corruption of original and authentic Chinese identity and values by the processes and influences of Western modernity" in Tay Teck Lock's *Money No Enough* (Tan, 2008, 155); the subtle homoeroticism of Victric Thng's short *Locust* (2004), K. Rajagopal's *Absence* (1997), and Royston Tan's *15* (2003) and *4:30* (2005); lesbianism as youthful passing in Eric Khoo's *Be With Me* (2005)[10]; the camp sensibilities of Royston Tan's short films *Cut* (2005), *Hock Hiap Leong* (2001), *Careless Whisperer* (2005), and *New York Girl* (2005), and feature film *881* (2007); queerness as sidekick or villainy in Ekachai Uekrongtham's *The Wedding Game* (2009); and homosexuality as failed filial piety in Kenneth Bi's *Rice Rhapsody* (2004), Royston Tan's *Mother* (2001),[11] Boo Junfeng's *Katong Fugue* (2007), and Loo Zihan's *Autopsy* (2008) and *Solos*, to which I will devote the final segment of this chapter. My quick cataloguing of these filmic tactics here is not to imbue them with a blanket notion of political negativity, but to suggest them as complex and conflicted configurations of queerness for others to unpack in the future, a critical enterprise beyond the scope of this short essay.

Solos: **Singapore's First Gay Feature**

I conclude my chapter by examining the beginnings[12] of a queer feature-length production culture in Singapore, both as celebration and critique, in the hopes of a grander and more open queer cinema to come. Kan Lume and Loo Zihan's *Solos* marks that beginning rather symptomatically from a political standpoint: according to producer Florence Ang, Red Dawn Productions pulled the film from the Singapore International Film Festival in 2007 when it refused to make the three edits demanded by the censorship board for the film's world premiere (Ang, 2008). This artistic gumption paid off, with *Solos* successfully touring some of the major film festivals. Constructing a dialogue-less, minimalist film where realist *mise-en-scènes* interact with artistically symbolic ones, the directors convey effectively an impossible presence of discursive articulation through vocalised linguistic absence, signifying the silencing of queer voices and those intimately connected to them within Singapore society.

What is also powerful about the film is that it gives voice to a rather identifiable experience among queer Singaporeans through a deceptively simple narrative that is complex in its emotional texture: the unnamed Boy (Loo Zihan) has a gay relationship with a Teacher (Lim Yu-Beng), while neglecting his Mother (Goh Guat Kian) to a lonely and restless existence. As the Boy and the Teacher wrestle with the boundaries of their relationship, a death in the Teacher's family crystallises for them their deep emotional connection to one another while bringing home for the Boy the indelible place that his Mother plays in his life. The deconstructed narrative structure and lack of dialogue leave much ambiguity to who has actually died. My reading that the death is someone dear in the Teacher's family suggests that the witnessing of this grief points the Boy to the fact that he has neglected his own Mother. My analysis of the film will not only take up the significance of the Mother in the ideological construction of the narrative, but will also return to Linda Williams' point of "innervation", which nicely connects *Solos* to the visual physicality of gay sexuality I first identified in *Saint Jack*.

By offering a number of gay sex scenes that are rather explicit in their configuration, the film is touching a nerve in queer audiences' painful cognizance of gay sexuality's impossibility in Singapore's public sphere (the uncut film is after all banned), while visualizing the very material and physical realities of gay sexual experience behind closed doors; thereby rupturing the public/private divide cinematically. The first sex sequence has the Teacher reaching out to a sleeping Boy in bed, by running his fingers teasingly around the latter's naked body, sexually arousing him. The nervous sensations generated by this visual synesthesia produce a complex rebounding ethical effect, particularly when the scene is preceded by a symbolic one with the Teacher and the Boy in what is seemingly a classroom setup in the middle of a forest, signifying a rewriting of the student-teacher relationship: isn't the Boy considered a minor? Are the two not related professionally as student and teacher? These ethical questions implicate the role homosexuality's illegality plays in proliferating an underground maze of other modes of illegalities and ethically questionable sexualities. My goal here is not to judge these sexualities but to suggest that freedom from legalistic structures of prohibition enables openness in dialogue and discussion of these very questions.

Conversely, the illegality of the Boy-Teacher liaison, especially when coupled with the film's later *ménage à trois* scene, invokes a certain naughty playfulness that queer cinema, from the outside in, can indulge in as a form of political résistance, a defiant thumbing the nose at the establishment. But as significant as this sexual-political play is, a point I do not wish to diminish in importance, the film must be credited for its willingness to confront the consequences of such representation, thereby rooting this signification in personal realities. For instance, the Teacher's seeming willingness to engage in the *ménage à trois* is framed by an initial hesitancy and tension, reflecting the extent to which people would go to satisfy their beloved. He does not only pretend to be asleep when the Boy has another go with the invited stranger in the bathroom, but also confronts the Boy in a fisticuffs, culminating in a beautifully composed image of alienation and pain representative of a lovers' quarrel. Here the Teacher occupies the top of the frame, with the Boy at the bottom, both having their bodies turned away from each other. This image creatively redeploys these same sexed bodies, with the earlier innervation of these bodies now retransmitting instead emotional estrangement, thus adding critical nuance to what would otherwise be just titillating soft-pornographic imagery.

Figure 9.1.
Teacher (Lim Yu-Beng), above, and Boy (Loo Zihan) in *Solos*. "Solos the Film", courtesy of Red Dawn Communications.

To conclude my analysis, I turn to an important scene where Teacher, Boy, and Mother all appear in the same frame near the beginning of the film. This scene is so essential in the narrating of their relationships that Kan and Loo repeat it close to the end of the film. Applying the rule of thirds in filmic composition, the filmmakers have the Teacher take up the left centre square of the screen, with the Boy assuming the middle focal square, and the Mother looming large in the lower right hand corner of the frame, all in deep focus. This somewhat diagonal construction of character placement not only establishes the tense relationship between the three but also foregrounds the Mother-Boy relationship as the emotional core and *telos* of the film. A shot of the Mother alone in bed opens the film, followed later by sequences of the Mother doing various tasks in the apartment in expression of her frustration with the son for ignoring her. Her love for the Boy is emphatically presented in various scenes, including one where she cleans away his earwax while he rests his head on her thighs, and another of a close-up of a post-it note asking "Boy [to] come home for dinner". The film ends with a symbolic scene where the mother wanders through the dilapidated void decks of Singapore's government-run apartment complexes to meet Boy playing his violin. The two stand at opposite ends of the widescreen frame and then come together, for the first time truly facing one another in emotional connection, as the Mother reaches out her hand to the Boy. The scenes of maternal domesticity mark a fascinating disruption of the innervation that the sexed gay bodies of the Boy-Teacher relationship disseminates, what one could characterize as an imagistic cold shower, so to speak. I prefer to understand, however, this maternal presence more as a socializing aura that anchors queer sexualities and its material practices in a socio-cultural context. Though the contrasting imageries may further spectacularize gay sex in this instance (because it is so rare that we see it in such overt display in Singapore cinema), the innervating energies sparked by the latter are rerouted and channeled by the Mother sequences into a cinematic conception of queer sexualities' integral place within and social connectedness to Singapore's body politic.

Even though the emotional resonance that the Mother-Boy relationship produces is clear, its narrative presence in gay Singapore cinema is unfortunately turning into a cliché: *Autopsy*, *Katong Fugue*, *Mother*, and *Rice Rhapsody* all incorporate the Mother figure as central to the narration of queer identities. Clearly, the maternal relation is an important one when it comes to gay characters coming out and searching for acceptance. Mothers undoubtedly suffer in desiring for their sons and daughters a certain kind of "normality" of existence that queer Singaporeans often do not experience. On the other hand, the frequent emphasis of maternal centrality in gay cinema is problematic on two levels. Firstly, the grieving Mother as figuration for the queer subject's failure to fulfill the demands of filial piety can lead to a relegation of queerness into the narrative margins of Singapore cinema (as made particularly evident in *Rice Rhapsody*). And, secondly, the presence of Mother takes the place of the conspicuously absent Father, patriarchy asserting its force field through the Mother, when it comes to confronting the question of homosexuality. Mothers are always blamed for queerness in her children,[13] so that Father's virile heterosexuality remains untainted despite biological and genetic connections. The maternal presence conveniently shields, while conveying, patriarchal imperatives. My specific criticism of *Solos'* dependence on the Mother motif is ultimately to tease out the unfolding contours of impossible presence as a necessarily conflicted and contradictory aesthetic that Singapore filmmakers must come to terms with.

Clearly, the imperfections of *Solos* reflect symptomatically the struggles that queer filmmaking consistently confront. Reviewers could generously read these struggles as among the many birth pangs necessary for queer cinematic culture to undergo before a mature queer Singapore cinema can emerge. The laudable bravery that Kan and Loo displayed in insisting on screening queer sex and sexuality cannot but innervate queer (or queer-identified) audiences and filmmakers to dare imagine and aspire toward a future (queer) Singapore cinema, where sexual marginality and an "impossible presence" will eventually be things of the past.

Filmography

4:30, Royston Tan, Zhao Wei Films, 2005.

15, Royston Tan, 27 Productions, 2003.

881, Royston Tan, Zhao Wei Films, 2007.

Absence, K. Rajagopal, 1997.

Army Daze, Ong Keng Sen, Cathay Asia Films, 1996.

Autopsy, Loo Zihan, 2008.

Be With Me, Eric Khoo, Zhao Wei Films, 2005.

Beautiful Boxer, Ekachai Uekrongtham, GMM Pictures Co., 2004.

Bishonen, Yonfan, Far Sun Film Company Ltd., 1998.

Bugis Street, Yonfan, Jaytex Productions, 1995.

Careless Whisperer, Royston Tan, 2005.

Color Blossoms, Yonfan, Far Sun Film Company Ltd., 2004.

Cut, Royston Tan, 2005.

Cut Sleeve Boys, Ray Yeung, Rice Is Nice Productions, 2006.

Forever Fever (also titled *That's the Way I Like It*), Glen Goei, Chinarunn Entertainment Inc., 1998.

Hock Hiap Leong, Royston Tan, 2001.

Katong Fugue, Boo Junfeng, Akanga Film Productions, 2007.

Liang Po Po The Movie, Teng Bee Lian, MediaCorp Raintree Pictures, 1999.

Locust, Victric Thng, 2004.

Lucky 7, various directors, Lucky 7 Film Company, 2008.

Money No Enough, Tay Teck Lock, JSP Group of Companies, 1998.

Mother, Royston Tan, 2001.

New York Girl, Royston Tan, 2005.

Perth, Djinn, Working Man Film Productions, 2004.

Pleasure Factory, Ekachai Uekrongtham, Fortissimo Films, 2007.

Rice Rhapsody, Kenneth Bi, JCE Entertainment Ltd., 2004.

Saint Jack, Peter Bogdanovich, Playboy Productions, 1979.

Solos, Kan Lume and Loo Zihan, Red Dawn Productions, 2007.

Tanjong Rhu (also titled *The Casuarina Cove*), Boo Junfeng, The Putnam School of Film, 2009.

Threshold, Loo Zihan, 2009.

Untitled, Loo Zihan, 2005.

The Wedding Game, Ekachai Uekrongtham, MediaCorp Raintree Pictures, 2009.

Women Who Love Women: Conversations in Singapore, Lim May Ling, 2006.

Yellow Fever, Ray Yeung, Sankofa Films, 1998.

10

The Kids Are *Not* All Right

The Curious Case of Sapphic Censorship in City-State Singapore

Loretta Chen

The recent banning of Lisa Cholodenko's *The Kids Are All Right* starring Julianna Moore, Annette Benning and Mark Ruffalo sparked off a furore in the Singapore Lesbian, Gay, Bisexual and Transsexual (LGBT) community.[1] The most talked-about movie at the 2010 Sundance Film Festival and the winner of the Teddy Award for Best Feature Film at the 2010 Berlin International Film Festival, the movie combines comedic surprise with scenes of poignant, raw emotion of a richly drawn portrait of a modern, urban lesbian family.

Nic and Jules (Annette Bening and Julianne Moore) are married and share a cosy suburban Southern California home with their teenage children, Joni and Laser (Mia Wasikowska and Josh Hutcherson). Both 'mums' have raised their children well. Mum Nic clearly wears the pants and is the sole breadwinner of the household. Mum Jules bore the children after having been artificially inseminated by an unknown sperm donor. However, as Joni prepares to leave for college, her 15-year-old brother, Laser, presses her for a big favour and enlists Joni's help to find their biological father, which of course sets the engine of the movie's narrative in full motion.

Members of the LGBT community and movie-goers alike were hugely anticipating the screening of the film at the Love and Pride Film Festival in one of Singapore's most popular movie theatres, Golden Village Grand on 7 November 2010 when the Media Development Authority (MDA) released a statement to unequivocally state the banning of the film, citing reasons "due to unforeseen circumstances". With no mention to specifics, this "rationale" given by the MDA is merely a politically correct, vague and imprecise way of indicating that the Film Festival has flouted the "guidelines which disallow the promotion, justification and glamorization of lesbian lifestyles and their explicit depictions" (MDA, 2006).

Having watched the movie myself, I can only postulate that the only reason the film was banned, aside from the fact it is set in a lesbian household which the MDA is already privy to, is the fact that the film portrays lesbianism in a healthy, acceptable, normal light thereby risking a "glamorization" of an alternative lifestyle. It is possible to argue that the only depictions of lesbians and gays in

Singapore that are sanctioned and tolerated, albeit with copious cuts and advisories, are if the portrayals of the LGBT community are unsavoury and contentious, thereby reifying the need for government scrutiny and public surveillance.

The Kids Meet *Silly Child*: Yet Another Instance of Sapphic Censorship

This controversial ban bears semblance to yet another incident. The last media episode that ignited much (on-line) dissent amongst the Singaporean lesbian community was over an ironically named *Silly Child* music video. Starhub Cable Vision (SCV) was fined by the Media Development Authority (MDA) for airing the music video by singer Olivia Yan on the MTV Mandarin Channel on 26 and 27 November 2007. In MDA's press statement, the music video was said to "portray romanticised scenes of two girls kissing" and highlighted that such behaviour was "unacceptable". This representation was "in breach of TV advertising guidelines which disallow advertisements that condone homosexuality" (*The Straits Times*, 2008).

The MDA had apparently consulted the Advisory Committee for Chinese Programmes which concurred that the commercial had promoted lesbianism as a romantic and acceptable lifestyle. The lyrics of Yan's song apparently further amplified this interpretation. Taking into account the severity of the breach, as well as the fact that the commercial was aired on a youth-oriented channel, the MDA found that a financial penalty was warranted and fined SCV S$10,000.

However, this writer argues that contrary to the MDA's simplistic reading, the music video actually rejects or is at best, ambivalent towards lesbianism as opposed to espousing the practice. What the video does do is to effectively foreground the tensions between sexuality, Chinese-ness and the queer lesbian body. In fact, there is a discernible narrative that charts this ambivalence or rejection of lesbianism which has been overlooked by the authorities.

The voice-over that precedes the song states, "This summer, I finally learnt what love as sung in love songs is all about." The video is seen through the eyes of Olivia, the singer, a fledgling undergraduate singer on the brink of a creative break who reminisces about a summer fling. During one particular band practice, she notices that a girl seems to be attracted to her. Both women are what can be conventionally described as "andro-femme", dressed casually in spaghetti strapped tops; cardigans, paired with military "cargo" pants or jeans and pretty dresses. The girls are seen frequently flirting, kissing and cuddling in the comfort of a typical undergraduate's room, replete with a Nirvana poster and Union Jack (Great Britain has legalised civil partnerships). There are also several shots of the girls in their burgeoning romance—practising and flirting in what can be interpreted as the campus green room, where the undergraduates apparently while their time away in band practice. There is also a clear shot of the girls sharing an intimate moment, kissing on the lips when one of the girls' boyfriend (presumably Olivia's) walks in on them. In the next shot, Olivia is seen talking to the boy. The couple look upset, with Olivia looking evidently sheepish. The duo embrace and Olivia then walks away. She breaks up with boy, presumably for the other girl thus foregoing heterosexuality for a potential homosexual encounter. There is no dialogue and nothing is made explicit.

From the brief four-minute video, it is clear that the girls were acquainted through their love for music and shared band sessions. Alternating between the quiet domesticity of home and the benign, progressive domicile of what can be interpreted as the university campus, Yan's video caused discomfort perhaps precisely because of its innocuous insidiousness.

What the Advisory Committee for Chinese Programmes and MDA failed to take notice was the fact that the song and its attendant suggestive lyrics seemed *not* to celebrate lesbianism but really could be read as a rejection of lesbianism. Olivia chose to be single and alone at the end of the song due to her own inability to decide (as suggested by the lyrics), the confusion and lack of personal conviction in pursuing a lesbian romance, thereby presumably caving into the pressures of a heteronormative society. In the final shot of the two women together, the other woman asks Olivia in hushed tones, "Can we still be friends?" The video ends with the women standing across each other in the far-flung corners of band practice room, exchanging wan and pained looks in what can be read as the "end of the affair". This interpretation lends itself very well to the opening preamble when we first hear of Olivia's 'Summer fling'. The ignorance and foolishness of the Summer fling is performed with Olivia self-reflexively calling herself, and perhaps the other infatuated girl a "Silly Child"—the title of the song.

This reading is altogether missed by the censors. In the MDA's and the Advisory Committee for Chinese Programmes' haste and discomfort in the very corporeal representation of the two female desiring bodies, they have ironically censored what could have been read as a flagrant rejection of lesbianism rather than a celebration of lesbianism. This erroneous censorship and logical gap is evidenced in yet another instance, *Cheaters*.

Bondage and Threesomes Do Not Make a Lesbian

The reality programme *Cheaters* features cases handled by the Cheaters private agency whose clients seek to find out if their respective partner has been unfaithful in their relationship. Despite the suggestive nature of the contents, the programme was allowed to be aired on cable provided by Starhub Cable Vision (SCV) on the Zone Reality Channel (Channel 83) as part of the Family Plus Tier subscription package that is aimed at a general audience.

The controversial episode was aired from 22 to 26 May 2006 and repeated on 29 August 2006. It had apparently contained footages of a woman engaging in lesbian sex acts with another woman. The programme also showed the woman tied to a bed in a bondage session with two other women. Although the scenes were deliberately pixellated, the MDA insisted that it was still obvious to viewers that the women were naked and engaging in "unnatural sex acts". SCV was subsequently cited for having breached the guidelines which disallow the promotion, justification and glamorization of lesbian lifestyles and their explicit depictions. In addition, MDA also found SCV's airing of this episode particularly offensive as it considered the fact that the channel is in SCV's Family Tier which is aimed at a general audience (MDA, 2006).

The Programme Advisory Committee for English TV and Radio Programmes (PACE) also agreed that the airing was objectionable. The Committee and MDA further argued that the woman featured in the programme had managed to get her boyfriend to accept her lifestyle and even invited other individuals to engage in threesomes with them. This portrayal was read by the authorities as promoting lesbianism as an acceptable lifestyle.

Interestingly, the very content of *Cheaters* is already predicated upon couples cheating on each other and yet MDA and PACE deemed it suitable for general 'family' viewing. However, a woman who cheats on her boyfriend with another woman is deemed unacceptable. It can be further argued that may have caused particular grief to the authorities would be the fact the woman in question actually persuaded the boyfriend to understand her attraction to the other woman and even successfully lures him into participating in a threesome. Not once did the authorities censure the threesome act as offensive but rather conflated the act of cheating, the threesome and the same-sex attraction as a single 'lesbian act'. In fact, the biggest irony is that the very presence of the boyfriend in the episode already renders the threesome act un-lesbian!

The authorities also made the sweeping assumption that all lesbians engage in threesomes. As a matter of fact, bondage is not part of a lesbian lifestyle but is a sexual preference that people can choose to engage in, regardless of sexuality. In fact, many lesbians engage in long-term monogamous relationships much as heterosexual couples do. Heterosexual bondage acts or threesomes are written about in female magazines and openly discussed with some local magazines such as the best selling women's magazine, *Her World*, even heralding the act as a means to spice up a staid heterosexual relationship.

In both instances highlighted above, what was objectionable was clearly the (mis)representation of lesbians as seductive or alluring bodies. However, it is arguable that the severity of both the indictment was really due to the (mis) representation of lesbianism as attractive and more importantly, accessible alternatives to what Adrienne Rich (1980) calls "compulsory heterosexuality".

MDA: Ministry of Discrepancies and Ambiguities

The Censorship Review Committee (CRC) (2003) is a government-appointed committee that reviews and makes recommendations regarding Singapore's censorship policies. Its mandate is to update censorship objectives and principles as society evolves while preserving Singapore's broader interests—national security, social cohesion, and community and family values. The range of media under the CRC's purview is free-to-air (FTA) television, cable television, theatre (classified as arts entertainment) and film amongst numerous others. The general rule of thumb for FTA television is that only NC15 programmes can be aired after 10pm while those classified as M18 are not allowed to be broadcast at all. Cable TV, on the other hand, is able to air M18 programmes after 10 p.m. on their international premium and Video-On-Demand (VOD) channels, subject to the appropriate advisory warnings given.

Clearly, the concerns of the MDA with regards to *Cheaters*, was with the promulgation of "unnatural sex". However, there is clear ambivalence (pun intended) in the treatment and outlook of these notions of morality and increasing liberalization. In particular, three sections of The Censorship Review appear to be in contention if not contradiction with each other. The detailed classification in The Censorship Review stipulates guidelines for "Media Content Standards" that proposes to:

- continue to disallow content that undermines public order and the nation's security, denigrates race and religion and erodes moral values through pornography, deviant sexual practices, sexual violence, child pornography, bestiality etc.
- gradually enlarge common space for discussion of racial and religious issues through the various mediums, as a long term approach in fostering racial and religious understanding and harmony.
- continue to strike a balance between allowing more space for creativity and maintaining moral standards (CRC, 2003: 15).

However, these guidelines are unclear especially when played out against two taxonomies: "homosexuality" and "sexual content and nudity". Under "homosexuality" the guidelines stipulate, "A more flexible and contextual approach when dealing with homosexual themes and scenes in content [and] allow greater leeway for adults, through suitable channels, to access such content provided it is not exploitative" (CRC, 2003: 15).

However, with regards to "sexual content and nudity", the guidelines are to "[allow] for greater leeway for non-exploitative sex and nudity relevant to context and content for adults. But, continue to impose stricter standards for such content in public spaces [and to] allow adults to access magazines such as

Cosmopolitan and programmes such as *Sex In The City* through suitable distribution channels" (CRC, 2003: 16).

Yet, the definitions of "flexible and contextual" and what can be defined as "exploitative" or even "greater leeway" remains ambivalent and normative, dependent upon highly personal preferences and viewpoints of the Committee members. The case with *Cheaters* highlights this increasing ambivalence and also performs a liminality—the state of being in the margins, the 'neither nor', as there is a clear conflict of priorities. From a mass broadcast media's standpoint however, the indication is clear—it is permissible to have a homosexual character as long as s/he does not perform the act on air. Indeed, it seems that the guidelines promote a culture that tolerates homosexuals but still condemns the act of homosexuality which is analogous to having lungs but being forbidden to breathe.

Time and Passion: How Many Seconds Doth a Lesbian Make?

I was personally embroiled in a long drawn out discussion with the MDA and the Esplanade over the staging of *251*, a play based on Singaporean pornographic star, Annabel Chong aka Grace Quek. The play staged in April 2007

Figure 10.1

Poster of *251*, written by Ng Yi-Sheng and directed by Loretta Chen.

drew abundant local and international media coverage owing to the sensation-alism and controversy surrounding Annabel Chong.

The officials from the Esplanade debated on the viability of the scene which shows Annabel Chong (played by Cynthia Lee Macquarrie) sharing an intimate moment with her secondary school fellow classmate and 'Friend' (name of the character in *251*) played by Cheryl Miles. The tender, fleeting kiss on the lips was integral to the play as it highlighted the first emotional entanglement and budding same-sex romance Annabel Chong had before she became a porn star. By January 2007, the authorities had already granted an R(21) rating to the play based on the draft script submitted, which meant only persons above the age of twenty one were allowed to be admitted. The play included the use of strong language, highly graphic sexual scenes and a much-touted topless scene.

Figure 10.2

Annabel Chong (played by Cynthia Lee Macquarrie) stands on a chair and readies herself for her "girl-on-girl" act with Porn Actress played by Eleine Ng.

Figure 10.3
Shows the infamous "triple-penetration" routine that was pioneered by Chong. It is typically featured in most hard-core pornography these days. The hard core porn scenes are symbolically staged in Singapore with the use of strategic lighting, music, costumes, sets and props.

As the performance date of the show drew closer however, the Esplanade officials began to request to sit in for rehearsals and also started sending e-mails and short message service (SMS) texts to ask for daily updates on the progress of the play. They were, in particular, concerned about the depiction of the "lesbian-kissing" scene and demanded to know the length of the kiss. I suggested that the authorities come up with guidelines to enable me to direct the "lesbian-kissing" scene and I also requested to know what the authorities regarded as an "acceptable length" for the "lesbian kissing scene". The personnel both at the MDA and the Esplanade did not provide an answer but placed an indefinite "embargo" on the scene. In the end, I decided to proceed with the "lesbian kiss" with a few small changes made. After all, the MDA has a track record of shutting down productions that they deem unfit for public viewing—even if it was opening night.

Instead of portraying the girls as 16-year-olds, I had them share an "innocent kiss" as young, 12-year-olds (with Madonna's iconic tune, *Like a Virgin* playing in the background). The actors "clocked in" at slightly under five seconds and we never heard from the authorities about this matter again. However, on opening night, yet another high ranking Esplanade official came to enforce the censorship of the first six words of the play, "In the beginning was the body" and insisted that the opening lines were religiously offensive even though the script has been submitted months prior and there had been no comment on this issue before. This incident also led to a series of other consternations and media frenzy which will not be discussed in this chapter.

Figure 10.4

"Friend" (played by Cheryl Miles) and Annabel Chong (Cynthia Lee Macquarrie) share a "girl-bonding" moment at home. As requested by the authorities, the characters who should have been 16-year-olds were infantilised as giggly 12-year-old girls so as to downplay the lesbian elements.

These separate incidents testify to the lack of transparency in the attitudes and treatment of lesbians and issues pertaining to their representation in Singapore. The first instance of Olivia Yan's *Silly Child* demonstrates the inability to read lesbians in Singapore, while the other two instances involving *Cheaters* and *251* indicate an anxiety over representation of lesbians in Singapore. Consequently, the ambiguous legal status of lesbian sex is also indicative of the ambivalent attitude to lesbianism *per se*.

The *Lack* as Cloak of Impenetrability

Jacqueline Lo, in an essay from *Interlogue* entitled 'Prison-house, Closet and Camp: Lesbian Mimesis in Eleanor Wong's Plays', points out that while homosexuality is amongst a list of sex offences made punishable by law under Section 377A of the Penal Code, lesbianism is not specifically mentioned since it is arguable as to whether sexual acts between lesbians involve "penetration" (Lo, 2000: 114). Yet, arguably, this lack of 'penetration' and lack of a "visible referent" raises the question of what Sue-Ellen Case cheekily calls "penis, penis, who's got the penis?" (Case, 1989: 291). This supposed "lack" has ironically abetted the invisibility of lesbians in the eyes of the law. Turning this line of argument on its head, it is possible to question the viability and ability of the authorities to penalise (pun intended) an act of lesbian representation when there is first and foremost nothing to (re)present, in which case how can lesbians be visibly represented in the first place on an island that does not even recognise its existence?

If the lesbian is *not* able to be visible in representation and has no referent in the eyes of the law, then just what makes the lesbian visible? Indeed, studies have shown that dress, deportment, language and mannerisms are determinants of lesbian identity and there exists a shared lesbian reservoir of knowledge that creates a particular lesbian iconicity. While there exists an unsaid code that governs lesbian corporeality, this is not a shared code with those outside the community, such as censorship review committees etc. This lack of knowledge of lesbian codes of behaviour may have led to the mis-readings, indecisions and ambiguities within the minds of the authorities in handling issues that deal with female homosexuality. Is there efficacy in ambiguity or should there be greater transparency of the lesbian codes of conduct to enable the authorities to make clearer and more informed judgment calls?

These are pressing and intricate issues that have to be stripped, teased and examined. The issue of lesbian iconicity, corporeality and subsequent representation needs to be raised and examined. Indeed, as much as Singapore is lauded internationally on the one hand for her tough stance on crime, she is also lambasted on the other for her intolerance of oppositional views. This nascent

State is truly awash with contradictions and paradoxes. We are in a country where chewing gum is banned but where meteorically rising casinos proudly emblazon its skyline; individual creativity is collectively incubated in State-run institutions; homosexuals 'tolerated' but sodomy criminalized. The lesbian is not recognised by the government and thus legally not in 'existence'. Yet there have been overt efforts and high-profile measures taken to censure and censor lesbian representations both on stage and on screen.

Indeed, the role of the performing arts is instrumental in creating or making (in)visible the lesbian body through a decisively Singaporean framework. Though aided and informed by Euro-American (and an increasing amount of Asian) lesbian scholarship, this exercise has contributed to the vibrancy of the lesbian community even as it remains unrecognized by the legal courts. Is there greater viability in remaining invisible or is there greater efficacy in being visible? There are no clear answers. But these four instances of Sapphic censorship have demonstrated that there is much ambiguity and inconsistency in the handling of the material at hand. The censorship authority is capable of misreadings, logical flaws and gaps in argument coupled with the over-eagerness to snip, censor and censure. Arguably, there is a gradual move towards increasing liberalisation but this will be a task that will take time. In the meantime, what is best is for us as artists, audience and readers alike is to continually read against the grain, between the gaps and to constantly engage, debate and critique the status quo. To quote Ng Yi-Sheng, playwright of *251*, where better to start than "in the beginning" and right here on our local stage.

11

"Singaporean by birth, Singaporean by faith"

Queer Indians, Internet Technology, and the Reconfiguration of Sexual and National Identity

Robert Phillips

On a warm evening in August of 2007, I made my way through the congested bylanes of Chinatown towards my familiar haunt, the Backstage Bar, one of Singapore's openly gay nightspots. I had been spending several evenings a week there in that it afforded me an easy way to network with openly gay men and most visits usually yielded at least one potential interview subject. I climbed the darkened stairway and entered the small smoke-filled room, decorated with old Broadway and film posters, took a seat at the main bar, and ordered a drink. Almost immediately, a Malay man in his mid-twenties came in from the balcony, took the stool next to mine, and struck up a conversation. After the obligatory small talk regarding where I was from and how I was getting on in Singapore, I told him of my ongoing research regarding the role of technology in national and sexual identity among queer Singaporeans. He seemed interested and, because I was eager to recruit more Malay informants for the project, I handed him my card. I encouraged him to call me should he be willing to give an interview. Moments later, as I was standing up to use the restroom, a young Chinese man who had been sitting across the room, approached the Malay man, rolled his eyes and said in a rather sarcastic voice, just loudly enough for me to hear, "Don't waste your time on him, he's only into 'black' guys." As I made my way through the crowded bar towards the restroom on the exterior of the building, I could not help but wonder what the Chinese man meant by his comment. Eventually I realized that he was not, as I had initially thought, implying that my sexual preference tended toward men whose ancestors hailed from Africa, but rather those whose origins lay in the Indian subcontinent. I am assuming that he had gotten this impression because many men who frequented Backstage Bar knew that my closest friend in Singapore, who accompanied me on most of my nights out at various pubs and clubs, was an expatriate Indian from New Delhi.

The Chinese man's comment is revealing on several levels, but of interest here is how it illustrates the racialized discourse of everyday life in Singapore. While making his comment, the Chinese man emphasized the word "black", seemingly to make clear his disdain for Indian-Singaporeans. The comment serves as an example of a dominant dynamic within this particular queer[1] community, which mimics Singapore's larger culture, one that relies heavily upon racial classification as a means of identification as well as exclusion. In this essay, I seek to expand this discussion by utilizing the experiences of self-identified queer Indian-Singaporean men as a lens through which to further explore these relationships. In doing so, I hope to think through some broader processes related to issues of ethnicity, sexuality, and the nation (see, for example, Boellstorff, 2004, 2005; Jackson, 2003; Manalansan, 2000).

My current research involves queer Singaporeans with the primary focus being the role of new and emerging technology in national and sexual identity. In this essay I am interested in sharpening the focus to think of those Singaporeans of Indian descent who self-identify as queer.[2] While conducting dissertation fieldwork from 2005 to 2007, I noticed an absence of queer Indian-Singaporean men in public spaces such as gay pubs and discos as well as semi-public spaces including gyms, saunas, and events organized by queer sociopolitical groups. In the process of searching for participants to interview for my study, I quickly realized that a vast majority of queer Indians in Singapore do not enact their sexual identities openly in the public sphere, choosing instead to live more private lives. As such, while I encountered most of my Chinese and Malay informants in pubs or in public gay 'cruising' areas, the bulk of Indian informants were met through references via informal social networks or while interacting in online chat rooms.[3] In this chapter, I do two things. First, I discuss the double minority status of queer Indian men in Singapore and examine some of the unique challenges that they face within the greater society. As with members of other diasporic communities around the globe, queer Indian-Singaporeans have assumed a unique type of identity forged through a combination of factors brought about by, among other things, processes of transnational migration. As Indians form one of the smallest ethnic communities in Singapore, they are far outnumbered by more dominant Chinese and Malay groups.[4] All of these ethnic groups share a type of ambiguous subjectivity, especially in terms of their relationship to the nation. Queer Indian-Singaporean men are both an ethnic and a sexual minority, further complicating this relationship. This dual-minority status has had a distinctive effect on the formation of this particular group's views on the nature of Singaporean national and sexual identity. Second, I examine two examples of online interaction, focusing on how queer Indian men in Singapore use the Internet as an alternative public sphere where they are able to construct and debate narratives of culture, identity, and national belonging. I conclude by suggesting that through the use of such practices, many queer Indian-Singaporeans have formed alternative narratives of self that confound the often conflicted and contested relationship between queer identity and national identity.

Marginal Subjects

Throughout dozens of interviews in Singapore, many informants, of all ethnic backgrounds, spoke of a general marginalization of non-Chinese within the greater society. Interviews also revealed that the exclusion of non-Chinese was particularly pronounced within Singapore's queer communities.[5] For example, a number of Indian-Singaporean interlocutors recounted stories of having satisfying intimate relationships with Chinese-Singaporeans. Yet, these relationships, for the most part, did not extend past the private realm of the bedroom or the semi-private realm of the sauna and into public spaces such as restaurants, pubs, and dance clubs. When asked about the dating scene in Singapore, Srini, a 25-year-old accountant, gave a response that spoke to the experiences of many of my Indian-Singaporean interlocutors. "You tend to be left out in the sexual sense, I think that people are not ready to acknowledge the fact that they have slept with a South Asian man, the majority, not openly. It's happened to me and my friends before. We think that they like us, but they are discreet about it." He continued, "I met this guy, a Chinese man, and he was all over me. But then two weeks later we met in a club and he came up to me and asked me not to tell his friends that he was with me for the last two weeks; he was not willing to acknowledge our relationship." Krishna, a 30-year-old bartender at one of Singapore's many queer bars was one of my key inform-ants for the project. We had many long conversations regarding all aspects of the place of minorities within Singaporean society. He spoke often of feeling like an outsider in his own country and community, especially in terms of the discrimination he felt from the majority Chinese:

> At the end of the day people tend to talk. I think that it has to do with their upbringing in the Chinese community, whether straight or gay, the parents make them think of everything in terms of race. It's stereotypical behaviour ... oh, the Indians smell of curry and coconut hair oil, the Malays all are after your money. So they (queer Chinese men) think that we are all supposed to be like that ... as they grow up they get the wrong impressions of us.

These stereotypes are perpetuated both within Singaporean society at large as well as within Singapore's queer communities and, according to many of my queer Indian interlocutors, made many feel that they were foreigners in their own country.

Chinese Entanglements

Because Singapore has a majority Chinese population, the everyday lives of Singaporeans of all ethnic backgrounds are affected by the multiple and potentially conflicting sources of self-understanding contained within the world views brought over by many Chinese migrants beginning in the mid-nineteenth century. Ethnic Chinese have settled in and around Southeast Asia for hundreds of years and have, in many respects, brought their homeland with them. When leaving their home country, emigrants often carry powerful and enduring cultural values with them and once in their new homeland, they utilize what has been referred to as "memory of place to construct imaginatively their new lived world" (Gupta and Ferguson, 1992: 11). In some instances, as is the case with many Chinese Singaporeans, association with the "homeland" grows that much stronger when it is absent. In fact, the association of Singapore with China is so compelling that some of my informants regularly spoke of Singapore as the "third China" or "Singapore, China".[6]

Because of Singapore's ethnically diverse population and the city-state's lack of history as an independent nation, the government is continually trying to forge one unified national identity, yet is caught between conflicting ideologies. While Singapore's government has consistently worked to inculcate ideas of modernity and technological prowess, many members of its majority-Chinese population are powerfully affected by contemporary ideologies of Confucianism (Lee, 1998, 2000). This powerful and deep-rooted ideological force is at once a global import to Singapore as well as one of the foundations of the current government. When Singapore's first government was formed by the People's Action Party (PAP) in 1954, the main goal was to form a political party that would be able to work effectively with the multicultural and multilingual population of Singapore.[7] During the formative years of the Singaporean nation, the new leaders had a surfeit of political and economic issues to deal with and had little time to devote to the instillation of cultural or moral values. Yet, when these crises had passed and the nation had gained some sense of stability, the PAP was more than eager to address issues surrounding cultural values. To this end "attention (was) translated into such actions as the introduction of moral education in schools … bilingualism, and the encouragement of cultural activities" (Tan, 1989: 14), the focus of which was very Sino-centric.

I suggest that this pragmatic discourse, which conflates China and Singapore on various levels, has had a significant effect on ideas of Singaporean national and sexual identity. In addition to this discourse, those dealing with other elements of Singaporean culture that have had a lasting impact on how Singaporeans construct ideas of the nation and what it means to be "authentically" Singaporean. Some of Singapore's religious and philosophical traditions, such as Hinduism, Buddhism, and Taoism, are rather tolerant of homosexuality, while others, such as Christianity and Islam, are less so. Dominating all these traditions, though, is politico-philosophical Confucianism, the ideals of which are emphasized by the current government as a way for Singaporeans to reclaim a cultural heritage that many see as having become diluted as it was transmitted over time and space. While the government of Singapore certainly appreciates the economic and technological progress that come with the adoption of Western values, many government officials nonetheless object to "practices of excessive individualism or excessive permissiveness, uncontrollable promiscuity and drug culture, sensual music and pornographic art, all of which could produce unhealthy and harmful effects in a culturally conservative but racially sensitive society like Singapore" (Tan, 1989: 14). This neo-Confucianism, then, "is also an attempt to reduce the influence of Western values which emphasize individualism and materialism" (Tan, 1989: 15). While this neo-Confucian discourse could be construed as going against Western values, I suggest that it is concomitantly about subtly opposing any non-Chinese ethnic culture by replacing it with a culture of "Chineseness".[8] Although the current racial make-up of Singapore is 74 per cent Chinese, 13 per cent Malay, 9 per cent Indian, and 4 per cent Other (Statistics Singapore, 2010), the founders of the nation assumed that the process of nation building necessitated the homogenization of language, ethnicity, and culture and the People's Action Party adopted "traditional Chinese values" as a cornerstone of this process.

These various actions by the government of Singapore, centered on ideas of Confucianism and "Chineseness", normalize the ethnic Chinese male, who is both heterosexual and Mandarin speaking, as the prototypical Singaporean citizen, increasing the alienation that many non-heterosexual non-Mandarin speaking Singaporeans feel. I suggest that it is a combination of these and other factors—marginalization along lines of race and language and an inability to publicly articulate non-normative sexual subjectivities that has led some queer Indian-Singaporean men to experiment with different ways of living. These alternatives revolve around issues of space and place and include migratory practices that transgress national borders and fixed locations (Manalansan, 2000).[9] In interview after interview, Singaporean interlocutors echoed the idea that in the context of their own nation, there was "no room" for ethnic and sexual minorities. When asked about solutions to this problem, a significant number of subjects spoke in terms of "travel" and recreating "home" and the concomitant new possibilities of self and identity that were believed to occur when able to leave Singapore, however briefly, in order to more easily experience alternative ways of life.

Many queer Indian-Singaporean men told me that they don't feel "at home" at home or in their homeland. As a corrective, they have turned to cyberspace in a search for queer authenticity. For these men, the virtual world of cyber-space is much more tolerant and forgiving; it serves as an anti-structure against the highly structured and regimented life of the centre. It also allows them to re-think and re-configure their relationship with their nation.

Queering the Nation, Online

The introduction of broadband Internet in 1998 ushered in a new era in Singapore. Although the government had intended that this new technology be used for educational and commercial purposes, Singaporeans of all persuasions quickly realized that, in addition to these government mandated purposes, the Internet was also the perfect tool with which to access information that had not appeared in government issued or controlled media.

It has also permitted Singaporeans to interact within a virtual public sphere, such as in the online forums of government-supervised newspapers or on sites dedicated to queer lifestyles and causes. These sites, made possible by the illiberal pragmatic political climate within which they operate, also allow for the discussion of a range of issues that affect their communities as well as the acquisition of information about rights struggles elsewhere. Interactions within these discursive sites also allow queer Singaporeans to network with one another as well as with those outside of their home communities. This includes Singaporeans abroad and non-Singaporeans, some of whom at one time lived or worked in Singapore. Perhaps most significantly, it allows for anonymous participation within a virtual public sphere. This is a crucial step for those, like many of the queer Indian-Singaporeans with whom I interacted, who were not comfortable interacting in the physical public sphere. These online interactions have opened up a new world in which queer Indian-Singaporean men can interact with one another as well as their fellow citizens. My research suggests that these interactions are empowering and have had a considerable effect on queer Indian-Singaporean subjectivities.

Thomas, a 50-year-old clerk who has been visiting queer sites since the late 1990s serves as a good example of the effects of interacting online, "When I first went online, it was eye opening and liberating to a certain extent ... inter-acting with other gay and lesbian Indians online has given me confidence as a person, an Indian person." He continued, "The flip side that you must look at is that as much as I see myself as a Singaporean, that I am still a minority. I'm also Christian and gay, so you know it is a triple whammy for me, you see? So in a way it did make me feel less unsure of myself as a person." For the most part, Thomas interacted on two online sites, *SiGNeL* and *Fridae*, which are discussed below.

SiGNeL

SiGNeL (Singapore Gay News List) is a Yahoo group and email forum that was founded in July of 1999 as an offshoot of the gay rights group People Like Us (PLU). At the time of writing this newsgroup has 2755 registered members. According to the PLU website, "*SiGNeL* is not a 'gay' group in the sense of being restricted to gay people. *SiGNeL* is open to everyone regardless of sexual orientation, to serve members who are interested in, and who confine discussions to gay issues pertaining to Singapore."[10] Postings range from queer themed articles taken from *The Straits Times* and other local newspapers to inquiries regarding legal rights in specific situations to movie reviews and announcements of public events of interest to the community. In most instances, a member posts an article or observation and the other members comment in an interactive and engaging manner. While the postings are moderated, the interference is quite limited and the moderator generally only disallows posts that are deemed defamatory to religious or ethnic groups (postings of this nature are prohibited by Singaporean law) or that do not pertain to gay, lesbian, bisexual or transgender issues.[11] The site is completely text based though many of the postings contain Internet links to more complex sites. The layout is quite simple as well as searchable. I was able to meet, both online and in the physical world, several of the regular queer Indian users of the forum. A vast majority of them used pseudonyms when posting in that they felt that using their real name or even a personal email address would put them at risk of being 'outed' to friends, family, or employer. Interactions on this forum allowed these queer men to actively but anonymously participate in ongoing debates dealing with issues of race, class, gender, and the role of queer Singaporeans within the greater culture.

Fridae

Stuart Koe, a Singaporean scientist and entrepreneur, founded *Fridae.com* in 2001. According to the website, the purpose of the site is to "build Asia's largest gay & lesbian community—united in diversity, and transcending geographical borders. *Fridae* empowers gay Asia to: come together, stay connected, be informed, overcome discrimination, nurture personal growth, and foster healthy relationships".[12] The site according to Koe, receives over 400,000 hits per month. While considered a Singaporean site, servers are based in Hong Kong in order to avoid the scrutiny of Singaporean authorities.[13]

Once the site is accessed, the user is given an array of choices. On the left side of the homepage is a bar that allows the user select from nine different options.

These are News/Features, Lifestyle, Personals, Agenda, Fotos@Fridae, Shop, City Guide, Perks, and Promotions. Many of the options are self-explanatory. Others such as Perks (giving the user the ability to join the site for a nominal fee) and Agenda (a listing of events of interest to the queer communities) are not. Until at least mid-2006, *Fridae* also had a highly trafficked Forum section where members could debate current events. While no reason was given for discontinuing the Forum section, users currently make use of the "comments" option provided with each article. While not as interactive as a traditional online forum, the "comments" section at the end of major articles is often the site of long-running debates among users.

At the time of writing, there were 119 profiles of men who described themselves as Indian, a small number in comparison with the countless thousands of profiles posted by Chinese-Singaporeans.[14] The most significant aspect of *Fridae*, for queer Indian-Singaporean men is that it allows them to meet other queer Indians, from both Singapore and abroad. I interviewed Vik, a labourer, several times during the course of fieldwork. He spoke often of the everyday difficulties he experienced in the physical world and with many other queer Indian men in Singapore had feelings of not belonging. In our first interview, I asked a question about *Fridae*, and he said that he had never heard of it. He eventually signed up and created a profile. During our final interview, he told me, "Once I discovered *Fridae*, I saw the world better. I read articles from all over the world and understood. Then I met a gay Indian friend on the site, he told me that he knew what I'm going through and made me feel better; it opened me up and made me come out of the closet discreetly."

Conclusions

The often-conflicted relationship between queer Indian-Singaporeans and their homeland is characterized by a long-standing desire to integrate into a nation that in many respects makes no room for minorities, sexual or otherwise. Yet, I suggest that web-based interactions have allowed queer Singaporeans to reimagine themselves as part of the national narrative, a narrative that is itself 'imagined'. Lian suggests that in the case of Singapore, there are four "cultural world orders superimposed on one society—namely Confucian-Chinese, Islamic-Malay, Hindu-Indian, and Christian-Anglo Saxon—out of which a common community has to be constructed" (Lian, 1999: 42). Anderson speaks to this constructed community identity within the nation by first acknowledging that, "[n]ation, nationality, nationalism—all have proved notoriously difficult to define, let alone analyze" (Anderson, 1983: 3). Nonetheless, he explains that what we conceptualize as the nation is neither a natural nor a real entity and is rather, an "imagined community". Anderson is putting forth the idea that the nation is in fact "an imagined political community—and imagined as both inherently limited and sovereign" (Anderson, 1983: 6). John Kelly (1995) bases his work on that of, among others, Anderson, when he suggests that we consider the "nation" as a narrative "constituted dialogically and useful and important politically, for a State trying to regulate a capitalist market, or for a people to contest politically within and against the institutional framework of a State" (Kelly, 1995: 257). I find this image of the "nation as narrative", especially compelling when thinking about the situation faced by many queer Indian-Singaporeans. When the nation is framed in this manner, in conjunction with web-based interventions, it allows for new conditions of possibility—especially in terms of re-writing the nation.

In combination with notions of queer identity, the idea of the "nation" thus becomes a useful tool with which to think about the impact of the Internet in Singapore. I argue that interactions on the Internet have allowed queer Indian-Singaporean men to stake a primary claim as *citizens* within the greater nation, rather than solely as queer Singaporeans. In doing so, they have begun to form their own unique type of identity that realigns the nation and national belonging with non-normative notions of gender, race, ethnicity, and class.

The men who told me their life stories and accounts of their interactions on the Internet represent ways in which many queer Indian-Singaporeans have formed alternative narratives that reflect the often-conflicted relationship between queer identity and national identity. Yet, through the transnational online practices described above, many of these minority Singaporeans have been able to leave the physical environment of their nation in order to enact new forms of citizenship that transcend geopolitical borders. Ideas of what it means to be queer, an ethnic Indian in Southeast Asia, and a citizen of Singapore are being reconstituted and given new meaning.

There is a concomitant shift in the way the nation is being viewed by these temporary transmigrants. Some would argue that processes associated with transnational migration could eventually lead to the dissolution of the nation-state and a concomitant loosening of national ties. My research suggests that, at least in the case of those queer Indian-Singaporeans with whom I interacted, these processes instead contribute to a reconstitution of national "space" as well as a desire to inhabit and take part in the political processes of their home country. Rather than viewing the Singaporean nation as a place from which to permanently escape, Singaporeans, particularly queer Indians, are using their experiences gained while interacting in cyberspace to re-think the way that they imagine their nation. More significantly, perhaps, is the effect these online prac-tices have had on the way queer Indian-Singaporeans view their relationship *to* the nation. I concluded each interview by asking my interlocutors to imagine what their life might be like if they were to emigrate from Singapore to a nation where they could experience a life free from marginalization based on race and sexual orientation. Although a hypothetical question, I was interested in determining whether or not these ethnic and sexual minorities had any real 'connection' to their nation. In a majority of cases, interlocutors looked at me with confusion; they were not interested in permanently emigrating from Singapore, but in fact longed to stay in Singapore in order to contribute to the nation-building process. The answer to my question provided by one queer Indian interlocutor speaks volumes and sums up the sentiments of many respondents: "Singaporean by birth, Singaporean by faith". This response plays into an overarching theme of this volume—that of illiberal pragmatics—and the fact that so much of the recently constructed Singaporean lifeworld, among citizens of all racial, ethnic, and sexual identities, is influenced by a logic of ambivalence. Through online interactions, the queer Indian-Singaporean men with whom I interacted were finding a renewed interest in claiming an identity that integrated a series of conflicting identities—that of being Singaporean, Indian, and queer, allowing them to generate alternative narratives through which they can re-imagine their relationship to the nation.

12

"We're the gay company, as gay as it gets"

The Social Enterprise of Fridae

Audrey Yue

Introduction

In 2001, the inception of the Singapore-based gay web portal, Fridae, created a buzz in the local gay and lesbian community.[1] Unlike the now delisted and then more ostentatious *PlanetOut* and *Gay.Com* which peaked alongside the dotcom bubble and queer commodity boom, Fridae sported a more subdued, and what some would hail, an understated design interface. With a logo and slogan on one end of the headbar championing the empowerment of 'gay Asia', and a series of polysexual animated stick figures on the other, the greyish blue tone of the homepage was minimalist and stylish. It had none of the hunky washboard stereotypes on display or the amateurish rainbow-lined graphics of other gay travel guides such as Utopia Asia. It was as if a front had surfaced to mark the arrival of the uniquely Singapore scene. Its almost reticent image seemed to embody the daily commonsensical expression of homosexuality in the country. Don't ask, don't tell, just be. Not quite the same mantra that bespeaks the West, this utterance refers to homosexuality's unofficial tolerance by the broader spectrums of the government and polity, resonating with the parlance, 'don't ask for gay rights, don't publicly announce your sexuality, and we will let you just be'.

What started as just another gay website selling personal profiles, marketing the occasional lifestyle accessory and publishing the select news stories, Fridae quickly expanded to become a key player for regional gay advocacy. Between 2001 and 2004, it organised the country's first public circuit parties. Aptly named the Nation Party strategically scheduled on the country's national day, the annual protest party grew so big that it became not only a main event in the regional 'pink' calendar, it also raised the ire of the authoritarian State who quickly banned the party after more than 8000 revellers attended the last bash. It was too big and too public, the organisers were told. By this time, the local scene had caught the gaze of the global press. "Got Pink Dollars to Spend?

Then Head for the Lion City. Singapore: It's In to be Out," *Time Asia* (Price, 2003) proclaimed. "Singapore Swing: The City's Gay Balancing Act," the *Wall Street Journal* (Prystay, 2007) exclaimed. Notwithstanding its short-lived public parties, Fridae diversified in the areas of the arts and public health. From 2005 to 2008, it was officially recognised as a supporter of the arts and received the highest commendation from the country's statutory arts organisation, the National Arts Council. By 2010, its online behavioural sex survey has become the world's largest and most multilingual, surpassing similar health reports in the UK and Australia.

In the last decade, the rise of Fridae coincided with many concurrent forces. Its new media commerce grew alongside the country's development of the creative economy. It tapped into a burgeoning regional subcultural market that was also emerging with queer social movements in Thailand, Taiwan, Hong Kong and China. Its platform is also especially suited to the pervasive network computing milieus that presently characterise Asia's prosumer media cultures. Against these forces, this chapter critically considers Fridae as a social enterprise by examining it as a hybrid business company with a social mission focus. This framework departs from orthodox studies of online gay personal ads and websites that focus on the construction of sexual identities; it provides a more pertinent way to understand the emergence of a gay social movement and queer entrepreneurship in a country where homosexuality is still illegal. As Geoff Mulgan suggests, "social entrepreneurship is part of the much broader story of democratization: of how people have begun to take control over their own lives, over the economy, and over society. It is, in some respects ... inseparable from the rise of social movements" (2006: 94). By providing social services, coordinating self-help resources and cultivating a volunteer culture, social enterprises facilitate a "governing rationality that values self-enterprise and personal responsibility" (Ouellette and Hay, 2008: 481). This chapter argues that Fridae's combination of business and social mission resonates with Singapore's neoliberal agenda; it further suggests that such a template provides the opportunity for the company to be a sustainable LGBT organization, thus serving as a model for the future of queer organizations in contemporary neoliberal economies.[2]

While this chapter's positive account of an expanding queer social movement and LGBT scene may seem to depart from this volume's earlier chapters that are more focussed on homosexual repression and restrictions, such an apparent disjuncture is not divergent. This pull/push, in/out feature of the community is characteristic of illiberal pragmatism. As this volume, and in particular, the book's introduction has shown, illiberal pragmatism is shaped by an ambivalent logic of liberalism and non-liberalism. Such a milieu supports the concurrent practices of closetedness and emancipation, in both official and unofficial forms of everyday life. As a social enterprise, Fridae's organisational model attests to this mode of governance, where, on the one hand, homosexuality is illegal but tolerated, and on the other hand, promoted through the cultural liberalisation of the creative economy.

Situating Fridae: New Media, Gay Businesses and Queer Consumption

Despite Fridae's influential role in shaping contemporary queer culture in Singapore, there is currently no sustained scholarship that examines its organisational structure or the specificity of its gay practice. One year after its launch, the US-based gay magazine, *The Advocate*, published a short profile of the website, lauding the English language portal for providing support resources to gays living in a conservative country (Mueller, 2002). As Fridae grew in popularity and expanded its activities, its Nation parties attracted the most controversy and preoccupied the bulk of scholarly writing. In a survey on the globalization of HIV/AIDS, Melinda Weiss (2006) shows how the conservative government sidesteps its health promotion responsibility by blaming the decadence of the parties as a potential cause for rising HIV/AIDS transmission in the country. Similarly, Eng Beng Lim (2005) shows how the images of gay masculinity promoted by these parties, what he calls Asia's 'Mardi Gras', mirror and also subvert their Western counterparts. These academic foci on the parties, rather the website, emphasize the influence of Fridae's diversified activities on public space and public health, rather than the impact of new media on the gay community.

It is now commonly acknowledged that the Internet has enabled the emergence of Singapore's local gay community (Berry et al., 2003). Since 2000 when the country became the first networked city in the world (Yue, 2006), the development of the creative media economy has encouraged the embrace of technological literacy through education, infrastructure and media capital. The subsequent globalisation of information has supported the rise of an unofficial and subcultural community despite the illegality of homosexuality and concerted rise in media surveillance.[3] Writings in this field have discussed how gays and lesbians use the Internet to organise and create sites of resistance that challenge the dominant Confucian and Christian family values of the status quo. Baden Offord (2003) examines *Yawning Bread*, a high profile blog by Singapore's foremost activist, Alex Au, to show how Au evokes the rhetoric of human rights in the fight for the liberation of gay rights. Kenneth Tan and Gary Lee (2007) examine how gay activists on the mailing list, *SiGNEL* (the Singapore Gay News List), are hailed by governmental discourses of economic liberalism that promote homosexuality on the one hand, and the neo-conservative religious majority that deplores homosexuality, on the other hand. The gay community, they argue, is imagined through these discourses: "homosexuals are 'interpellated' as gay Singaporean subjects who are part of a community that is rejected by an imaginary mainstream and yet grudgingly relied upon by a State anxious to appear sufficiently open-minded in order to attract global capital and talent" (Tan and Lee, 2007: 184). For them, the Internet and the tools it offers allow the scene to become "a more self-conscious gay community" and "also a more politically oriented movement" (Tan and Lee, 2007: 187). Instead of the linear developmental model of the scene, community and activism suggested by Russell Heng (2001), the Internet has allowed homosexuals to strategically locate themselves in all discourses of homosexuality, ranging from oppositional voices, coalitional networking and outreach, to literally writing the history of its nascent movement. On Wikipedia and influential gay and lesbian websites, e-lists and blogs such as People Like Us (PLU), RedQuEEn!, Herstory, sgbutterfly, Trevvy and sayoni, every discourse of Singapore's gay and lesbian history and everyday life is meticulously documented: colonial sex narratives, fiction and cinema, development of bars and scenes, letters to the government, activism, support groups, public parties and pride events. Academic writings such as those discussed above (e.g. Offord; Tan and Lee; Heng) analyse these sites predominantly through their resistive forces as a nascent social movement imbricated in the State's illiberal and yet pragmatic regime of regulation and liberation.

Fridae is unique and departs from these sites. Trading under its parent organisation, Jungle Media, it began boldly as a gay Internet start-up, a for-profit business company based in Singapore but registered in Hong Kong. Until its recent move to a Texas server, its content, from the beginning, was also hosted in Hong Kong. These off shore practices are pragmatic business strategies, as prevention measures against the country's notorious regime of online censorship and gay business raids.[4] As its CEO Dr Stuart Koe explains,

> Regulations in Singapore are soft. The official line is anything that does not end with a dot sg falls outside the guidelines. They don't scrutinise. They don't even care where you are hosted. There are porn sites that are hosted in Singapore. Just like [there are] porn magazines that are printed in Singapore. So long as we can have the semblance that the primary market is not Singapore. You don't have to say what you are doing when you register a business … you [just] say what sector you are in, web development …. To have a server elsewhere was done as a hedge, just in case, but we've never been called on that. The server is still outside because there's better data centres elsewhere so it's a business consideration (Yue, 2010a).

Fridae's birth follows the global trend that saw the visible rise in queer commodity consumption in the early years of the new millennium.[5] From lifestyling and pink tourism to gay-related marketing and diversity employment practices, the gay corporate business sector, estimated then in 2001 to be worth US$490 billion in America alone (Prince, 2002), has expanded from its subcultural origins in cafés, bars and saunas. With a market group renowned for its early adoption of technology, social media has become the most conspicuous site of gay consumption. The high profile ascent and bust of the publicly-listed *PlanetOut* and *Gay.Com*, together with their subsidiaries that include Liberation publications such as *The Advocate* and *Out*, and *RSVP Vacations*, attest to the volatility of a market that mainstream businesses are keen to woo but loathe to invest.

Fridae commenced in a Singapore gay business environment that was beginning to come alive with State rental subsidies and entrepreneurial incentives designed to encourage a creative night-time economy. Bars, clubs and saunas, initiated by individuals, groups of friends and events management companies, surfaced almost overnight and flourished as new subcultural icons. Zouk, Cows and Coolies, Taboo, and Butch Hunt are but some clubs and events that have become household names in the local gay and lesbian imagination. At its height the queer business community boasted more venues, media companies and restaurants in the gay cluster of Chinatown, a five-kilometre downtown riverside precinct, than their counterparts in the Australian major cities combined, a country where the author resides.[6] During this period between 2001 and 2005, there were about 120,000 registered users on Fridae, with the Singapore market accounting for about 90 per cent of its traffic.

Fridae currently oversees five broad activities: website, media company, gay-related marketing, Internet producer of HIV programming, and community cultural development. In the following, this chapter critically introduces the specificities of these practices using organizational sociology, under the conceptual framework of social entrepreneurial theory.

The Social Enterprise

The social enterprise forms part of the larger discourse on social entrepreneurship. The term was coined by Joseph Banks (1972) who proposed that business organizations, when managed differently, can solve social problems. It gained traction when Amitai Etizioni (1973) nominated it as a third sector between the State and market. In recent years, it has become a global phenomenon as a result of the growing needs of ever expanding marginalised communities, increased dominance of multinational corporations and withdrawal of the State from public service and provision (Drayton, 2002; Greiner, 2006). The success of organisations such as the Grameen Bank, *Big Issue* and Youth United have inspired new forms of operational structures that can also effectively fulfil social responsibilities. Unlike philanthropy or corporate social responsibility where the main motivation for giving is ultimately to increase economic profits (Valor, 2006), social entrepreneurship is conceptually characterised by market orientation, innovation and sociality (Nicholls, 2006).

Market Orientation

The social enterprise is different from social and business organizations because it has mixed economic and social objectives. Driven by its need to maintain a double or triple bottom line, it seeks to recover its full cost so it can continue to deliver its social mission focus. In this context it aims to develop independent economic projects that can sustain social service delivery.

Fridae's hybrid mode of business operation reflects the market orientation of the social enterprise. Its main product is a website that sells personal profiles through a range of membership subscriptions. Like most online dating services, free membership provides access to viewing while paid membership offers search and reply privileges. In 2007, Fridae reached the 200,000-profile mark for its English site and 50,000-profile mark for its Chinese site. It is currently Asia's largest gay website with over two million visits per month. This service has generated a viable income stream of over S$1 million per annum, enough for co-founder Koe to be hired as a CEO, as well as run a full-time office of over twelve staff that includes designers, reporters and translators. It currently publishes in English, with site translations into Chinese, Korean and Thai, with Japanese in the pipeline. When it first started, Singapore subscriptions formed at least half of its membership base. Since the launch of the Chinese site in 2004, Chinese membership (China, Hong Kong and Taiwan) has grown exponentially and now dominates the site.

Fridae complements this service with an online shop that opened in 2003, first selling tickets for its circuit parties, and gradually clothes, sex toys, books, DVDs and other miscellaneous gift items. Products are sourced mostly from local independent artists, and even include in-house compilations of dance music and charity donations to regional HIV/AIDS organizations. Such retailing decisions offer a glimpse into its social setting agenda where the platform is harnessed to promote gay photographers, DJs, and fashion designers, as well as increase the profiles of non-government funded health promotion agencies. It further mobilises the community through its 'Directory' listings where user-generated content allows other gay and lesbian and queer friendly businesses to advertise and tap into the distributive reach of the site. This synergy works well with its travel portal that promotes the major cities of Asia as destinations of gay tourism. Often, the company also partners with major airlines and hotels for cheap party circuit deals. All these are anchored through the 'Lifestyle' link that further showcases films, exhibitions and media gadgets.

Fridae's social setting objectives are most distinct through its other activities. Its media company hires local and offshore journalists to provide news stories on the regional queer community. Covering politics, social movement, media and lifestyle, these are often breaking news that materialise not only the presence of regional communities but also mark the milestones of nascent social movements. On the website is an archive portal that provides one of the most comprehensive accounts of LGBT developments in the region in the last decade.

Fridae also offers its platform for gay-related marketing. While affiliates and stakeholders include small commercial gay businesses or gay friendly brands such as those discussed above, it is the primary conduit for government and public health organisations that may have specific reasons to want to reach out to the constituency, for example, in the areas of HIV prevention and outreach.

Fridae produces Internet-related HIV programs for health promotion, research and education. In 2006, it launched Singapore's third and then largest Behavioural Surveillance Survey in partnership with the charity and community-based organisation, Action for AIDS, and 'Think Again', the first HIV prevention campaign in the country. Its annual survey is now conducted in ten languages and has 14,000 respondents. In 2005, it started its community cultural development arm, now called Fridae Foundation, that has since raised and disbursed about S$70,000 to local initiatives. This funding source has allowed the local community to start IndigNation, Singapore's annual Pride Month, and has also sponsored Rascals Prize, a biennial award for Singapore LGBT research, as well as support independent filmmakers and artists like Boo Junfeng who could not raise money because of the gay content of his films and the country's stringent censorship.

Fridae's mixed model format has raised concerns about business ethics, especially in the context of minority community formation and social services delivery (Crane and Matten, 2010). As Koe reveals,

> In the early days it created a lot of distrust because the activists saw me as a businessman; the commercial people didn't trust me because they think I have a political agenda. And so in many ways we were seen as outsiders and no one understood where we were coming from and couldn't understand the vision. From my point of view, it has always made sense. We needed to do both and all of it in order to be successful because if you focus on one aspect, you will be much more narrow in scope, and the possibility of success is also much smaller. The gay community is small and if you relied on it to make a living you wouldn't be able survive, prospects are limited and you have to be creative how you operate [sic]. So we had to be regional to begin with, if we didn't do HIV work we won't have the credibility (Yue, 2010a).

The question of business ethics is especially evident in debates on online communities, and the roles played by commercial gay and lesbian websites.

While computer mediated communication has lent itself well to the many dynamics of gays and lesbians, such as connecting isolated and closeted individuals, meeting other gays and lesbians, community building, political mobilising and identity play, the question of whether it can be a 'real' community in a structure of relative anonymity has led to concerns about the appropriation of the discourse of 'online virtual community' by commercial businesses. There is no agreement on what constitutes an online community; while this debate continues, it is also acknowledged that there are heterogeneous queer communities, and that gays and lesbians use online services not to replace but enhance offline interactions. However, despite such prolific debates, similar websites like *PlanetOut* still insist on such marketing and in fact "replicate this virtual community model within a commercial context" (Gudelunas, 2005: 8).

Fridae markets itself with its mission of 'empowering gay Asia' through what it calls "a potent mix of Content, Community and Commerce" (Fridae, 2010). Although it is not clear what proportion it actually reaches of the total estimated Asian gay and lesbian population despite its staggering monthly hits, it is clear that if online content is considered, the community is primarily constituted through pure economy. This is also apt for its offline Nation parties where tickets can cost as much as US$40 for local residents and exponentially more for regional visitors. Likewise, its community activities, including IndigNation's events, have often been criticised for its proclivity towards the arts and serving only a very small (and usually 'converted') audience base, usually LGBTs in the higher-income and professional tiers, and men. This is evident from Fridae's membership which consists of predominantly educated, middle-class gay men; of those with a university degree: 55 per cent of Singapore subscribers, 80 per cent of subscribers from Hong Kong, Taiwan, East and Southeast Asia, and 90 per cent of China subscribers (Yue, 2010a). Of the Singapore subscribers, approximately 60 per cent are Chinese, while other racial groups such as Malays, Indians and Eurasians make up the rest of the 40 per cent. Compared to the Chinese hegemony of mainstream Singapore, this distribution reflects a less marked Chinese dominance. The male bias of the website reflects the sometimes separatist nature of the Singaporean LGBT culture where popular websites and events among lesbians are Herstory and Two Queens, rather than Fridae and Nation (Yue, 2011). Where the latter may favour more highly produced circuit parties (and this is not an unusual stereotype of the global gay scene), the former are more predisposed to women's nights at local clubs and pubs. The class and gender privilege of Fridae's community strongly reflects the Internet's capacity to create highly niche communities based on tastes (*Gesellschaft*) rather than kinship and solidarity (*Gemeinschaft*). Fridae's bulletin board entitled 'tribes' indeed attests to its self-awareness of such a community as networked, individualised and compartmentalised (Maffesoli,

1996; Castells, 2000). This may also explain why it charges a premium for 'perk' privileges and its latest beta version incorporates a more sophisticated personality-driven software to highly define the search capacity through in-depth questionnaires. While Fridae's financial support of community events may be similar to *PlanetOut*'s sponsorship of offline gay and lesbian neighbourhoods, it has resisted the compulsion to join the monopoly of gay media when the then conglomerate *PlanetOut* partners offered to buy the company, and it is this independence, as the following sections will critically illustrate, that has allowed the social enterprise to remain innovative and true to its sociality.

Innovation

The social entrepreneur is a civic innovator (Emerson, 2003). S/he brings "an innovative approach to achieving its [social] mission" (Nicholls, 2006: 13). By disrupting old techniques and introducing new models to improving society, new models potentially improve society and bring about social change (Nicholls, 2006: 101). Seen in this way, innovation involves the process of creative destruction when new combinations are formed as a result of employing existing resources in a different way and doing new things with them (Schumpeter, 1934). This discourse of innovation also lies at the heart of the creative economy (Pol and Carroll, 2004: 195).

Fridae flourished in a national environment just when the government was embarking on its creative economy blueprint. The new creative clusters—design, media and arts—identified in its 2001 *Creative Industries Development Strategy* (Media Development Authority, 2001) suited Fridae as a company in the sector of information technology. Although Fridae did not seek venture capital from government-initiated incentives, its civic innovations were indirect beneficiaries of this policy. This is evident in its creative labour and operational processes.

Creative labour process is defined as a perspective that "looks inside the experience or actuality of production processes and reveals how inputs of human labour, machinery and 'raw materials' are transformed into finished products" (Smith and McKinlay, 2009: 5). This approach shows how innovation is harnessed for the purpose of producing more capital by transforming use value into high value for producers and consumers. In a social enterprise that is also part of the creative economy, this means looking at the work *content*, employment *contract* and management *control* (Smith and McKinley, 2009: 29–50), in order to consider how sociality can be accumulated across the value chain. Such operational processes incorporate three types of innovation (Alvord, Brown and Letts, 2004). First, innovation is transformational when it has the ability to build capacity to change cultural contexts; second, innovation is economic when tools and resources can be customised to increase profit and productivity; third, innovation is political when it builds local movements and empowers marginalised groups to increase their political influence.

Content, commonly referred to as the intangibles that form the basis of intellectual property rights (Howkins, 2001), is often the most valued product of the creative economy. Content, the work performed by creative labour, is characterised by Marx's social relations of production (Smith and McKinley, 2009: 35). This mode identifies the skills that the worker brings in order that different workers can be stratified into different classes, according to assets, value and hence, social status.

The production of content at Fridae is most explicit through its gay media channel where writers are hired to generate and publish content, translators for its non-English websites and, designers and programmers to create and maintain the websites. These professions have gained high profiles in the last decade as a result of the government's objective to build capacity that saw arts and multimedia training embedded at all levels of education. Higher degree qualifications are also encouraged through cultivating the city-state as an education hub for the knowledge economy. Media schools, competitions and university programs have mushroomed and been established over this decade. At Fridae, the twelve staff, in the thirty-something age bracket, belong to this first generation of digital natives who have benefitted from such initiatives.

The work that goes into creating content at Fridae is innovative in many ways: the staff are creative workers whose work demands innovation on a regular basis; they also work in a new media environment that is new and constantly changing, and this demands not only keeping up with the requisite skills but also finding new ways of working with the evolving technology. While these innovations are not entirely specific to Fridae and are perhaps more endemic to the new media industry, the most significant form of innovation with the production of content is transformational innovation. The work has allowed young activists, graphic designers and journalists—about 80 per cent of workers at Fridae are gay or lesbian identified—to build capacity as individuals through the social recognition of their professional status. This is also socially innovative as it allows workers to create "new career biographies, new practices of learning [and] new patterns of work organization across time, space and social relations" (Gill, 2009: 161).

Creative queer biography is evident in the life and work experiences of Sylvia Tan, Fridae's website editor and longest serving employee. Tan is the company's second website editor and has helmed this position since 2000 when she responded to an ad posted on the RedQuEEn mailing list. After graduating with a journalism and public relations degree from an Australian university, she returned to Singapore where she worked briefly as an IT reporter for a government news television channel before joining Fridae. As website editor, she works with freelance reporters and writers from Asia. She is also the Singapore news correspondent and has the responsibility of commissioning work. When Fridae's news coverage began to change from 'soft' lifestyle topics to more political stories, at the time when, as Tan says, "Singapore became more exciting" (Yue, 2010b), Tan's approach to the job became more activist-oriented. That she is one of the few journalists in the country barred from applying for an official press permit has not deterred the scope of her investigative reporting. She would regularly call upon censorship and police authorities for comments when there are controversies that involve the LGBT community. She broke news stories about Christian fundamentalism and ex-gay conversions that were later picked up by mainstream media. She covered gay and lesbian conferences and queer film festivals across Asia, news items that would not or rarely make mention in other channels of gay media. When she started at Fridae, she was only 23 years old, and was out about her sexuality in a social context. Ten years into the job, it has not only politicised her; she now uses her professional skills to actively advance the community's claims to rights. This new capacity in her work experience has enabled her to craft a new creative queer biography that began as a part-time co-owner of an Internet café serving the heartlands and making websites for gay saunas, and an internee at one of Australia's most established (now defunct) gay press, *Brother Sister*. While the 10–8 working hour day at a fixed office location is far from the cool bohemia associated with the industry, it is a full time position that allows her to exploit her everyday butch embodiment and expand her community networks that comes with the informality and sociality of the job. For Singapore workers at Fridae's office, the stability of a long-term full-time work is indeed a possibility as it is the company's mixed market orientation that has allowed it to be sustainable.

Transformational innovation is also evident on a larger scale across the community and in the region. The specificity of Fridae's content—knowledge about gay Asia—is unmatched across the global terrain of gay media. Apart from the academic Queer Asia series at Hong Kong University Press and the porn magazine genre, there is no other English-language media dedicated to the knowledge production of these emerging minority groups, especially from a region where homosexuality is, for the most part, still a criminal offence. Fridae's distributive reach is also unprecedented. This has furthered its capacity to literally imagine, make present and unite the disparate 'collective', gay Asia, through the structure of its virtual community. The timeliness of the term has also coincided with the rise of 'gay Asian' books and events across the region. The co-edited *Gay and Lesbian Asia: Culture, Identity, Community* (Jackson and Sullivan, 2001) was one of the first publications to use the collective rubric of 'gay Asia', not in an attempt to define what constitutes this collective, but to produce innovative approaches in Malaysia, South Korea,

India, China, Thailand and the Philippines that decenter metropolitan sexual identities (see also Phillips et al., 2000). Common here are the shared histories of postcoloniality, nationalism and developmentalism that shape local conditions of emergence. The term gained momentum in 2005 when the first queer Asian studies conference was held in Bangkok; it resulted in the publication of *AsiaPacifiQueer: Rethinking Genders and Sexualities* (Martin et al., 2008) where the co-editors highlight the theoretical complexity of hybrid sexualities for the Asia Pacific region. These social and political imaginations, as well as conceptual novelties, are reflected in Fridae's naming of the website. Inspired by the nativist figure of Friday in Daniel Defoe's *Robinson Crusoe* (Defoe, 1965; see Fridae, 2010), Fridae is symbolic of the challenge to Eurocentric sexualities, as well as recuperation of local hybrid identities that arise as a consequence of global modernization and indigenization.

Fridae's transformational innovation of content is not without its organizational drawbacks. Apart from the twelve full-time work positions at the Singapore office, all other work are contract-run and based on commissions. As this is usually recruited through recommendations, the networking that comes with the LGBT community is increasingly valued as a useful resource for securing work. With contracted offshore positions mostly based in Beijing and Bangkok (and usually paid less than the general market rate [Yue, 2010b]), Fridae replicates the international division of cultural labour that also characterises first world knowledge economies. For these freelancers, working for Fridae can be sometimes undervalued and precarious. This hierarchy reflects the regional cultural hegemony of Singapore's arts and cultural policies that have been criticised for presenting an epistemological discontinuity with its ASEAN neighbours (Kawasaki, 2004).

Management control at Fridae replicates the hierarchical ordering of mainstream organizations. Although the office is designed as an open plan concept, Koe occupies the main desk at a corner in the front, much like his symbolic status as the company's official spokesperson. Koe's status reflects the person-centred perspective that characterises early research on social entrepreneurship where the focus is on the business hero, who is described through a portrait of social leadership and business aptitude, as one presenting a certain degree of risk-taking but also demanding a strong desire to control the environment (Casson, 1982; Leadbeater, 1997; Prabhu, 1999). While staff defers to Koe through the distinction of organizational roles, the congenial office layout ensures that coordination of work processes in the office is intimate rather than opaque. This spatial specificity is important to maximise the frequency of interaction and enhance the productivity of all staff across all levels, especially as it relates to the larger place-bound making of the LGBT community. As Sarah-Anne Munoz (2010) suggests, a discussion of management operation in terms of spatial scale can bring cultural geography to bear on social and economic impacts through the way social enterprises engender the imagination of place in their regeneration of community.

Spatial analyses of new media companies tend to use cluster theory to show how agglomeration can enhance the economic and social value chain (Pratt, 2009). Fridae's spatial distinction, however, is located through its micro-geography, at the level of how bodies, individuals and communities are beneficiaries of the activities conducted in the office space. At the heart of this space is the seed of Fridae's political innovation.

Fridae's office is located in an industrial park away from the country's nominated creative precincts or gay clusters. Tucked in a nondescript multi-storey building, the office is known only through its small 'Jungle Media' signage by the side of the door. Sharing the building with other tenants including pipe makers, garment factories and caretakers, Fridae's cheap rent allows it to command a bigger office space (Yue, 2010a). While this affords employees more personal workspace, the expansive office has served as the headquarters of recent high profile political organising. In particular, during the heated two-year period between 2007 and 2009 when the country debated to overturn the 377A Penal Code that criminalises homosexuality, Fridae was active, not only in its news reporting, but the office was used by activists to coordinate the Repeal 377A campaign. With access to media equipment and networks, and with cheap parking, good public transport and easy access to low cost hawker food, the office became a hotbed of gay activism. This campaign witnessed Koe putting his name as one of the three high profile signatories in an open letter to the government; it also saw the coming-of-age of the Singapore gay and lesbian Internet community. From online petitions, to debates on morality, family values and religion, the local cyberspace became a repository for the making of a democratic civil society.[7] In 2009, Fridae's office also became the headquarters of the Pink Dot campaign, an annual one-day event where people, dress in pink, gather at the country's only government-designated Speakers Corner at Hong Lim Park, to form a pink dot to celebrate the freedom to love.[8] What began as a town hall meeting quickly evolved to become one of the largest grassroots-initiated public gatherings ever seen in the country, with more than 4000 straights and queers and their families turning up in 2010 to show support for the LGBT community. From within the office space of Fridae, coordinators were able to oversee the supervision of equipment and performances, the making of videos, and the dissemination of the event, practices that mobilize and galvanize the community at large. Political innovation is clearly evident in Fridae's ability to scale up and build a movement with external alliances. It uses the vision of its management control to focus on interventions in the gay movement designed to raise consciousness about the decriminalisation of homosexuality, the acceptance and recognition of same sex love and ultimately, to empower the constituency. Rather than relying on the spatial agglomeration of the gay cluster that it lacks, it creates a micro-geography that further nurtures and sustains the wider gay and lesbian community. Examining the spatial context of the social enterprise shows how new spaces and practices are created which in turn bring new experiences that can transform others who are impacted by such activities (Munoz, 2010: 307).

Clearly, the transformational and political innovations at the heart of Fridae's organizational and creative labour processes—from content, contract and management control—are sustained by its economic innovation. The same leveraging capacities discussed thus far also drive its economic innovation. The key to Fridae's business strategy is its ability to customise new tools and resources to increase economic and social productivity. This is especially evident in the programming of its Internet-based HIV/AIDS surveys and campaigns where the same structures that are designed for the marketplace of personal ads are used to implement survey and campaign instruments. This strategy allows the organisation to tender for public health projects from within Singapore and across the region, including collaboration with non-government AIDS organisations in Asia, Australia and the USA. It provides value to all stakeholders: for the community, a bespoke package for safe-sex awareness and education; for the government, a ready-made constituency for health prevention and promotion. With a doctorate in pharmacy and research expertise on HIV medicine, Koe, a long time AIDS activist and current director of various AIDS organisations, also adds value to these strategies. These deeply embedded community origins allow Fridae to further develop creative networks that not only help increase economic opportunities but also deliver impact and create new social value. An example of such impact is evident in the evaluation and subsequent follow-up to its 2006 online behavioural sex survey. The survey was conducted for three weeks and 45 per cent of the responses received were from Singapore residents. The evaluation report, focusing on Singapore and written by Koe himself, noted an increase in high-risk sexual practices despite sound knowledge of safe sex practices (Koe, 2006). Using the survey and the report to further lobby for safe sex education, Fridae, together with a local independent AIDS organisation, was able to design, promote and launch Singapore's first safe-sex campaign a few months later through the same portal. New configurations such as these across the whole value chain have clearly enabled Fridae to market a new consumption model that can also create innovative social value. Unlike other online gay personals portals, Fridae maintains competitive advantage and stays relevant through its social legitimacy.

Conclusion: Legitimating Sociality

The concept of the social lies at the heart of the social enterprise yet the pre-dominant rational and instrumental approaches to this field have been criti-cised for taking the social for granted (Nicholls and Cho, 2006). Thinking about sociality means thinking about how social objectives are defined, negotiated and pursued (Cho, 2006). It also means thinking about how social enterprises are legitimated as organisations through the ways assets and resources are acquired to maintain and influence social behaviour (Dart, 2004).

From the critical analysis of the five activities pursued by Fridae presented in this chapter, it is not hard to ascertain the nature of Fridae's sociality. As the title of this essay suggests, and what Koe maintains in an interview, "it is a gay company, as gay as it gets" (Yue, 2010a). It markets gay products to a gay constituency, nurtures the gay community through its media and marketing arms, and from its HIV programming and community cultural development projects, builds gay social capital. Despite Koe's monological vision, it serves a multiplicity of social movement objectives that are participatory and commu-nity-based. Central to this innovation is the way it legitimises the organization.

Two forms of legitimacy that underpin the institutional foundation of the social enterprise are relevant to Fridae. Pragmatic legitimacy refers to "the kind of exchange calculation of the expected value of a focal organization's activity to immediate stakeholder groups" (Dart, 2004: 416). Fridae's program-related investment and its social impact returns to its stakeholders, for example, can be considered as this form of legitimacy. As Alex Nicholls and Albert Cho suggest, this form of legitimacy is "based on simple exchange calculations where the external actor asks the questions, what did I get from this organization and does it conform to my expectations?" (Nicholls and Cho, 2006: 113). While it is hard to accurately assess social performance, it is clear from activities like Pink Dot, Nation Party and IndigNation, and even through the high response rate to the HIV surveillance surveys, that it has engaged the broader social constituency.

Moral legitimacy refers to legitimacy that is "based on an evaluation of whether an activity of a focal organization is the proper one rather than whether it specifically benefits those who are making the evaluation" (Dart, 2004: 416–17). Moral legitimacy has been seized upon as a mode of organi-sational justification in the neoliberal economy where the welfare state is in decline and the social welfare sector is encouraged to pursue market-based business approaches and solutions. Similarly, the ideological ascent of the corporate social responsibility discourse has also prompted business organisa-tions to take a more active role in the social. In Asia, the rise of neoliberalism has been boosted by new governmental models such as the creative economy where knowledge workers and small business organisations alike are encouraged to refashion themselves as innovatively as possible in all manner of ways for the new economy (Ong, 2006). In a non-welfare state like Singapore where the moral legitimacy of the social enterprise has emerged as a flag bearer of such an economy, it is not surprising that Fridae has been able to successfully negotiate the contradictions between the illegality of homosexuality and the promotion of a self-regulating homosociality.

By critically situating Fridae as a social enterprise rather than through gay and lesbian new media cultural studies that consider new discourses of gay Asian sexual identity enabled by online informationality and interactivity, this chapter hopes it has provided another approach to understanding the new institutional modes that can sustain LGBT organizations and social movements. This approach is relevant to a country where homosexuality is illegal and social organisations cannot be officially registered. It is precisely through the illiberal yet pragmatic moral legitimacy of Fridae that has allowed it to flourish as Asia's largest gay website in Singapore's neoliberal economy. Through its social innovations, Fridae has indeed, in the last decade, made visible its gay constituency, both in the country and regionally, serving as a template for the future of queer institutions.

Notes

Introduction: Queer Singapore

1. A longer and earlier version of this section has been published in the *Gay and Lesbian Issues and Psychology Review* (see Yue, 2007). The author thanks the Journal for permission to reprint parts of the article here.

2. Although a considerably larger number of gender reassignment surgeries have been conducted in Bangkok over this period (see Aizura, 2011), in Singapore, these surgeries are State-sanctioned. Through these surgeries, Singapore has become one of the first countries in the region to legally recognise transsexual status.

Chapter 1: How to Bring Singaporeans Up Straight (1960s–1990s)

1. For a detailed history of the Nation Party, see Audrey Yue's introduction in this volume.

2. The telemovie was broadcasted on 30 December 2007 on Arts Central, a T.V. channel in Singapore and is available at: http://www.youtube.com/watch?v=hjo28ya5rDI (accessed on 14 September 2009).

3. See International Monetary Fund (2009); World Bank (2009); Central Intelligence Agency (2004).

4. Three SDP supporters were charged for contempt of court when they turned up in identical t-shirts with a print of a kangaroo dressed in a judge's robe to hear a defamation suit against Dr. Chee by Lee and his son, Lee Hsien Loong. See Koh (2008).

5. See *BBC* (2008).

6. In recent years, these institutions have allowed public feedback on issues such as the building of a casino or the repeal of the sodomy law, 377A, but such acts are gestural and act as strateges to retain electoral votes. Authority and deciding power are still incumbent on the State: the casino is still a go-ahead and 377A still stands despite public opinion.

7. For censorship in films, see Kenneth Chan's chapter in this book.

8. See Chris K. K. Tan's chapter in this book.

9. The stories during the 'Stop at Two' campaign, surfacing only now in the age of digital reproduction, are devastating. Miss Rebecca Lim (2008) writes, "My mother was pressurized heavily when she was pregnant with her third child. Whether it was a boy or girl, she never got to find out as the pressure on her was so great (nurses chiding her to follow the law, having to pay a fine should she produce more

than two) that she had an abortion a few weeks after she found out about her pregnancy." In an article in *The Straits Times*, Mavis Toh (2008) reports on the plight of
several women who lived through that period: Margaret Chua, who had a tubal
ligation, said, "The pressure was high. The Government clearly didn't want us to
have more than two … Now, more than 30 years later, I wish I had more"; Teo Gek
Eng was lambasted by doctors and nurses for her third pregnancy and was asked
if she wanted an abortion; Mary Koh aborted her third child because she could not
afford to pay the fine; Dr. Paul Tan claims to have performed as many as 9 steriliza-
tion operations a day. He said, "Pregnant women came in saying, 'Doctor, I think
I'm pregnant again' as if they committed a crime."

Chapter 2: Enforcement of 377A

1. Singapore's Penal Code borrowed heavily, and often in a word-for-word fashion,
    from the Indian Penal Code, the imported section 377 which had criminalised
    "carnal intercourse against the course of nature" (which was judicially interpreted
    to include same sex intercourse); a statement that was eventually repealed in 2007.
    Remaining in the books was 377A, which had been introduced into the Penal Code
    some decades later, apparently inspired by contemporaneous legislation in England.
2. The context was a piece of legislation intended to reform the Penal Code (which
    houses 377A). Anti-377A activists had urged the government to include the repeal
    of 377A in the reform. The essentially religiously motivated pro-377A lobby was
    spurred into action to oppose such a move.
3. The most prominent of whom is Alex Au (2010a), who has been making this
    argument for years.
4. See also the unreported decision (i.e., a judicial decision which did not find its way
    into the official reports) of Mohamed Ibrahim Mohamed Hussain where a reli-
    gious teacher was charged with 377A for an act with a 16-year-old, although there
    appeared also to have been elements of non-consent (*The Straits Times*, 2006).
5. The idea of taking into consideration (popularly known as 'TIC') additional charges
    is actually at heart a humane policy of both reducing the punishment and sparing
    the accused of a longer criminal record where he is indeed properly prosecuted for
    several offences. It is not so when the accused ought not to have been prosecuted for
    the additional offences.
6. Five others were punished for soliciting the same boy (*The Straits Times*, 2009). I do
    not discuss the three who were charged under the now defunct section 377. It is to
    be noted that the absence of 377 does not disconcert the prosecution or the police.
    As we have seen, they can easily be charged under alternative provisions now.
7. See, for example, Au (2010b).
8. In *Chief Military Prosecutor v CPL Ang Eng Sui* (2001), the accused was convicted of
    a 377A offence for consensual activity in a detention barracks gym with a fellow
    military policeman; refer 'Man abetted indecent act in public pool' (*The Straits Times*,
    1999), the accused had allowed another man to perform oral sex on him in a public
    pool. More recently, 377A was used in the "toilet sex" case of Muhammad Noor
    Izuan Saad and Timothy Ang Ah Sai (*Channel News, Asia*, 2010). Both appeared to
    have pleaded guilty; Timothy Ang was sentenced to two weeks' imprisonment, and
    Muhammad to four weeks' imprisonment (apparently for subsequently alleging
    that Ang had molested him).

9. See the 'One Seven' case (Au, 2010b) for which I could uncover no other source, but have no reason to doubt the authenticity of. This scenario was to be replayed in the case of Tan Eng Hong where 377A was again the officially preferred provision for what was alleged to have been sexual activity in a public toilet (see *Fridae*, 2010). The 377A charge was eventually substituted for a charge under section 294 of the Penal Code:

> Whoever, to the annoyance of others does any obscene act in any public place … shall be punished with imprisonment which may extend to 3 months, or with fine, or with both.

The reason for the substitution was again unclear. There is no evidence of a plea bargain; at the time of writing the accused has not pleaded guilty. It is possible that the accused's threatened challenge to the constitutionality of 377A prompted the prosecution to act in order to deprive the accused *locus standi* (a doctrine which allows someone to challenge the constitutionality of a law only if he or she is sufficiently affected) to take up the challenge.

The choice of section 294 of the Penal Code (public obscenity) over section 20 of the MOPOA (public indecency) is interesting. It is unclear if the prosecutorial mind was directed at this choice. Section 294 is apparently the more serious offence (see the punishment structures in footnote 26), but its requirements are also higher. "Annoyance" to at least one other person is necessary. The act must also be "obscene" and not merely indecent. Section 42 of the Penal Code defines "obscene" in these terms:

> any thing or matter the effect of which is, if taken as a whole, such as to tend to deprave and corrupt persons who are likely, having regard to all relevant circumstances, to read, see or hear the matter contained or embodied in it.

Whilst "indecency" is commonly thought to be something merely offensive, "obscenity" appears to require evidence of some sort of pernicious effect on the observer. Sex in a locked cubicle of a public toilet is much more clearly an indecency and much less clearly an obscenity.

10. Unlike the situation of sex with minors, the potential use of 377A as a bargaining chip in public sex cases has real bite; imprisonment is mandatory for 377A and the maximum term is two years. In comparison, Section 294 of the Penal Code (public obscenity) permits either a fine, imprisonment of up to 1 year, or both, while Section 20 of the MOPOA (public indecency) permits either a fine of up to S$1000, or imprisonment up to 1 month (but apparently not both), with those limits rising to S$2000 and 6 months for subsequent offending.

11. Sexual activity inside a motor vehicle parked in a public car park is apparently not considered by law enforcers to be deserving of prosecution, at least if such activity cannot be perceived with the naked eye (because of makeshift curtains, or the lack of illumination). There is no obvious reason why this is different from sexual activity in a locked cubicle of a public toilet.

12. Section 23, carries a maximum penalty of ten years imprisonment, five times more than the maximum for 377A.

13. Famously showcased in *Public Prosecutor v Tan Boon Hock* (1994) (see also Au, 2010b). Oddly, the charges preferred were not under 377A, but outrage of modesty.

14. See the relevant extract (*Parliamentary Debates*, 2007: 52). I do not pretend to comprehend these terms beyond the general sentiment that homosexuals are not to be too

publicly assertive about their sexuality. But even that is sufficient for the purposes of this discussion.

15. I have argued elsewhere that even the symbolic use of 377A is constitutionally questionable (see Hor, 2010). The fact that its existence provides the opportunity for actual illegitimate and unconstitutional prosecutions bolsters that proposition, and it is open to the courts to declare the retention of 377A itself to be unconstitutional. Since the writing of this chapter, an application has been made to the court to declare 377A unconstitutional. That application was denied in the High Court on the ground that the applicant, once but no longer charged under 377A, did not have the standing to make such an application (*Tan Eng Hong v Attorney-General*, 2011). The appeal from this decision has been heard and the Court of Appeal has reserved judgment (see Petrat, 2011).

Chapter 5: Transnational Lesbian Identities

1. See Manalansan, 1997; Wieringa, et al. 2007; Boellstorff, 2007; Leung, 2008; Cruz-Malavé and Manalansan, 2002 among others.

2. See Chalmers, 2008; Bacchetta, 2002; Bhaskaran, 2004; Blackwood, 1999, 2005, 2008; Sinnott, 2004; Chao, 2000.

3. After Singapore gained independence in 1965, the postcolonial state maintained the law, Section 377A, instituted by the British colonial government in the 19th century, which prohibits 'gross indecency' between two men. Although targeted at male same-sex relations, this law could be widely interpreted as making same-sex sexual lives illegal in Singapore.

4. In some of these non-Western contexts, women who love women do not identify with the term 'lesbian' or 'queer'. These terms, for example, are either absent or as yet uncommon in the local lexicon of India (Bacchetta, 1999, 2002) and Indonesia (Blackwood, 2008). In Thailand, women who love women completely resist the term 'lesbian' (Sinnott, 2004). Researchers have resorted in various ways to represent this reality by either referring to "lesbian" women in inverted commas (see for example Bacchetta, 2002: 954) or italicising the indigenised term to underscore its distinction with English terms (see for example Boellstorff, 2005: 8).

5. Bunzl's made a similar albeit more eloquent point for the case of Austria, observing that "homosexuals became central players in the social drama of modernity. Constituted as always already outside the margins of respectability, their abjection gave coherence to the fiction of German nationness" (2004: 13).

6. In 2009, local gay activists organised what was the first public gathering of the community at a national park. Up to 2,500 members and friends of the gay community wore pink to form a human dot. 'Pink Dot', as it is called, has since become an annual event with over 4,000 people attending in 2010, and over 8,000 in 2011. The 'Pink Dot' draws on the global gay signifier 'pink' as the colour is often associated with the global gay LGBT community. But 'more importantly', the Singaporean organisers say, pink 'is the colour of our national identity cards and it is what you get when you mix the colours of our national flag' (Pinkdotsg 2009). The idea of a 'dot' is drawn from the representation of Singapore as a red dot on the world map, a geographic imaginary frequently appropriated by the State in its nationalistic discourse emphasising the fragility of the nation and the need to defend it.

7. Yue relies on Cornel West's (1989) philosophy of pragmatism to expound her argument in relation to queer cultural productions in Singapore. For the full theoretical treatise, see Yue (2007: 155–58).

Chapter 6: Both Contagion and Cure

1. Other contemporary instances of sovereign city-states are the Vatican City State and the Principality of Monaco. Neither of these functions as a global city to the extent Singapore does (despite the Vatican's influence globally over members of the Roman Catholic faith). Conversely, while Macau and Hong Kong are similar to city-states, enjoying a high degree of legal, political and economic autonomy as Special Administrative Regions of the People's Republic of China (under the one-country two-systems arrangement), and Hong Kong confidently asserts its role as a global city, unlike Singapore, Monaco and the Vatican City State, they are not sovereign entities.

2. In this, the understandings of cosmopolitanism are quite similar to those developed by Ulf Hannerz who distinguishes between cosmopolitans and locals within the world cultures created by globalizing processes (See Hannerz, 1996: 102–11, 27–39).

3. The other is Kuala Lumpur, the capital of neighbouring, and predominantly Muslim, Malaysia. It is worth noting the extensive shared histories—colonial and postcolonial—that link these two cities.

4. The interview from which this quote is drawn was reported by Reuters (2007) and Trevvy (Team Trevvy, 2007), among others. A transcript of the relevant part of the interview was provided by Au (2007a).

Chapter 8: The Negative Dialectics of Homonationalism, or Singapore English Newspapers and Queer World-Making

1. For more information, please access 'Singapore Pages/NewspaperSG' at http://newspapers.nl.sg/.

2. For the historical illustrations and justifications, see George, 2007.

3. According to Turnbull, the number of English, Chinese, Malay and Tamil dailies stood at 4, 2, 2 and 3 respectively. See Turnbull, 2009: 323.

4. For a similar appraisal on the reproductive role of women, see Heng and Devan, 1992.

5. For essays on these matters, see Goh, 2008 and Amirthalingam, 2009.

6. For a heteronormative treatment of Singapore's economy, see Chua, 2003.

7. In the first volume of his *Parerga and Paralipomena*, Schopenhauer (1974) states that "the cheapest form of pride is national pride; for the man affected therewith betrays a want of individual qualities of which he might be proud, since he would not otherwise resort to that which he shares with so many millions" (Schopenhauer, 1974: 360).

8. Two criticisms against the bias of the local press stems from Prof. Thio Li-Ann's speech, which can be obtained from the Hansard (2009), as well as from Au (2010).

9. If the accused is proven to be a homosexual psychopath, as justified by the American Psychiatric Association's *Diagnostic and Statistical Manual of Mental Disorders I* (1952), he could plead for 'diminished responsibility' and receive pardon from capital punishment. Then, he would only be charged for manslaughter (which was the case) and the illegal act of gross indecency between two male persons as stipulated in

section 377A of the 1938 Straits Settlements Penal Code, which remained in the 1955 Singapore Penal Code. It is significant to also note that the removal of homosexuality as a mental disorder in 1974 was not reported in *The Straits Times*.

10. For an exposition of the film *Saint Jack*, refer to the chapter by Kenneth Chan in this volume.

Chapter 9: Impossible Presence

1. While the Uhdes are more generous in their assessment of the government's role in fostering the revival of the film industry, they acknowledge that Singapore's economic "success" led to "a relative neglect of the arts, considered inessential by the government" (Uhde and Uhde, 2010: 54).

2. My characterization of these complex institutional entities here is somewhat unfairly reductive. For a more nuanced narration of the Singapore Film Commission, see Millet, 2006: 100–1. Millet credits the Singapore Film Commission for supporting, for instance, Djinn's edgy *Perth* (2004) and Royston Tan's subtly homoerotic paean to Singapore's violent gangster youth culture in *15* (2003). See also the Uhdes' interview with Daniel Yun, who heads MediaCorp Raintree Pictures, for a more conflicted understanding of the organization's economic imperative (Uhde and Uhde, 2010: 68–70).

3. For "how sexuality functions as technology for cultural policy" in Singapore as a "creative city", see Yue, 2007: 366.

4. Spatial constraints do not permit me to indulge in extended reflections on this matter, an issue that my fellow contributors in this collection have delved into with greater efficacy and rigor. From a personal observational standpoint, I have noticed growing public usage of "queer" in Singapore, as a mode of complicating essentialist identity categories. Because I am not of the theoretical mind that rejects Western theory *in toto* as a mode of cultural nationalist politics, I pragmatically embrace "queerness" as a theoretically useful paradigm within a Singapore context.

5. Williams cites Benjamin, 1999.

6. I am in happy possession of a DVD copy distributed legally in Singapore by an Australian company, Umbrella Entertainment. See especially the DVD's extra feature "Interview with Director Peter Bogdanovich" as he describes in his own words the production's struggles with the Singapore censors. *Saint Jack*, dir. Peter Bogdanovich, 112 min., Umbrella Entertainment, 2004, DVD. In chapter eight of this book, Jun Zubillaga-Pow also references the Singapore government's official take on *Saint Jack*, as represented by the country's main English-language newspaper *The Straits Times* in 1980.

7. Lim, 2004. For gay prostitution, see pages 105–23.

8. Millet suggests that *Saint Jack*'s "1970s American independent filmmaking … style … would resurface 10 to 15 years later in the works of young local filmmakers like Djinn, who were attracted by the fringes and underbelly of Singapore society" (Millet, 2006: 77).

9. Because of its soft-core sexuality, DVDs of the film are not available in Singapore.

10. It is both interesting and perplexing to note that lesbian cinematic representations have thus far been limited in Singapore.

11. In his excellent analysis of Royston Tan's oeuvre, political scientist Kenneth Paul Tan alludes subtly to the queer possibilities in Tan's films. He notes how *15* offers a "homoerotic subtext [that] is clear and poignant" despite the filmmaker's disavowal of such a reading (Tan, 2008: 240). He also characterizes Tan's autobiographical confessions in *Mother* as references to the filmmaker's "vaguely implied homosexuality" (Tan, 2008: 236).

12. The Uhdes label *Solos* as "the first gay fiction feature" (Uhde and Uhde, 2010: 154) and praise it as "one of the best films the city has produced" (Uhde and Uhde, 2010: 153).

13. In her trenchant analysis of the "revisionist, ego-based psychoanalytic" work of Richard C. Friedman and Richard Green in the 1980s (Sedgwick, 1993: 70), Eve Kosofsky Sedgwick critiques the notion that "mothers … have nothing to contribute to this process of masculine validation [in gay boys], and [points out how] women are reduced in the light of its urgency to a null set: any involvement in it by a woman is overinvolvement; any protectiveness is overprotectiveness; and, for instance, mothers 'proud of their sons' nonviolent qualities' are manifesting unmistakable 'family pathology'" (Sedgwick, 1993: 75; Sedgwick quotes from Friedman, 1988: 193).

Chapter 10: The Kids Are *Not* All Right

1. An earlier version of this essay appears as 'Censure and Censor', 19 March 2010, in *S/PORES: New Directions in Singapore Studies*, http://s-pores.com/page/3/?s. I thank the editors for allowing me to reproduce the ideas introduced in that paper here.

Chapter 11: "Singaporean by birth, Singaporean by faith"

1. One preliminary note on terminology: In my time doing fieldwork in Singapore, I found that for the most part, the individuals with whom I interacted used the terms "LGBT", "gay", "lesbian", "bisexual" or "queer" when referring to themselves and to those in their social and activist circles. Some informants did speak in local terms such as *ah qua* (a derogatory Hokkien term for gay men) or *pondan* (Malay for effeminate male) at different times and in different contexts. For the sake of consistency, simplicity, and inclusivity, I utilize queer. My research in Singapore suggests that the logic of enumeration, in which potentially endless number of initialisms such as LGBT, LGBTQ, and LGBTQI etc. is insufficient to capture the "unstable identity process" (Phelan, 1997: 60) demonstrated by many of my Singaporean interlocutors. Additionally, most names and many identifying details have been changed to protect the anonymity of informants.

2. In my research, I have interacted with numerous Singaporean men of Indian descent who have sex with other men (MSM), a majority of whom are married with children. While their sexual behaviour may be etically perceived and described as bisexual or even gay, this particular group of men does not self-identify in this manner. As such, their experiences are not represented in the current essay.

3. Due to the relative anonymity that comes with communications that occur in cyberspace, it was impossible to definitively determine if the persons with whom I were interacting online were truly Indian-Singaporeans. However, most of the men and women whom I encountered online eventually agreed to meet offline. In these instances, their identity was verified.

4.   It should be emphasised that a vast majority of current Singaporeans are the product of diasporic migrations that have taken place since the early nineteenth century. In addition to the minority ethnic Indians, ethnic Malays are a minority in Singapore despite being politically portrayed as indigenous *bumiputras*. Singapore's majority Chinese are themselves a minority within the greater Southeast Asian region.

5.   While this essay primarily examines marginalization of queer Indian-Singaporeans, it should be noted that in many instances queer Malay-Singaporeans face similar problems.

6.   The People's Republic of China (PRC) is viewed as the "first" China whereas Taiwan (Republic of China) is seen as the "second" China. Depending on the perspective of the speaker, Singapore or Hong Kong is often spoken of as the "third" China.

7.   There are four official languages in Singapore. English is the language of administration and commerce. Among the other languages, Malay is the national language and Mandarin and Tamil are considered official languages.

8.   For more on the idea of "Chineseness" see Chun 1996. For a comparative discussion of the idea of "Americanness" see Grewal, 2005.

9.   The marginalization encountered by queer Indian-Singaporeans is, of course, not unique (See, for example, Bhaskaran, 2004; Gopinath, 2005; Ratti, 1993). In addition to the interviews conducted in Singapore, I conducted abbreviated interviews with queers of Indian origin in other cosmopolitan cities including Kuala Lumpur, Bangkok, and Hong Kong. While the content of these interviews varied widely, interlocutors in all locations spoke of marginalization along racial lines.

10. People Like Us (2011), http://www.plu.sg/society/?p=39 (accessed on 13 October 2011).

11. For a full listing of content guidelines see People Like Us (2011), http://www.plu.sg/society/?p=40 (accessed on 13 October 2011).

12. Fridae (2011), http://www.fridae.com/aboutus/ (accessed on 13 October 2011).

13. The other site discussed in this chapter, *SiGNeL*, is a Yahoo group and as such, the servers are located in the United States.

14. At the time of writing there were approximately 350 profiles posted by men who identify as Malay.

Chapter 12: "We're the gay company, as gay as it gets"

1.   Although the official website is known as 'Fridae.com', this chapter uses 'Fridae' rather than 'Fridae.com' to refer to how the website has become a 'brand' or 'cultural icon' for other offline and online practices. This usage is also consistent with how the company names itself on its website. See Fridae (2010).

2.   See Davis (2008) for a toolkit for sustainable LGBT businesses that includes a short profile on Fridae.

3.   On how the State embraces new media and suppresses the civil society, see Rodan (2003).

4.   On the legal and political ramifications of Singapore's Internet censorship laws, see Hogan (1999) and Rodan (1998). On gay business raids, see Anonymous (2010).

5. Queer consumption studies is a burgeoning field that includes niche marketing, pink tourism, gay advertising and the media commodification of sex and sexual identity. Recent studies here include Branchik (2006); Gobe (2001); Fejes (2002); Sender (2004); and Streitmatter (2004).

6. For a history of these developments and the specificities of lesbian consumption practices, see Yue (2011).

7. For a useful representation of these debates, see groyn88 (2010).

8. The Speaker's Corner is the only place in the country where public assembly and public speaking are allowed without a police permit.

References

Introduction: Queer Singapore

Aizura, A. 2011. The Romance of the Amazing Scalpel: 'Race', Labour, and Affect in Thai Gender Reassignment Clinics. In *Queer Bangkok: 21st Century Markets, Media, and Rights*, ed. P. Jackson. 143–62. Hong Kong: Hong Kong University Press.

Ang, P. H. and Nadarajan, B. 1996. Censorship and the Internet: A Singapore perspective. *Communications of the ACM* 39(6): 72–78.

Ang, P. H. and Min, Y. T. 1998. *Mass Media Laws and Regulations in Singapore*. Singapore: Asian Media Information and Communications Centre.

Berry, C., Martin, F. and Yue, A. (eds.) 2003. *Mobile Cultures: New Media in Queer Asia*. Durham: Duke University Press.

Bhabha, H. 1999. Arrivals and Departures. In *Home, Exile, Homeland: Film, Media, and the Politics of Place*, ed. H. Naficy. vii–xii. New York: Routledge.

Chan, K. 2004. Cross-Dress for Success: Performing Ivan Heng and Chowee Leow's 'An Occasional Orchid' and Stella Kon's 'Emily of Emerald Hill' on the Singapore Stage. *Tulsa Studies in Women's Literature* 23(1): 29–43.

———. 2008. Gay Sexuality in Singaporean Chinese Popular Culture: Where Have All the Boys Gone? *China Information* 22(2): 305–29.

Chan, K. and Heng, I. 2004. Drag and the Politics of Identity and Desire in Singapore Theatre: A Conversation with Ivan Heng. *Tulsa Studies in Women's Literature* 23(1): 121–34.

Chong, T. 2005. From Global to Local: Singapore's Cultural Policy and Its Consequences. *Critical Asian Studies* 37(4): 553–69.

———. 2010. 'Back Regions' and 'Dark' in Singapore: The Politics of Censorship and Liberalisation. *Space & Polity* 14(3): 235–50.

Chua, B. H. 1995. *Communitarian Ideology and Democracy in Singapore*. London: Routledge.

———. 1997. *Political Legitimacy and Housing: Stakeholding in Singapore*. London: Routledge.

———. 2003. *Life Is Not Complete without Shopping: Consumption Culture in Singapore*. Singapore: Singapore University Press, National University of Singapore.

———. 2004. Cultural Industry and the Next Phase of Economic Development of Singapore. Paper presented at the Workshop on Port Cities and City-States in Asia, Europe, Asia-Africa Institute, University of Hamburg, Germany, 4–7 November 2004.

———. 2007. Political Culturalism, Representations and the People's Action Party of Singapore. *Democratization* 14(5): 911–27.

———. 2008. Singapore in 2007: High Wage Ministers and the Management of Gays and Elderly. *Asian Survey* 48(1): 55–61.

Cowan, R. 2003. *Cornel West: The Politics of Redemption*. Cambridge: Polity Press.

Detenber, B. H. Cenite, M., Ku, M. K. Y, Ong, C. P. L., Tong, H. Y, and Yeow, M. L. H. 2007. Singaporeans' Attitudes towards Lesbians and Gay Men and Their Tolerance of Media Portrayals of Homosexuality. *International Journal of Public Opinion Research* 19(3): 367–79.

De Waal, C. 2005. *On Pragmatism*. Belmont, CA.: Wadsworth.

Dowsett, G. W. 1993. 'I'll Show You Mine, If You Show Me Yours': Gay Men, Masculinity Research, Men's Studies, and Sex. *Theory and Society* 22: 697–709.

Florida, R. 2002. *The Rise of the Creative Class: And How It's Transforming Work, Leisure, Community and Everyday Life*. New York: Basic Books.

Foucault, M. 1979. *The History of Sexuality*, vol. 1–3. London: Allen Lane.

Frank, D. J. and Mceneaney, E. H. 1999. The Individualization of Society and the Liberalisation of State Policies on Same-Sex Sexual Relations, 1984–1995. *Social Forces* 77(3): 911–43.

Gea, S. J. 2006. Razzle dazzle em!. *Fridae.com*, 7 July. http://www.fridae.com/newsfeatures/printer.php?articleid=1710 (accessed on 28 September 2007).

Gibson, C. and Kong, L. 2005. Cultural economy: A critical review. *Progress in Human Geography*, 29(5): 541–61.

Global Alliance for Cultural Diversity. 2006. *Understanding Creative Industries: Cultural Statistics for Public-Policy Making*. Paris: UNESCO.

Goh, D. 2008. It's the Gays' Fault: News and HIV as Weapons against Homosexuality in Singapore. *Journal of Communication Inquiry* 32(4): 383–99.

Heng, R. 2001. Tiptoe Out of the Closet: The Before and After of the Increasingly Visible Gay Community in Singapore. *Journal of Homosexuality* 40(3–4): 81–97.

Herndl, C. G. and Bauer, D. A. 2003. Speaking Matters: Liberation Theology, Rhetorical Performance, and Social Action. *College Composition and Communication* 54(4): 558–85.

Howkins, J. 2001. *The Creative Economy: How People Make Money from Ideas*. London: Allen Lane.

Jackson, P. 2001. Pre-gay, Post-queer: Thai Perspectives on Proliferating Gender/Sex Diversity in Asia. *Journal of Homosexuality* 40(3–4): 1–25.

Koh, A. 1995. *Glass Cathedral*. Singapore: EPB Publishers.

Kymlicka, W. 1995. *Multicultural Citizenship: A Liberal Theory of Minority Rights*. Oxford: Oxford University Press.

Lee, J. S. 1992. *Peculiar Chris*. Singapore: Cannon International.

Lee, T. 2000. Internet Regulation in Singapore: A Policy/ing Discourse. *Media International Australia Incorporating Culture and Policy*, 95: 147–69.

Leong, L. W. T. 1997. Singapore. In *Sociolegal Control of Homosexuality: A Multi-nation Comparison*, eds. D. West and R. Green. 127–44. New York: Plenum Press.

Leung, H. H. S. 2008. *Undercurrents: Queer Culture and Postcolonial Hong Kong*. Vancouver and Hong Kong: UBC Press and Hong Kong University Press.

Lim, E. B. 2005a. Glocalqueering in New Asia: The Politics of Performing Gay in Singapore. *Theatre Journal* 57: 383–405.

———. 2005b. The Mardi Gras Boys of Singapore's English-Language Theatre. *Asian Theatre Journal*, 22(2): 293–309.

Lim, K. F. 2004. Where Love Dares (not) Speak Its Name: The Expression of Homosexuality in Singapore. *Urban Studies* 41(9): 1759–877.

Lim, V. K. G. 2002. Gender Differences and Attitudes towards Homosexuality. *Journal of Homosexuality* 43(1): 85–97.

Low, L. 2001. The Singapore Developmental State in the New Economy and Polity. *The Pacific Review* 14(3): 411–41.

Martin, F. 2010. *Backward Glances: Contemporary Chinese Cultures and the Female Homoerotic Imaginary*. Durham: Duke University Press.

Martin, F., P. Jackson, M. McLelland and A. Yue, eds. 2008. *AsiaPacifiQueer: New Genders and Sexuality*. Illinois: University of Illinois Press.

Media Development Authority. 2002. *Creative Industries Development Strategy: Propelling Singapore's Creative Economy*. Singapore: Ministry of Information, Communication and the Arts.

Mills, C. W. 2001. Prophetic Pragmatism as Political Philosophy. In *Cornel West: A Critical Reader*, ed. G. Yancy. 192–223. Malden: Massachusetts.

Ministry of Public Management, Home Affairs, Posts and Telecommunications. 2001. *Information and Communications in Japan*. Tokyo: Japan Copyright Institute.

Moo, J. 1990. *Sisterhood: The Untold Story*. Singapore: Times Editions.

———. 1993. *Sisterhood: New Moons in San Francisco*. Singapore, Times Editions.

Munt, S. 1998. Introduction. In *Butch/Femme: Inside Lesbian Gender*, ed. S. Munt. 1–11. London and Washington: Cassell.

The New Shorter Oxford English Dictionary. 1993. Oxford: Oxford University Press.

Ong, A. 1999. Cultural Citizenship as Subject Making: Immigrants Negotiate Racial and Cultural Boundaries in the United States. In *Race, Identity and Citizenship: A Reader*, eds. R. D. Torres, L. F. Miron and J. X. Inda. 262–94. Massachusetts: Blackwell.

———. 2006. *Neoliberalism as Exception: Mutations in Citizenship and Sovereignty*. Durham: Duke University Press.

Oswin, N. 2010. The Modern Model Family at Home in Singapore: A Queer Geography. *Transactions of the Institute of British Geographers* 35(2): 256–68.

Pakulski, J. 1997. Cultural Citizenship. *Citizenship Studies* 1(1): 73–86.

Price, D. C. 2003. Singapore: It's In to Be Out. Got Pink Dollars to Spend? Then Head for the Lion City. *Time Asia*, 18–25 August.

Prystay, C. 2007. Singapore Swing: The City's Gay Balancing Act. *The Wall Street Journal*, 10 August. http://online.wsj.com/article/SB118667829527493165.html (accessed on 8 October 2010).

Putnam, H. W. 2001. Pragmatism Resurgent: A Reading of *The American evasion of philosophy*. In *Cornel West: A Critical Reader*, ed. G. Yancy. 19–37. Malden: Massachusetts.

Rodan, G. 2003. Embracing Electronic Media But Suppressing Civil Society: Authoritarian Consolidation in Singapore. *The Pacific Review* 16(4): 503–24.

Rosaldo, R. 1999. Cultural Citizenship, Inequality, and Multiculturalism. In *Race, Identity and Citizenship: A Reader*, eds. R. D. Torres, L. F. Miron and J. X. Inda. 253–61. Massachusetts: Blackwell.

Ross, A. 2009. *Nice Work If You Can Get it: Life and Labor in Precarious Times*. New York: New York University Press.

Schein, R. E. 1997. *Strategic Pragmatism: The Culture of Singapore's Economic Development Board*. Cambridge, MA. and London: MIT Press.

Seidman, S. 2005. From Outside to Citizen. In *Regulating Sex: The Politics of Intimacy and Identity*, eds. E. Bernstein and L. Schaffner. 225–45. New York: Routledge.

Signorile, M. 1993. *Queer in America: Sex, the Media, and the Closets of Power*. New York: Random House.

Stevenson, N. 2003. *Cultural Citizenship: Cosmopolitan Questions*. Maidenhead, Berkshire: Open University Press.

Tan, K. P. 2007. Imagining the Gay Community in Singapore. *Critical Asian Studies* 39(2): 179–204.

UNESCO. 2005. *Asia-Pacific Creative Communities: Promoting the Cultural Industries for Local Socio-Economic Development—A Strategy for the 21st Century*. Bangkok: UNESCO.

Warner, M. 1999. *The Trouble with Normal: Sex, Politics, and the Ethics of Queer Life*. New York: The Free Press.

West, C. 1989. *The American Evasion of Philosophy: A Genealogy of Pragmatism*. Madison, Wisconsin: University of Wisconsin Press.

———. 1993. *Race Matters*. Boston: Beacon Press.

Westbrook, R. B. 2005. *Democratic Hope: Pragmatics and the Politics of Truth*. Ithaca and London: Cornell University Press.

Wood, M. D. 2000. *Cornel West and the Politics of Prophetic Pragmatism*. Illinois: University of Illinois Press.

Yeoh, P. 2006. Writing Singapore Gay Identities: Queering the Nation in Johann S. Lee's *Peculiar Chris* and Andrew Koh's *Glass Cathedral*. *The Journal of Commonwealth Literature* 41(3): 121–35.

Yue, A. 2007. Creative Queer Singapore: The Illiberal Pragmatics of Cultural Production. *Gay and Lesbian Issues and Psychology Review* 3(3): 149–105.

———. 2011. Doing Cultural Citizenship in the Global Media Hub: Illiberal Pragmatics and Lesbian Consumption Practices in Singapore. In *Circuits of Visibility: Gender and Transnational Media Cultures*, ed. R. Hegde. 250–67. New York: New York University Press.

Chapter 1: How to Bring Singaporeans Up Straight (1960s–1990s)

Althusser, L. 1997. *Lenin and Philosophy, and Other Essays*. Translated from French by Ben Brewster. London: NLB.

APF. 2008. Opposition Would Ruin Singapore: Lee Kuan Yew. 25 June. http://afp. google.com/article/ALeqM5hO5GOaqrgGNspmaeLjs7LFRH6Fsw (accessed on 14 September 2009).

BBC. 2008. Editor "defamed" Singapore Leader. 24 September. http://news.bbc.co.uk/ 2/hi/asia-pacific/7632830.stm (accessed on 9 May 2009)

Berlant, L. 2008. *The Female Complaint*. USA: Duke University Press.

Bristow, J. 1991. *Empire Boys: Adventures in a Man's World*. Great Britain: HarperColllins Academic.

Central Intelligence Agency. 2004. Country Comparison–GDP–Per Capital, https://www.cia.gov/library/publications/the-world-factbook/rankorder/2004 rank.html (accessed on 9 May 2009).

Chang, A. 2009. MM's Reassuring Comments Seals Researcher's Move Here. *The Straits Times*, 29 March. http://pluralsg.wordpress.com/2008/04/13/mms-reassuring-comments-seal-researchers-move-here (accessed on 14 September 2009).

Chou, W. 2000. *Tongzhi: Politics of Same-Sex Eroticism in Chinese Societies*. New York: Haworth.

Cook, M. 2003. *London and the Culture of Homosexuality, 1885–1914*. United Kingdom: Cambridge University Press.

Deacon, E. E. 1999. Digest of the Criminal Law of England. In *Nineteenth-Century Writings on Homosexuality: A Sourcebook*, ed. Chris White. 27. London and New York: Routledge (original work published 1831).

Douglas, Lord Alfred (1892 [1894]), 'Two Loves', *The Chameleon*, December. From Two Loves (1894 poem), *Wikisource*, http://en.wikisource.org/wiki/Two_Loves_%281894_poem%29 (accessed on 13 October 2011).

Fanon, F. 1996. *Fanon: A Critical Reader*. Gordon, L. et al. eds. Great Britain: Blackwell.

Forbes. 2006. Singapore Bans Far Eastern Economic Review Magazine. 28 September. www.forbes.com/feeds/afx/2006/09/28/afx3051478.html (accessed on 9 May 2009).

Forster, E. M. 1993. *Maurice*. USA: Norton (original work published 1971).

Foucault, M. 1990. *The History of Sexuality, Vol. 1: An Introduction* (trans. R. Hurley). USA: Vintage Books (original work published 1976).

———. 1995. *Discipline and Punish: The Birth of the Prison* (trans. A. Sheridan). USA: Second Vintage Books (original work published 1975).

Gramsci, A. 2000. *The Antonio Gramsci Reader: Selected Writings 1916–1935*. New York: NYU Press.

Grice, K. and Drakasi-Smith, D. 1985. The Role of State in Shaping Development: Two Decades of Growth in Singapore. *Transactions* 10, 347–59.

Hall, S. 2004. *Stuart Hall*, ed. Procter, J. London, Great Britain: Routledge.

Hebdige, D. 1979. *Subculture: The Meaning of Style*. London and New York: Routledge.

Heng, R. 2001. Tiptoe Out of the Closet: The Before and After of the Increasingly Visible Gay Community in Singapore. In *Gay and Lesbian Asia: Culture, Identity, Community*, eds. G. Sullivan and P. A. Jackson. 81–96. New York: Haworth.

Hinsch, B. 1992. *Passions of the Cut Sleeves: The Male Homosexual Tradition in China*. USA: University of California Press.

Holden, P. 2001. A Man and an Island: Gender and Nation in Lee Kuan Yew's *The Singapore Story. Biography* 24, 401–24.

Holloway, R. 1999. The White Swan. In *Nineteenth-Century Writings on Homosexuality: A Sourcebook*, ed. Chris White. 13. London and New York: Routledge (original work published 1813).

International Monetary Fund. 2009. World economic outlook database, April 2009, http://www.imf.org/external/index.htm (accessed on 9 May 2009).

Jackson, P. A. 2001. Pre-gay, Post-queer: Thai Perspectives on Proliferating Gender/Sex Diversity in Asia. In *Gay and Lesbian Asia: Culture, Identity, Community*, eds. G. Sullivan and P. A. Jackson. 1–26. New York: Haworth.

Koh, G. Q. 2008. Three Face Court over Kangaroo T-shirts. *Reuters UK,* 14 October. http://uk.reuters.com/article/oddlyEnoughNews/idUKTRE49D3XB20081014 (accessed on 9 May 2009).

Lee, J. S. 1992. *Peculiar Chris.* Singapore: Cannon International.

Lee, K. Y. 2005. Speech by Minister Lee Kuan Yew in parliament on the proposal to develop integrated resorts. http://stars.nhb.gov.sg/stars/public (accessed on 14 Oct 2009).

Library of Congress. 1989. Singapore: Population Control Policies. http://www.country-data.com/cgi-bin/query/r-11807.html (accessed on 14 Oct 2009).

Lim, R. 2008. Regrets of a Child of "Stop-at-Two" Era. *The Straits Times,* 6 September. http://www.straitstimes.com/ST+Forum/Online+Story/STIStory_275523.html (accessed on 10 May 2009).

Media Development Authority, Singapore. 2008. MediaCorp TV Channel 5 Fined for Breaching Programme Code. http://www.mda.gove.sg/wms.www/thenewsdesk.aspx?sid=869 (accessed on 14 September 2009).

Ministry of Education, Singapore (MOE). 2009. Desired Outcomes of Education. www.moe.gov.sg/education/desired-outcomes (accessed on 14 September 2009).

The Morning After. 2007. http://www.youtube.com/watch?v=hjo28ya5rDI (accessed on 14 September 2009).

Reporters Without Borders. 2008. Press Freedom Index 2008. http://en.rsf.org/press-freedom-index-2008,33.html (accessed on 14 September 2009).

Rich, A. 1980. Compulsory Heterosexuality and Lesbian Existence. *Signs* 5(4), 631–60.

Sa'at, A. 2001. *A History of Amnesia.* Singapore: Ethos Books.

Sa'at, A. 2008. Chiam See Tong on Malays in the SAF. http://www.blurty.com/talkread.bml?journal=sleepless77&itemid=205338 (accessed on 14 September 2009).

Sadasivan, B. 2005. The AIDS Epidemic. Speech in parliament. http://stars.nhb.gov.sg/stars/public (accessed on 14 September 2009).

Schaffer, T. 1994. "A Wilde Desire Took Me": The Homoerotic History of *Dracula. ELH* 61(2), 381–425.

Sinfield, A. 1994. *The Wilde Century.* London: Cassell.

Singapore Democratic Party. 2009. Truth about Elections. http://yoursdp.org/index.php/truth-about/elections (accessed on 14 September 2009).

Stoker, B. 1997. *Dracula.* USA: Norton (original work published 1897).

Toh, M. 2008. Two Is Enough. *The Straits Times,* 24 August. http://chutzpah.typepad.com/slow_movement/2008/08/st-two-is-not-enough.html (accessed on 10 May 2009).

Turnbull, C. M. 1989. *A History of Singapore, 1819–1988* (2nd ed.). Singapore: Oxford University Press.

Wilson, A. N. 2002. *The Victorians.* USA: W. W. Norton.

Wong, T. and Yeoh, B. S. A. 2003. Fertility and the Family: An Overview of Pro-natalist Population Policies in Singapore. *Asian Metcentre Research Paper,* 12. http://www.populationasia.org/Publications/RP/ AMCRP12.pdf (accessed on 14 September 2009).

World Bank. 2009. *Gross Domestic Product,* http://siteresources.worldbank.org/DATA STATISTICS/Resources/GDP_PPP.pdf (accessed on 9 May 2009).

Zakaria, F. 1994. Culture is Destiny: A Conversation with Lee Kuan Yew. http://www.lee-kuan-yew.com/leekuanyew-freedzakaria.html (accessed on 14 September 2009).

Chapter 2: Enforcement of 377A

Attorney-General's Chambers, 29th January 2009. Proceedings for Unnatural Offences Against Ng Geng Whye, Quek Hock Seng, Song Choong Chen Thomas, Balasundaram S/O Suppiah, Muhammad Hafashah bin Mohd Aslam and Ng Yong You Victor. http://www.agc.gov.sg/docs/Pau-Media_BackgroundBrief_Unnatural_Offences_2.pdf (accessed on 11 October 2011).

Au, Alex. 2010a. *Yawning Bread*. http://www.yawningbread.org/index2.htm (accessed on 1 October 2011).

Au, Alex. 2010b. The "One Seven" Case. *Yawning Bread*. http://www.yawningbread.org/arch_2001/yax-248.htm (accessed on 28 October 2010).

Channel News Asia. 2009. Singapore Won't Repeal Homosexual Law. 5 July. http://www.channelnewsasia.com/stories/singaporelocalnews/view/440540/1/.html (accessed on 28 October 2010).

Channel News Asia. 2010. Man Jailed for Four Weeks for Having Sex with Another Man. 23 September. http://www.channelnewsasia.com/stories/singaporelocalnews/view/1082967/1/.html (accessed on 28 October 2010).

Chief Military Prosecutor v CPL Ang Eng Sui [2001] SGMCA 3. Magistrates Court: Singapore.

Children and Young Persons Act. Chapter 38, Singapore Statutes: Section 7.

Fridae. 2010. http://www.fridae.com/newsfeatures/2010/09/27/10325.singapore-gay-advocacy-group-questions-use-of-section-377a?n=sec (accessed on 28 October 2010).

Hor, M. 2010. The Penal Code Amendments of 2007—Lessons in Love. In Management of Success: Singapore Revisited, ed. Terence Chong. 335–54. Singapore: Institute of Southeast Asian Studies.

Infectious Diseases Act. Chapter 137, Singapore Statutes: Section 23.

Law Society of Singapore v Tan Guat Neo Phyllis [2007] 2 SLR(R) 239; SGHC 207. High Court: Singapore.

Miscellaneous Offences (Public Order and Nuisance) Act. Chapter 184, Singapore Statutes: Section 20.

Ng Huat v Public Prosecutor [1995] 2 SLR(R) 66; SGHC 124. High Court: Singapore.

Parliamentary Debates. 2007. 23 October. http://www.parliament.gov.sg/parlweb/get_highlighted_content.jsp?docID=390554&hlLevel=Terms&links=MUST,PLACE,MUST,PLACE&hlWords=%20they%20too%20must%20have%20a%20place%20&hlTitle=&queryOption=5&ref=http://www.parliament.gov.sg:80/reports/public/hansard/title/20071023/20071023_S0003_T0002.html#1 (accessed on 28 October 2010).

Parliamentary Debates. 2008. 21 July. http://www.parliament.gov.sg/parlweb/get_highlighted_content.jsp?docID=520779&hlLevel=Terms&links=HOMOSEXU,ACTIV&hlWords=%20homosexual%20activities%20&hlTitle=&queryOption=1&ref=http://www.parliament.gov.sg:80/reports/public/hansard/title/20080721/20080721_S0007_T0002.html#1 (accessed on 28 October 2010).

Penal Code. Chapter 224, Singapore Statutes: Sections 90(a)(ii), 294 and 375–377D.

Petrat, C. 2011. Exorcising Specters: The Issue of 377A. *The Online Citizen*. 4 October. http://theonlinecitizen.com/2011/10/exorcising-specters-the-issue-of-377a/ (accessed on 5 October 2011).

Public Prosecutor v Adam Bin Darsin [2000] SGHC 267. High Court: Singapore.

Public Prosecutor v Amayapan Kodanpany [2010] SGHC 52. High Court: Singapore.

Public Prosecutor v Chan Mun Chiong [2008] SGDC 189. District Court: Singapore.

Public Prosecutor v Lim Beng Cheok [2003] SGHC 54. High Court: Singapore.

Public Prosecutor v Rahim bin Basron [2010] SGHC 90. High Court: Singapore.

Public Prosecutor v Soo Hwee Keong [2007] SGDC 262. District Court: Singapore.

Public Prosecutor v Tan Boon Hock [1994] 2 SLR(R) 32; [1994] SGHC 101. High Court: Singapore.

Public Prosecutor v Teo Kern Yiam [2005] SGDC 88. District Court: Singapore.

Public Prosecutor v ZQ [2009] SGDC 4. District Court: Singapore.

The Straits Times. 1999. Man Abetted Indecent Act in Public Pool. 12 October.

———. 2006. Religious Teacher Sexually Abused Teen. 11 February.

———. 2008. Human Rights Label Often Abused. 4 July.

———. 2009. Two Jailed for Gay Sex with Teen. 6 August.

———. 2010. Producer Jailed for Sex with Boy. 8 July.

Tan Eng Hong v Attorney-General [2011] 3 SLR 320; SGHC 56. High Court: Singapore.

Chapter 3: Sexual Vigilantes Invade Gender Spaces

Ang, B. 2009. Whatever You Can Think of, They Did. *The New Paper*, 4 May.

Baca Zinn, M., Eitzen, D. S., Wells, B. 2010. *Diversity in Families*. Boston: Allyn & Bacon.

Basu, R. 2009a. Long-Time Member and New Exco Lock Horns. *The Straits Times*, 24 April.

Basu, R. 2009b. The Awareness to Right a Wrong. *The Sunday Times*, 3 May.

Becker, H. 1963. *Outsiders: Studies in the Sociology of Deviance*. New York: Free Press.

Burack, C. 2008. *Sin, Sex and Democracy: Antigay Rhetoric and the Christian Right*. Albany: State University of New York Press.

Cahn, N. and Carbone, J. 2010. *Red Families V. Blue Families*. New York: Oxford University Press.

Chan, L. G. 2009. Schools Should Stop Offering Them Altogether. *The Straits Times* (Forum), 9 May.

Chan, P. C. W. 2010. Psychosocial Implications of Homophobic Bullying in Schools. In *Protection of Sexual Minorities since Stonewall*, ed. Phil C. W. Chan. 143–75. London: Routledge.

Chan, R. 2009a. Old Guard Takes Battle Online. *My Paper*, 27 April.

———. 2009b. How I Became Aware. *My Paper*, 4 May.

———. 2010. More Girls under 14 Having Sex. *My Paper*, 9 February. http://www.asiaone.com/Health/News/Story/A1Story20100209–197553.html (accessed on 2 April 2010).

Chin, Y. L. A. 2007. Beware the High-Risk "Gay Lifestyle". *The Straits Times* (Forum), 7 August. http://www.yawningbread.org/apdx_2007/imp-348.htm (accessed on 1 March 2010).

Chong, E. 2010. Ex-waiter Gets Jail for Sexual Grooming. *The Straits Times*, 23 September.

Chua, M. H. 2009. AWARE Saga: A New Militancy Emerges. *The Straits Times*, 25 April, p. 2.

Cobb, M. 2006. *God Hates Fags: The Rhetorics of Religious Violence*. New York: New York University Press.

Escoffier, J. 1996. Culture Wars and Identity Politics: The Religious Right and the Cultural Politics of Homosexuality. In *Radical Democracy: Identity, Citizenship and the State*, ed. David Trend. 165–78. New York: Routledge.

Gardner, R. 2009. Schools must teach pupils about babies, Aids and sex. *The Independent*, 28 April. http://www.independent.co.uk/news/education/education-news/schools-must-teach-pupils-about-babies-aids-and-sex-1675189.html (accessed on 28 April 2009).

George, C. 2006. *Contentious Journalism and the Internet Advantage: Democratizing Public Discourse in Malaysia and Singapore*. Singapore: Singapore University Press.

Gilboa, E. (ed.) 2002. *Media and Conflict*. Ardsley, New York: Transnational.

Govindan, R. 2009. Govt Should Ensure AWARE Stays Secular. *The Straits Times* (Forum), 24 April.

Han, F. K. 2009. Why We Covered AWARE Saga the Way We Did. *The Straits Times*, 30 May. http://www.ngejay.com/?p=2851 (accessed on 1 April 2010).

Herman, D. 1998. *The Antigay Agenda: Orthodox Vision and the Christian Right*. Chicago: University of Chicago Press.

Holden, P. 2009. Is New Guard Believable on Inclusiveness? *The Straits Times* (Forum), 1 May 2009.

Humphreys, L. 1970. The Breastplate of Righteousness. In *Social Perspectives in Lesbian and Gay Studies*, eds. Peter M. Nardi & Beth E. Schneider. 29–37. London: Routledge.

Hunter, J. D. 1991. *Culture Wars: The Struggle to Define America*. New York: Basic Books.

Hussain, Z. 2009. Coup Leader Comes Open. *The Straits Times*, 24 April.

Hussain, Z. and Wong, K. H. 2009. Churches Should Stay Out of AWARE. *The Straits Times*, A6, 1 May.

Jacob, P. 2009. Dangerous Turns in Domestic Dispute. *The Straits Times*, 20 April.

John, A. 2009. Too Many Questions Left Unanswered. *The Straits Times*, 23 April.

Leong, L. W. T. 2008. Decoding Sexual Policy in Singapore. In *Social Policy in Post-Industrial Singapore*, eds. Lian Kwen Fee and Tong Chee Kiong. 279–308. Leiden: Brill.

Lyons, L. 2004. *A State of Ambivalence: The Feminist Movement in Singapore*. Leiden: Brill.

Ministry of Education. 2009a. *MOE Statement on Sexuality Education Programme*, 6 May. http://www.moe.gov.sg/media/press/2009/05/moes-statement-on-sexuality-ed.php (accessed on 27 October 2009).

Ministry of Education. 2009b. *Policies on Sexuality Education*, 15 July. http://www.moe.gov.sg/education/programmes/social-emotional-learning/sexuality-education/policies/ (accessed on 18 October 2011).

Narayanan, G. 2008. *Policing Marital Violence in Singapore*. Leiden: Brill.

The New Paper. 2009. Most Hated: Feminist Mentor No More. 3 May.

Othman, D. 2009. AWARE Sex Guide Suspended. *The Straits Times*, 6 May.

Pilger, J. 2004. *Tell Me No Lies: Investigative Journalism and Its Triumphs*. London: Jonathan Cape.

Quek, C. and Spykerman. K. 2009. Sharp Rise in Girls under 16 Having Sex. *The Straits Times*, 9 February.

Quigley, W. P. 2003. *Ending Poverty as We Know It: Guaranteeing a Right to a Job at a Living Wage*. Philadelphia: Temple University Press.

Rubin, G. 2002. Thinking Sex: Notes for a Radical Theory of the Politics of Sexuality. In *Sexualities: Critical Concepts in Sociology, vol. 2*, ed. Ken Plummer. 188–241. London: Routledge.

Serrenti, A. 2009. Will Programmes Continue to Be Neutral? *The Straits Times* (Forum), 24 April.

Shoemaker, P. and Cohen, A. 2006. *News around the World.* New York: Routledge.

Siow, L. S. 2008. Online Campaign Leads to Rethink at DBS. *The Business Times*, 5 December. http://www.yawningbread.org/apdx_2008/imp-392.htm (accessed on 1 March 2010).

Smith, R. and Windes. R. 2000. *Progay/Antigay: The Rhetorical War over Sexuality.* Thousand Oaks, California: Sage.

Stein, A. 2001. *The Stranger Next Door: The Story of a Small Community's Battle over Sex, Faith and Civil Rights.* Boston: Beacon Press.

The Straits Times. 2010. Sex Infections on the Rise. 14 January.

Sudderuddin, S. 2009a. More Teens Hit by Sexual Infections. *The Sunday Times*, 25 October.

———. 2009b. When Teens Have Consensual Sex. *The Sunday Times*, 1 November.

Suhaimi, N. D. 2009a. Way Power Was Seized Is Criticized. *The Straits Times*, 25 April.

———. 2009b. Church against Homosexuality as "Normal Alternative Lifestyle". *The Straits Times*, A6, 1 May.

Sum, C. W. 2009. MOE: No Complaints from Parents, Dr Thio. *The Straits Times* (Forum), 29 April.

The Sunday Times. 2009. Claire Nazar: Why I Quit as AWARE President. 20 April.

Talbot, M. 2008. Red Sex, Blue Sex: Why Do So Many Evangelical Teenagers Become Pregnant? *The New Yorker*, 3 November.

Tan, A. 2009. Get Facts on Sex Ed Right: Ministry Hasn't Received Any Complaints about AWARE Programme. *The Straits Times*, 29 April.

Tan, P. 2009a. Concern over Sexuality Programme in Schools: 1,300 Sign Online Petition. *The New Paper*, 1 May.

———. 2009b. She Puts AWARE Quotes on T-shirts for Sale. *The New Paper*, 7 May.

Tan, T. L. 1990. *The Singapore Press: Freedom, Responsibility and Credibility.* Singapore: Times Academic Press.

Teo, W. G. and Soh. E. 2009. Face-off: The White Shirts v. the Red Shirts. *The Sunday Times*, 3 May.

Thio, S. M. 2009. Gay Activists a Key Constituency of AWARE. *The Straits Times* (Forum), 18 May.

Toh, M. and Thomas. S. 2010. More Minors Having Sex: A Trend That's Likely to Continue. *The Straits Times*, 9 February.

Vasundhra, D. 2009. What the School Programme Teaches Students. *The Straits Times* (Forum), 29 April.

Weiss, M. 2006. *Protest and Possibilities: Civil Society and Coalitions for Political Change in Malaysia.* Stanford, California: Stanford University Press.

Wong, K. H. 2009a. Unknowns Knock Out Veterans at AWARE Polls. *The Straits Times*, 10 April.

———. 2009b. New Guard Ousted. *The Sunday Times*, 3 May.

Yeo, A. 2009. Concerns Addressed. *The Straits Times* (Forum), 30 April.

Yong, D. 2009. Men Played Active Role in Meeting. *The Sunday Times*, 3 May.

Chapter 4: "Oi, Recruit! Wake Up Your Idea!"

Alexander, J. 2006. *The Civil Sphere*. Oxford: Oxford University Press.

Daniels, T. 2005. *Building Cultural Nationalism in Malaysia: Identity, Representation, and Citizenship*. New York: Routledge.

Donzelot, J. 1979. *The Policing of the Family*. Paris: Gallimard Editions.

Hefner, R. 2001. Introduction: Multiculturalism in Malaysia, Singapore, and Indonesia. In *The Politics of Multiculturalism: Pluralism and Citizenship in Malaysia, Singapore, and Indonesia*, ed. Robert W. Hefner. 1–58. Honolulu: University of Hawai'i Press.

Lim C.-S. 2002a. *Serving Singapore as a Gay Man, Part 1*. www.yawningbread.org/guest_2002/guw-080.htm (accessed on 17 October 2009).

———. 2002b. *Serving Singapore as a Gay Man, Part 2*. www.yawningbread.org/guest_2002/guw-081.htm (accessed on 17 October 2009).

Lister, R. 1998. *Citizenship: Feminist Perspectives*. New York: New York University Press.

Mann, M. 1987. Ruling Class Strategies and Citizenship. *Sociology* 21(3): 339–54.

Marshall, T. H. 1950. *Citizenship and Social Class and Other Essays*. Cambridge: Cambridge University Press.

Ong, A. 1996. Cultural Citizenship as Subject-Making: Immigrants Negotiate Racial and Cultural Boundaries in the United States. *Current Anthropology* 37(5): 737–62.

———. 1999. *Flexible Citizenship: The Cultural Logics of Transnationality*. Durham; London: Duke University Press.

Rosaldo, R. 1994. Cultural Citizenship in San Jose. *PoLAR: Political and Legal Anthropology Review* 17: 57–63.

Scott, J. 1998. *Seeing Like a State: How Certain Schemes to Improve the Human Condition Have Failed*. New Haven: Yale University Press.

Shafir, G. 1998. *The Citizenship Debates: A Reader*. Minneapolis: University of Minnesota Press.

Siim, B. 2000. *Gender and Citizenship: Politics and Agency in France, Britain, and Denmark*. New York: Cambridge University Press.

Tan, C. K. K. 2009. 'But They Are Like You and Me': Gay Civil Servants and Citizenship in a Cosmopolitanizing Singapore. *City and Society* 21(1): 133–54.

Turner, B. 2009. and Marshall, T. H. Social Rights and English National Identity. *Citizenship Studies* 13(1): 65–73.

Wheeler, C. C. and Schaefer, L. C. 1988. Harry Benjamin's First Ten Cases 1938–1953: Historical Influences. In *Sexology*, ed. W. Eicher and G. Kockott. 179–82. Berlin: Springer-Verlag.

World Health Organization. 1977. *International Statistical Classification of Diseases and Related Health Problems, 9th Revision*. Geneva: World Health Organization.

———. 1992. *International Statistical Classification of Diseases and Related Health Problems, 10th Revision*. Geneva: World Health Organization.

Chapter 5: Transnational Lesbian Identities

Anderson, B. 1983. *Imagined Communities: Reflections on the Origins and Spread of Nationalism.* London: Verso.

Au, A. 2009. Soft Exterior, Hard Core. In *Impressions of the Goh Chok Tong Years in Singapore,* eds. B. Welsh, J. Chin, A. Mahizhnan and T.H. Tan. 399–409. National University of Singapore: NUS Press.

Bacchetta, P. 1999. When the Hindu Nation Exiles Its Queers. *Social Text* 61: 141–66.

———. 2002. Rescaling Transnational "Queerdom": Lesbian and "Lesbian" Identitary-Positionalities in Delhi in the 1980s. *Antipode,* 34(5): 947–73.

Balaji, S. 2005. Speech in Parliament. Singapore. 9 March.

Berry, C., Martin, F. and Yue, A. 2003. *Mobile Cultures: New Media in Queer Asia.* Durham, London: Duke University Press.

Bhaskaran, S. 2004. *Made in India: Decolonizations, Queer Sexualities, Trans/National Projects.* New York: Palgrave Macmillan.

Blackwood, E. 1999. Tombois in West Sumatra: Constructing Masculinity and Erotic Desire. In *Female Desires: Same-Sex Relations and Transgender Practices across Cultures,* eds. E. Blackwood and S. E. Wieringa. 181–206. New York: Columbia University Press.

———. 2002. Reading Sexuality across Cultures: Anthropology and Theories of Sexuality. In *Out in the Field: Reflections of Lesbian and Gay Anthropologists,* eds. E. Lewin and W.L. Leap. 69–92. Urbana: University of Illinois Press.

———. 2005. Gender Transgression in Colonial and Postcolonial Indonesia. *The Journal of Asian Studies* 64(4): 849–79.

———. 2008. Transnational Discourses and Circuits of Queer Knowledge in Indonesia. *GLQ: A Journal of Lesbian and Gay Studies* 14(4): 482–507.

Boellstorff, T. 2005. *The Gay Archipelago: Sexuality and Nation in Indonesia*: Princeton University Press: Princeton and Oxford.

———. 2007. Queer Studies in the House of Anthropology. *Annual Review of Anthropology* 36: 17–35.

Brown, P., Green, A. and Lauder, H. 2001. *High Skills: Globalization, Competitiveness, and Skill Formation.* Oxford and New York: Oxford University Press.

Bunzl, M. 2004. *Symptoms of Modernity: Jews and Queers in Late-Twentieth-Century Vienna.* Berkeley: University of California Press.

Chalmers, S. 2002. *Emerging Lesbian Voices from Japan.* London and New York: Routledge-Curzon.

Chan, K. 2008. Gay Sexuality in Singaporean Chinese Popular Culture: Where Have All the Boys Gone? *China Information* XXII(2): 305–29.

Chao, A. 2000. Global Metaphors and Local Strategies in the Construction of Taiwan's Lesbian Identities. *Culture, Health and Sexuality* 2(4): 377–90.

Chua, B. H. 1995. *Communitarian Ideology and Democracy in Singapore.* London and New York: Routledge.

Cruz-Malavé, A. and Manalansan, M. F. 2002. Introduction. In *Queer Globalizations: Citizenship and the Afterlife of Colonialism.* 1–10. New York: New York University Press.

Dasgupta, R. 2009. The 'Queer' Family in Asia. In *Inter-Asia Roundtable 2009: Gender Relations in the 21st Century Asian Family.* 115–47. Singapore: Asia Research Institute, National University of Singapore.

Davies, S. 2010. Social-Political Movements: Homosexuality and Queer Identity Movements—Southeast Asia. In *Encyclopedia of Women and Islamic Cultures*, ed. Joseph Saud, not paginated. Leiden: Brill Academic Publishers.

———. 2010. *Gender, Diversity in Indonesia: Sexuality, Islam, and Queer Selves*. London: Routledge Curzon.

Elegant, S. 2003. A Lion in Winter. *Time*. 30 June.

Foucault, M. 1980. *The History of Sexuality*. Vol. 1. New York: Vintage.

Goh, C. T. 1990. Speech on President's Address. Singapore. 13 June.

———. 2003. Speech at the National Day Rally. Singapore. 17 August.

Gopinath, G. 2005. *Impossible Desires: Queer Diasporas and South Asian Public Cultures*. Durham: Duke University Press.

Grewal, I. and Kaplan, C. 1994. Introduction: Transnational Feminist Practices and Questions of Postmodernity. In *Scattered Hegemonies: Postmodernity and Transnational Feminist Practices*, eds. I. Grewal and C. Kaplan. 1–33. Minneapolis: University of Minnesota Press.

———. 2001. Global Identities: Theorizing Transnational Studies of Sexuality. *GLQ: A Journal of Lesbian and Gay Studies*, 7(4): 663–79.

Hill, M. 2000. 'Asian Values' as Reverse Orientalism: Singapore. *Asia Pacific Viewpoint* 41(2): 177–90.

Housing and Development Board. 2008. *Public Housing in Singapore: Residents' Profile, Housing, Satisfaction and Preferences: HDB Sample Household Survey 2008*. Singapore: Housing and Development Board.

———. 2010. *Eligibility to Buy New HDB Flat*. http://www.hdb.gov.sg/fi10/fi10321p.nsf/w/BuyingNewFlatEligibilitytobuynewHDBflat?OpenDocument#FamilyNucleus (accessed on 18 August 2010).

Kam, L. 2008. Recognition through Mis-recognition: Masculine Women in Hong Kong. In *AsiaPacifiQueer: Rethinking Genders and Sexualities*, eds. F. Martin, P. A. Jackson, M. McLelland and A. Yue. 99–116. Urbana and Chicago: University of Illinois Press.

Khor, D. and Kamano, S. eds. 2006. *Lesbians in East Asia: Diversity, Identities and Resistance*. Binghamton, NY: Harrington Park Press.

Kim, H. S., Puri, J. and Kim-Puri, H. J. 2005. Conceptualizing Gender-Sexuality-State-Nation: An Introduction. *Gender and Society* 19(2): 137–59.

Koh, D. 2010. CEO of Fly Entertainment, Irene Ang. *I-S Magazine Online*. http://is.asia-city.com/movies/article/ceo-fly-entertainnment-irene-ang (accessed on 21 August 2010).

Lee, H. L. 2007. Speech to Parliament on Reading of Penal Code (Amendment) Bill. Singapore. 22 October.

Leung, H. 2008. *Undercurrents: Queer Culture and Postcolonial Hong Kong*. Vancouver: University of British Columbia Press.

Lim, S. S. 2000. Letter—All Can Be Part of Singapore 21. *The Straits Times*, 6 June.

Manalansan, M. F. 1997. In the Shadows of Stonewall: Examining Gay Transnational Politics and the Diasporic Dilemma. In *The Politics of Culture in the Shadow of Capital*, eds. L. Lowe and D. Lloyd. 485–505. Durham, NC: Duke University Press.

Marte, R. 2006. *L Talk: Eileena Lee on the Challenges of GLBT Activism in Singapore*. http://www.isiswomen.org/index.php?option=com_content&task=view&id=268&Itemid=135 (accessed on 17 August 2010).

Martin, F., Jackson, P. A., McLelland, M. and Yue, A. eds. 2008. *AsiaPacifiQueer: Rethinking Genders and Sexualities*. Urbana and Chicago: University of Illinois Press.

Oswin, N. 2010. Sexual Tensions in Modernizing Singapore: The Postcolonial and the Intimate. *Environment and Planning D: Society and Space* 28: 128–41.

Pinkdotsg. 2009. Pink Dot FAQ, May 5. http://pinkdotsg.blogspot.com.au/2009/05/pink-dot-faq.html (accessed on 16 August 2010).

Povinelli, E. A. and Chauncey, G. 1999. Thinking Sexuality Transnationally. *GLQ: A Journal of Lesbian and Gay Studies* 5(4): 439–50.

Salaff, J. 1988. *State and Family in Singapore: Restructuring a Developing Society.* Ithaca: Cornell University Press.

Sayoni. 2005. *About Sayoni.* http://www.sayoni.com/index.php?option=com_content&view=article&id=337&Itemid=61 (accessed on 17 August 2010).

Silvio, T. 2008. Lesbianism and Taiwanese Localism in *The Silent Thrush*. In *AsiaPacifiQueer: Rethinking Genders and Sexualities*, eds. F. Martin, P. A. Jackson, M. McLelland and A. Yue. 217–34. Urbana and Chicago: University of Illinois Press.

Sinnott, M. 2004. *Toms and Dees: Transgender Identity and Female Same-Sex Relationships in Thailand*. Honolulu: University of Hawai'i Press.

Spivak, G. C. 1988. Can the Subaltern Speak? In *Marxism and the Interpretation of Culture*, eds. C. Nelson and L.Grossberg. 271–313. Basingstoke: Macmillan Education.

Tan, K. P. 2007. Singapore's National Day Rally Speech: A Site of Ideological Negotiation. *Journal of Contemporary Asia* 37(3): 292–308.

Tan, K. P, and G. J. J. Lee. 2007. Imagining the Gay Community in Singapore. *Critical Asian Studies* 39(2): 179–204.

Tong, C. 2008. Being a Young Tomboy in Hong Kong: The Life and Identity Construction of Lesbian Schoolgirls. In *AsiaPacifiQueer: Rethinking Genders and Sexualities*, eds. F. Martin, P. A. Jackson, M. McLelland and A. Yue. 117–30. Urbana and Chicago: University of Illinois Press.

West, C. 1989. *The American Evasion of Philosophy: A Genealogy of Pragmatism*. Madison, Wisconsin: University of Wisconsin Press.

Wieringa, S. E., Blackwood, E., and Bhaiya, A. eds. 2007. *Women's Sexualities and Masculinities in a Globalizing Asia*. New York: Palgrave Macmillan.

Yue, A. 2007. Creative Queer Singapore: The Illiberal Pragmatics of Cultural Production. *Gay and Lesbian Issues and Psychology Review* 3(3): 149–60.

———. 2011. Doing Cultural Citizenship in the Global Media Hub: Illiberal Pragmatics and Lesbian Consumption Practices in Singapore. In *Circuits of Visibility: Gender and Transnational Media Cultures*, ed. R. Hegde, 250–67. New York: New York University Press.

Chapter 6: Both Contagion and Cure

Acharya, A. 2008. *Singapore's Foreign Policy: The Search for Regional Order*. Hackensack: Institute of Policy Studies/World Scientific.

Adam, B. D., Duyvendak, J. W., and Krouwel, A. eds. 1999. *The Global Emergence of Gay and Lesbian Politics: National Imprints of a Worldwide Movement*. Philadelphia: Temple University Press.

Aldrich, R. 2004. Homosexuality and the City: An Historical Overview. *Urban Studies* 4 (9): 1719–37.

Alexander, M. J. 1994. Not Just (Any)*Body* Can Be a Citizen: The Politics of Law, Sexuality and Postcoloniality in Trinidad and Tobago and the Bahamas. *Feminist Review* 48: 5–23.

Altman, D. 1995. The New World of 'Gay Asia'. In *Asian and Pacific Inscriptions: Identities, Ethnicities, Nationalities*, ed. S. Perera. 121–38. Bundoora: Meridian.

———. 1997. Research and Its Discontents. *Melbourne Journal of Politics* 24: 41–43.

———. 2001. *Global Sex*. Crows Nest: Allen and Unwin.

Ang, I. and Stratton, J. 1995. Straddling East and West: Singapore's Paradoxical Search for National Identity. In *Asian and Pacific Inscriptions: Identities, Ethnicities, Nationalities*, ed. S. Perera. 179–92. Bundoora: Meridian.

Au, A. W. 2004. *Sycophancy: Our Unique Tourist Draw. Yawning Bread*, March. http://www.yawningbread.org/arch_2004/yax-370.htm (accessed on 1 November 2010).

———. 2007a. *"Eventually" said Lee Kuan Yew. Yawning Bread*. http://www.yawning-bread.org/apdx_2007/imp-347.htm (accessed on 5 September 2010).

———. 2007b. *Reading the Tea Leaves: MM Lee Kuan Yew on Homosexuality in Singapore. Fridae*, 24 April. http://www.fridae.com/newsfeatures/2007/04/24/1834.reading-the-tea-leaves-mm-lee-kuan-yew-on-homosexuality-in-singapore (accessed on 20 October 2010).

Bech, H. 1997. *When Men Meet: Homosexuality and Modernity*, trans. T. Mesquit and T. Davies. Chicago: University of Chicago Press.

Berry, C. 1994. *A Bit on the Side: East-West Topographies of Desire*. Sydney, New South Wales: EMPress.

Betsky, A. 1997. *Queer Space: Architecture and Same-Sex Desire*. 1st ed. New York: William Morrow & Co.

Boey, D. 2003. What Fewer Babies May Mean for SAF Planners. *The Straits Times*, 17 December.

Carver, T. 2007. Materializing the Metaphors of Global Cities: Singapore and Silicon Valley. *School of Sociology, Politics and International Studies, University of Bristol— Working Papers* (01–07), http://www.bristol.ac.uk/spais/research/workingpapers/wpspaisfiles/carver0107.pdf (accessed on 12 July 2011).

Chang, T. C. 2000. Renaissance Revisited: Singapore as a 'Global City for the Arts'. *International Journal of Urban and Regional research* 24(4): 818–31.

Chang, T. C. and B. S. A. Yeoh. 1999. "New Asia—Singapore": Communicating Local Cultures through Global Tourism. *Geoforum* 30: 101–15.

Chang, T. C. and Lee, W. K. 2003. Renaissance City Singapore: A Study of Arts Spaces. *Area* 35(2): 128–41.

Chasing the pink dollar. 2003. *The Straits Times (Sunday Times)*, 17 August.

Chiu, S. W.-K., Ho, K. C. and Lui, T.-L. 1998. *City States in the Global Economy: Industrial Restructuring in Hong Kong and Singapore*. Boulder: Westview Press.

Chua, B. H. 1998. World Cities, Globalisation and the Spread of Consumerism: A View from Singapore. *Urban Studies* 35(5–6): 981–1000.

———. 2000. *Consumption in Asia: Lifestyles and Identities*. London; New York: Routledge.

———. 2003. *Life Is Not Complete without Shopping: Consumption Culture in Singapore*. Singapore: Singapore University Press.

Chua, M. H. 2003. It's not about gay rights—it's survival. *The Straits Times*, 9 July.

Clark, D. 2003. *Urban World/Global City*. 2nd ed. London: Routledge.

Connors, M. 1997. Prefacing Research on the Global Gay. *Melbourne Journal of Politics* 24: 44–48.

da Cunha, D. 2010. *Singapore Places Its Bets: Casinos, Foreign Talent and Remaking a City-State*. Singapore: Straits Times Press.

D'Emilio, J. 1983. Capitalism and Gay Identity. In *Powers of Desire: The Politics of Sexuality*, eds. A. Snitow, C. Stansell and S. Thompson. 100–13. New York: Monthly Review Press.

Dreher, C. 2002. Be Creative—or Die. *Salon Media Group*, 6 June 2002 http://www.salon.com/books/int/2002/06/06/florida/print.html (accessed on 31 May 2010).

Economic Strategies Committee. 2010. Report of the Economic Strategies Committee: High Skilled People, Innovative Economy, Distinctive Global City. Singapore: Economic Strategies Committee.

Fairclough, G. 2004a. Cover Story—Gay Asia: Tolerance Pays. *Far Eastern Economic Review*, 28 October, 52–60.

———. 2004b. For its own reasons, Singapore is getting rather gay friendly: tourist dollars are a part of it, but there are still limits; renaming a 'military' ball. *The Wall Street Journal*, 22 October, A1.

Florida, R. L. 2002. *The Rise of the Creative Class: And How It's Transforming Work, Leisure, Community and Everyday Life*. New York: Basic Books.

———. 2005a. *Cities and the Creative Class*. New York: Routledge.

———. 2005b. *The Flight of the Creative Class: The New Global Competition for Talent*. 1st ed. New York: HarperBusiness.

Foreign Policy. 2010. Metropolis Now: The 2010 Global Cities Index. *Foreign Policy* September/October: 124–28.

Friedmann, J. 1986. The World City Hypothesis. *Development and Change* 17: 69–93.

Ganesan, N. 1992. Singapore's Foreign Policy Terrain. *Asian Affairs* 19(2): 67–79.

George, C. 2005. Calibrated Coercion and the Maintenance of Hegemony in Singapore. In *Asia Research Institute Working Paper Series*, eds. G. Wade, T. Winter, H.-H. Shen and M. Kaur. (No. 48) 19 September 2005. Singapore: National University of Singapore.

Globalization and World Cities Research Network. 2008. *The World According to GaWC 2008*. Loughborough University. http://www.lboro.ac.uk/gawc/world2008t.html (accessed on 23 October 2010).

Goh, C. T. 2000. *Transforming Singapore: Prime Minister Goh Chok Tong's National Day Rally 2000 Speech in English*. Media Division, Ministry of Information and the Arts, Government of Singapore. http://www.gov.sg/nd/ND00.htm (accessed on 2 November 2004).

———. 2010. *Speech by Mr Goh Chok Tong, Senior Minister, at NTU Students' Union Ministerial Forum, Nanyang Technological University—Singapore: Global City of Buzz, Home for Us*. Ministry of Information, Communications and the Arts Communications Support Department, Singapore Government, 29 October. http://www.news.gov.sg/public/sgpc/en/media_releases/agencies/micacsd/speech/S-20101029–1.html (accessed on 31 October 2010).

Goh, D. 2008. It's the Gays' Fault: News and HIV as Weapons against Homosexuality in Singapore. *Journal of Communication Inquiry* 32(4): 338–99.

Goh, R. B.H. 2003. Things to a Void: Utopian Discourse, Communality and Constructed Interstices in Singapore Public Housing. In *Theorizing the Southeast Asian City as Text: Urban Landscapes, Cultural Documents, and Interpretive Experiences*, eds. R. B.H. Goh and B. S.A. Yeoh. 51–72. Singapore: World Scientific Publishing.

Goldberg, J. 1992. *Sodometries: Renaissance Texts, Modern Sexualities*. Stanford: Stanford University Press.

Gross, J. S. and Hambleton, R. 2007. *Governing Cities in a Global Era: Urban Innovation, Competition and Democratic Reform*. Basingstoke: Palgrave Macmillan.

Hack, K., Margolin, J.-L., and Delaye, K. eds. 2010. *Singapore from Temasek to the 21st Century: Reinventing the Global City*. Singapore: NUS Press.

Hannerz, U. 1996. *Transnational Connections: Culture, People, Places*. London and New York: Routledge.

Hawley, J. C. 2001a. *Postcolonial and Queer Theories: Intersections and Essays*. Westport and London: Greenwood Press.

———. 2001b. *Postcolonial, Queer: Theoretical Intersections*. Albany: State University of New York Press.

Heng, G. and Devan, J. 1992. State Fatherhood: The Politics of Nationalism, Sexuality and Race in Singapore. In *Nationalisms and Sexualities*, eds. A. Parker, M. Russo, D. Sommer and P. Yaeger. 343–64. New York and London: Routledge.

Hing, A. Y. 2008. Evolving Singapore: The Creative City. In *Creative Cities, Cultural Clusters and Local Economic Development*, eds. P. Cooke and L. Lazzeretti. 313–37. Cheltenham: Edward Elgar Publishing.

Huang, T.-y. M. 2000. Hong Kong Blue: Flâneurie with the Camera's Eye in a Phantasmagoric Global City. *Journal of Narrative Theory* 30(3): 385–402.

———. 2004. *Walking between Slums and Skyscrapers: Illusions of Open Space in Hong Kong, Tokyo, and Shanghai*. Hong Kong: Hong Kong University Press.

———. 2006. The Cosmopolitan Imaginary and Flexible Identities of Global City Regions: Articulating New Cultural Identities in Taipei and Shanghai. *Inter-Asia Cultural Studies* 7(3): 472–91.

Huxley, T. 2000. *Defending the Lion City: The Armed Forces of Singapore*. St. Leonards: Allen & Unwin.

Isin, E. F. 2000. *Democracy, Citizenship, and the Global City*. New York: Routledge.

Kong, L. 2000. Cultural Policy in Singapore: Negotiating Economic and Socio-Cultural Agendas. *Geoforum* 31(4): 409–24.

———. 2007. Cultural Icons and Urban Development in Asia: Economic Imperative, National Identity, and Global City Status. *Political Geography* 26: 383–404.

Kotkin, J. 2006. *The City: A Global History*. London: Phoenix.

Ku, A. S. M. and Tsui, C. H.-c. 2009. The "Global City" as a Cultural Project: The Case of the West Kowloon Cultural District. In *Hong Kong Mobile: Making a Global Population*, eds. H. Siu and A. Ku. 343–65. Hong Kong: Hong Kong University Press.

Kwok, K.-W. and Low, K.-H. 2002. Cultural Policy and the City-State: Singapore and the 'New Asian Renaissance'. In *Global Culture: Media, Arts, Policy and Globalization*, eds. D. Crane and N. Kawashima. 149–68. New York: Routledge.

Lee, H. L. 2007. *Speech during the Second Reading of the Penal Code (Amendment) Bill*. Singapore Parliament Reports, 23 October 2007. http://www.parliament.gov.sg/

parlweb/get_highlighted_content.jsp?docID=390527&hlLevel=Terms&links=&
hlWords=%20%20&hlTitle=&queryOption=1&ref=http://www.parliament.gov.
sg:80/reports/public/hansard/title/20071023/20071023_S0003_T0002.html#1
(accessed on 1 November 2010).

Lee, K. C. 1993. *Diplomacy of a Tiny State*. 2nd ed. Singapore: World Scientific.

Leifer, M. 2000. *Singapore's Foreign Policy: Coping with Vulnerability*. London: Routledge.

Lek, A. and Obendorf, S. 2004. *Contentment or Containment? Consumption and the Lesbian and Gay Community in Singapore*. *James Gomez News*. http://eprints.lincoln.ac.uk/3539/ (accessed on 31 November 2010).

Leong, L. W.-T. 1995. Walking the Tightrope: The Role of Action for AIDS in the Provision of Social Services in Singapore. *Journal of Gay and Lesbian Social Services* 3(3): 11–30.

———. 1997. Singapore. In *Socio-Legal Control of Homosexuality*, eds. D. J. West and R. Green. 127–44. New York: Plenum Press.

Levett, C. 2004. Pink Pride of Lion City Glows a Patriotic Red and White. *Sydney Morning Herald*, 14 August, 19.

Lim, K. F. 2004. Where Love Dares (Not) Speak Its name: The Expression of Homosexuality in Singapore. *Urban Studies* 41(9): 1759–88.

Lion Television. 2005. *The History of Singapore: Episode 3—Lion City, Asian Tiger [videorecording]*: Discovery Networks Asia (Producer).

Low, L. 1998. *The Political Economy of a City-State: Government-Made Singapore*. Singapore: Oxford University Press.

———. 2002. The Limits of a City-State: Or Are There? In *Singapore in the New Millennium: Challenges Facing the City-State*, ed. D. da Cunha. 221–22. Singapore: Institute of Southeast Asian Studies.

Lyons, L. 2004. Sexing the Nation: Normative Heterosexuality and the "Good" Singaporean Citizen. In *The Nation of the Other: Constructions of Nation in Contemporary Cultural and Literary Discourses*, eds. A. Branach-Kallas and K. Wieckowska. 79–96. Torun: Uniwersytet Mikolaja Kopernika.

McGirk, J. 2004. Gum, Gays and Gambling. *The Independent*, 26 August.

Ministry of Information and the Arts, Singapore. 2000. *Renaissance City Report: Culture and the Arts in Renaissance Singapore*. Singapore: Ministry of Information and the Arts.

Murray, G. and Perera, A. 1996. *Singapore: The Global City-State*. New York: St Martin's Press.

National Security Coordination Centre. 2004. *The Fight Against Terror: Singapore's National Security Strategy*. Singapore: National Security Coordination Centre.

Ng, H. R. E. 2008. *The Singapore Heartland: The Performing Identities of Local Landscapes*. Asian Film Archive 2008. http://www.asianfilmarchive.org/cineodeon2008/document/Tertiary%20Winner.pdf (accessed on 12 July 2011).

Ng, K. K. 2008. *Born This Way but…: The Changing Politics of Male Homosexuality in Contemporary Singapore*. Singapore: KangCuBine Publishing.

Ng, Y.-S. and Wee, J. 2006. *SQ21: Singapore Queers in the 21st Century*. Singapore: Oogachaga Counselling and Support.

Noland, M. 2004a. Popular Attitudes, Globalization, and Risk (WP 04–2). In *Working Papers*. Washington: Institute for International Economics.

———. 2004b. Tolerance Can Help Countries to Achieve Prosperity. *The Financial Times*, 19 August, 17.

Obendorf, S. 2006. Sodomy as Metaphor. In *Postcolonizing the International: Working to Change the Way We Are*, ed. P. Darby. 177–206. Honolulu: University of Hawai'i Press.

Offord, B. 1999. The Burden of (Homo)sexual Identity in Singapore. *Social Semiotics* 9(3): 310–16.

Olds, K. and Yeung, H. 2004. Pathways to Global City Formation: A View from the Developmental City-State of Singapore. *Review of International Political Economy* 11 (3): 489–521.

Ortmann, S. 2003. Legitimacy and the National Threat in Singapore (Legitimität und die nationale Gefahr in Singapur). Magisterarbeit, Political Science (Politische Wissenschaft in der philosophischen Fakultät 1), Friedrich-Alexander Universität Erlangen-Nürnberg, Erlangen.

Panthera, J. 2008. *Leaving Singapore for Pinker Shores*. Yawning Bread, 4 February 2008 [cited]. http://www.yawningbread.org/guest_2008/guw-148.htm (accessed on 1 November 2010).

Reuters. 2007. Singapore Considers Legalizing Homosexuality: Lee. *Reuters [Newswire]*, 24 April.

Sandercock, L. 2006. Cosmopolitan Urbanism: A Love Song to Our Mongrel Cities. In *Cosmopolitan Urbanism*, eds. J. Binnie, J. Holloway, S. Millington and C. Young. 37–52. London: Routledge.

Sanders, D. E. 2009. 377 and the Unnatural Afterlife of British Colonialism in Asia. *Asian Journal of Comparative Law* 4(1): 1–51.

Sassen, S. 1996. Whose City Is It? Globalization and the Formation of New Claims. *Public Culture* 8(2): 205–23.

———. 2001. *The Global City: New York, London, Tokyo*. 2nd ed. Princeton, N.J. ; Oxford: Princeton University Press.

Scott, A. J. 2001. *Global City-Regions: Trends, Theory, Policy*. Oxford: Oxford University Press.

Sim, L.-L., Ong, S.-E, Agarwal, A., Parsha, A. and Keivani, R. 2003. Singapore's Competitiveness as a Global City: Development Strategy, Institutions and Business Environment. *Cities* 20(2): 115–27.

Singapore 21 Committee. 1999. Singapore 21: Together We Make the Difference. Singapore: Singapore 21 Committee.

Singh, B. 1988. *Singapore: Foreign Policy Imperatives of a Small State*. Singapore: Centre for Advanced Studies, National University of Singapore.

———. 2007. The Military and Small States: The Role of Hard Power in Singapore's Domestic and Foreign Policy. Paper read at Sixth Pan-European International Relations Conference, 12–15 September, Turin, Italy.

Tan, C. K.K. 2009. "But They Are Like You and Me": Gay Civil Servants and Citizenship in a Cosmopolitanizing Singapore. *City and Society* 21(1): 133–54.

Tan, K. P. 2003. Sexing up Singapore. *International Journal of Cultural Studies* 6(4): 403–23.

Tan, K. P. and Lee, G. J. J. 2007. Imagining the Gay Community in Singapore. *Critical Asian Studies* 39(2): 179–204.

Taylor, P. J. 2004. *World City Network : A Global Urban Analysis*. London: Routledge.

Team Trevvy. 2007. *Lee Kuan Yew: No Option but to Legalize Homosexual Sex*. Trevvy.com, 25 April. http://www.trevvy.com/scoops/article.php?a_id=144 (accessed on 5 September 2010).

Thio, L.-a. 2006. "Pragmatism and Realism Do Not Mean Abdication": A Critical and Empirical Inquiry into Singapore's Engagement with International Human Rights Law. *Singapore Year Book of International Law*, 8: 41–91.

Tong, S. 2007. *Ian McKellen Wades into Singapore Gay Rights Debate*. *Reuters*, 19 July. http://www.reuters.com/article/idUSSIN7694520070719 (accessed on 1 November 2010).

Tremewan, C. 1994. *The Political Economy of Social Control in Singapore*. Basingstoke: Macmillan in association with St Antony's College, Oxford.

Wee, C.J. W.-L. 2002. National Identity, the Arts, and the Global City. In *Singapore in the New Millennium: Challenges Facing the City-State*, ed. D. da Cunha. 221–42. Singapore: Institute of Southeast Asian Studies.

Wong, C. Y. L., J. C. Chong and C. C. J. M. Millar. 2006. The Case of Singapore as a Knowledge-Based City. In *Knowledge Cities: Approaches, Experiences, and Perspectives*, ed. Francisco Javier Carrillo. 87–96. Burlington: Butterworth-Heinemann.

Wong, K. S. 2009. *Comments by DPM and Minister for Home Affairs Wong Kan Seng in Response to Media Queries Related to AWARE*. Ministry of Home Affairs: Press Releases, 15 May. http://www.mha.gov.sg/news_details.aspx?nid=MTQ0MA%3d%3d-H1aIkd I4Ksw%3d (accessed on 2 November 2010).

Wu, W. 2004. Cultural Strategies in Shanghai: Regenerating Cosmopolitanism in an Era of Globalization. *Progress in Planning* 61: 159–80.

Yen F. 2009. Unite Against Alternative Values, Anglicans Urged. *The Straits Times*, 30 November.

Yeoh, B. S. A. and Chang, T. C. 2001. Globalising Singapore: Debating Transnational Flows in the City. *Urban Studies* 38(7): 1022–44.

Youngblood, R. 2007. Singapore Sends Mixed Signals on Homosexuality. *Deutsche Presse-Agentur [Newswire]*, 5 October.

Yue, A. 2006. Cultural Governance and Creative Industries in Singapore. *International Journal of Cultural Policy* 12(1): 17–33.

———. 2007a. Creative Queer Singapore: The Illiberal Pragmatics of Cultural Production. *Gay and Lesbian Issues and Psychology Review* 3(3): 149–60.

———. 2007b. Hawking in the Creative City. *Feminist Media Studies* (4): 365–80.

Chapter 7: Photo Essay

Bugge, O. M. 2009. This is Singapore (posting on 6 September). http://www.captain-svoyage-forum.com/showthread.php?773-This-is-Singapore/page2 (accessed on 1 February 2010).

Heng, R. 2005. Where Queens Ruled!—A History of Gay Venues in Singapore. *Yawning Bread*. August. http://www.yawningbread.org/guest_2005/guw-101.htm (accessed on 1 February 2010).

Hite, S. 1981. *The Hite Report on Male Sexuality*. London: Macdonald.

Melnick, R. 2001. Odeon Theatre. *Cinema Treasures*. http://cinematreasures.org/theater/1536/ (accessed on 1 February 2010).

Tangawizi. 2009. Is Singapore Unique? *Asia Finest Discussion Forum*, 18 August, http://www.asiafinest.com/forum/lofiversion/index.php/t210654.html (accessed on 1 February 2010).

Tania. 2006. http://www.myspace.com/zultania (accessed on 1 February 2010).

Chapter 8: The Negative Dialectics of Homonationalism, or Singapore English Newspapers and Queer World-Making

Adorno, T. W. 1990. *Negative Dialectics*, trans. E. B. Ashton. London and New York: Routledge.

Ahmed, S. 2004. *The Cultural Politics of Emotion*. London and New York: Routledge.

———. 2010. *The Promise of Happiness*. Durham: Duke University Press.

Amirthalingam, K. 2009. Criminal Law and Private Spaces: Regulating Homosexual Acts in Singapore. In *Regulating Deviance: The Redirection of Criminalisation and the Futures of Criminal Law*, eds. B. McSherry, A. W. Norrie and S. Bronitt. 185–212. Portland: Hart.

Au, A. 2010. Journalists Should Not Retail Government's Disinformation. *Yawning Bread*, 22 June. http://yawningbread.wordpress.com (accessed on 31 August 2010).

Barr, M. D. 2002. *Cultural Politics and Asian Values: The Tepid War*. London and New York: Routledge.

Berlant, L. and Warner, M. 1998. Sex in Public. *Critical Inquiry* 24(2): 547–66.

Chua, B. H. 1985. Pragmatism of the People's Action Party Government in Singapore: A Critical Assessment. *Southeast Asian Journal of Social Science* 13(2): 29–46.

———. 2003. *Life Is Not Complete without Shopping: Consumption Culture in Singapore*. Singapore: Singapore University Press.

Duggan, L. 2002. The New Homonormativity: The Sexual Politics of Neoliberalism. In *Materializing Democracy: Toward a Revitalized Cultural Politics*, eds. R. Castronovo and D. Nelson. 175–94. Durham: Duke University Press.

Floyd, K. 2009. *The Reification of Desire, Toward a Queer Marxism*. Minneapolis: University of Minnesota Press.

Foucault, M. 1990. *The History of Sexuality, vol. 2: The Use of Pleasure*, trans. R. Hurley. New York: Vintage Books.

George, C. 2007. Consolidating Authoritarian Rule: Calibrated Coercion in Singapore. *The Pacific Review* 20(2): 127–45.

Goh, D. 2008. It's the Gays' Fault: News and HIV as Weapons against Homosexuality in Singapore. *Journal of Communication Inquiry* 32(4): 383–99.

Hansard (Singapore). 2009. Debate on President's Address. Parliament 11, Session 2, Vol. 86, Sitting 3, 26 May.

Harvey, D. 2007. *A Brief History of Neoliberalism*. Oxford: Oxford University Press.

Heng, G. and Devan, J. 1992. State Gatherhood: The Politics of Nationalism, Dexuality, and Race in Singapore. In *Nationalisms and Sexualities*, eds. A. Parker et al. 343–64. London and New York: Routledge.

Hennessy, R. 2000. *Profit and Pleasure: Sexual Identities in Late Capitalism*. London and New York: Routledge.

Khoo, B. L. 1972. The Outsiders: New Nation Looks at Lesbianism in Singapore, *New Nation*, 16 October.

Klesse, C. 2007. *The Spectre of Promiscuity: Gay Male and Bisexual Non-monogamies and Polyamories*. Aldershot: Ashgate.

Lee, K. Y. 1977. Interview: 'We Want a Balance of Power', *Newsweek*, 12 December, 64.

Leong, L. W.-T. 2005. The 'Straight' Times: News Media and Sexual Citizenship in Singapore. In *Journalism and Democracy in Asia*, eds. A. Romano and M. Bromley. 159–71. Abingdon and New York: Routledge.

The Lycan Times. 2011. http://www.nowhere.per.sg/pics2/old_sg2/QE_walk2n.jpg (accessed on 2 May 2011).

McCarthy, S. N. 2006. *The Political Theory of Tyranny in Singapore and Burma: Aristotle and the Rhetoric of Benevolent Despotism.* London and New York: Routledge.

Munt, S. 2008. *Queer Attachments: The Cultural Politics of Shame.* Aldershot: Ashgate.

Mutalib, H. 2000. Illiberal Democracy and the Future of Opposition in Singapore. *Third World Quarterly* 21(2): 313–42.

Perlman, F. 2002. *The Continuing Appeal of Nationalism* (1984). Detroit: Black & Red.

Plummer, K. 2003. *Intimate Citizenship: Private Decisions and Public Dialogues.* Seattle: University of Washington Press.

Puar, J. 2006. *Terrorist Assemblages: Homonationalism in Queer Times.* Durham: Duke University Press.

Rodan, G. 2004. *Transparency and Authoritarian Rule in Southeast Asia.* London and New York: Routledge.

Sadiki, L. 2004. *The Search for Arab Democracy, Discourses and Counter-discourses.* New York: Columbia University Press.

Schopenhauer, A. 1974. Aphorisms on the Wisdom of Life. In *Parerga and Paralipomea,* vol. I, trans. E.F. J. Payne. Oxford: Oxford University Press.

Sim, S.-F. 2005. Social Engineering the World's Freest Economy: Neo-liberal Capitalism and Neo-liberal Governmentality in Singapore, *Rhizome: Cultural Studies in Emerging Knowledge* 10. http://www.rhizomes.net/issue10/sim.htm (accessed on 10 October 2011).

The Straits Times. 1968. 'Manslaughter, not murder', claim by defence. 10 July.

———. 1970. Children's books aren't kid stuff anymore. 13 September.

———. 1980. Whose business is show business? 29 November.

———. 1992. Half say 'no' to homosexual and lesbian materials. 5 August.

———. 2003. National Day Rally Speech. 23 August.

Tan, K. P. 2008. Religious Reasons in a Secular Public Sphere: Debates in the Media about Homosexuality. In *Religious Diversity in Singapore,* ed. L. A. Eng. 413–33. Singapore: Institute of Southeast Asian Studies and the Institute of Policy Studies.

Tan, S.-K. 2009. Singapore as a Society of Strangers. In *Chinese Connections: Critical Perspectives on Film, Identity, and Diaspora,* eds. S.-K. Tan, P. X. Feng and G. Marchetti. 205–19. Philadelphia: Temple University Press.

Turnbull, C. M. 1995. *Dateline Singapore: 150 Years of The Straits Times.* Singapore: Singapore Press Holdings.

———. 2009. *A History of Modern Singapore, 1819–2005.* Singapore: NUS Press.

Yeo, T. J., Khoo, B. L. and San, L. C. 1972. They are different. *New Nation,* 25 July.

Chapter 9: Impossible Presence

Ang, F. 2008. Producers' notes. *Solos Movie.* http://www.solosmovie.com/notes.html (accessed on 9 October 2011).

Au, A. 2006. The Cinematic Road to the Future. *Fridae,* 16 October. http://www.fridae.com/newsfeatures/2006/10/16/1721.the-cinematic-road-to-the-future (accessed on 9 October 2011).

Benjamin, W. 1999. The Work of Art in the Age of Its Technological Reproducibility: Second Version. In *Selected Writings, vol. 3, 1935–1938*, eds. H. Eiland and M. W. Jennings, trans. E. Jephcott and H. Zohn. 101–33. Cambridge: Belknap.

Films Act (Chapter 107). 1981. Revised 1998. http://agcvldb4.agc.gov.sg/non_version/ cgi-bin/cgi_retrieve.pl?actno=REVED-107&doctitle=FILMS ACT&date=latest& method=part (accessed on 10 October 2011).

Friedman, Richard C. 1988. *Male Homosexuality: A Contemporary Psychoanalytic Perspective*. New Haven: Yale University Press.

Hansen, M. B. 1999. Benjamin and Cinema: Not a One-Way Street. *Critical Inquiry* 25(2): 306–43.

Lim, G. 2004. *Invisible Trade: High-Class Sex for Sale in Singapore*. Singapore: Monsoon Books.

Lim, S. H. 2006. *Celluloid Comrades: Representations of Male Homosexuality in Contemporary Chinese Cinemas*. Honolulu: University of Hawai'i Press.

Media Development Authority. 2011. Classification Ratings for Films and Videos. http:// www.mda.gov.sg/Industry/Films/Classification/Pages/ClassificationRatings. aspx (accessed on 9 October 2011).

———. 2004. Free-to-Air Television Programme Code. http://www.mda.gov.sg/ Documents/PDF/industry/Industry_TV_ContentGuidelines_FTATVProgCode. pdf (accessed on 4 October 2011).

Millet, R. 2006. *Singapore Cinema*. Singapore: Editions Didier Millet.

People Like Us. 2006. Short Circuit 2006—Another First by People Like Us. http://www. plu.sg/society/?p=60 (accessed on 9 October 2011).

Sedgwick, E. K. 1985. *Between Men: English Literature and Male Homosocial Desire*. New York: Columbia University Press.

———. 1993. How to Bring Your Kids up Gay. In *Fear of a Queer Planet: Queer Politics and Social Theory*, ed. Michael Warner. 69–81. Minneapolis: University of Minnesota Press.

Tan, K. P. 2008. *Cinema and Television in Singapore: Resistance in One Dimension*. Leiden: Brill.

Tan, S. 2009. 'Tanjong Rhu' and 'Threshold' Cut from Short Film Festival in Singapore. *Fridae*, 14 August. http://www.fridae.com/newsfeatures/2009/08/14/8780. tanjong-rhu-and-threshold-cut-from-short-film-festival-in-singapore (accessed on 9 October 2011).

Uhde, J. and Y. N. Uhde. 2010. *Latent Images: Film in Singapore*. 2nd ed. Singapore: Ridge Books.

Williams, L. 2008. *Screening Sex*. Durham: Duke University Press.

Yue, A. 2007. Hawking in the Creative City: *Rice Rhapsody*, Sexuality and the Cultural Politics of New Asia in Singapore. *Feminist Media Studies* 7(4): 365–80.

Zubillaga-Pow, J. 2010. The Irony of Censorship. *Fridae*, 25 August. http://www.fridae. com/newsfeatures/2010/08/25/10247.the-irony-of-censorship (accessed on 9 October 2011).

Chapter 10: The Kids Are *Not* All Right

251. 2007. Ng Y.-S. Dir. Loretta Chen. Performed by Cynthia Lee-Mcquarrie, Cheryl Miles and Amy Cheng. Toy Factory Productions. Esplanade Theatre Studios, Singapore. 7 April.

Butler, J. 1993. *Bodies That Matter*. New York: Routledge.

Case, S.-E. 1989. Towards a Butch-Femme Aesthetic. In *Making a Spectacle: Feminist Essays on Contemporary Women's Theatre*, ed. L. Hart. 282–99. Ann Arbor: The University of Michigan Press.

Censorship Review Committee (CRC). 2003. *Report on Censorship Review Committee 2003*. Singapore.

Invitation to Treat: The Eleanor Wong Trilogy. 2004. By Eleanor Wong. Dir. Claire Wong. Perf. Tan Kheng Hua, Lim Yu-Beng, Janice Koh. Wild Rice. Drama Centre Theatre, Singapore. 24 April.

Lo, J. 2000. Prison House, Closet and Camp: Lesbian Mimesis in Eleanor Wong's Plays. In *Interlogue*, ed. S. Kirpal. 99–116. Singapore: Ethos Books.

Media Development Authority (MDA). 2006. SCV Fined for Breaching Programme Code on Its Reality Zone Channel. http://www.mda.gov.sg/wms.www/thenewsdesk.aspx?sid=747 (accessed on 23 October 2006).

Ng, Y.-S. 2007. *251* (unpublished play script).

———. 2007. *The Forbidden City: 2006 Singapore censorship report* (unpublished manuscript).

Rich, A. 1980. Compulsory Heterosexuality and Lesbian Existence. *Signs: Journal of Women in Culture and Society* 5: 631–60.

The Straits Times. 2008. Starhub Cable Vision Fined for Breaching the TV Advertising Code. 9 April.

Wong, E. 2005. *Invitation to Treat: The Eleanor Wong Trilogy*. Singapore: Firstfruits Publications.

———. 2007. Re: Lesbians in Singapore. E-mail interview, 23 April.

Chapter 11: "Singaporean by birth, Singaporean by faith"

Anderson, B. 1983. *Imagined Communities: Reflections on the Origin and Spread of Nationalism*. London: Verso.

Bhaskaran, S. 2004. *Made in India: Decolonizations, Queer Sexualities, Trans/national Projects*. New York: Palgrave Macmillan.

Boellstorff, T. 2004. The Emergence of Political Homophobia in Indonesia: Masculinity and National Belonging. *Ethnos* 69(4): 465–86.

———. 2005. *The Gay Archipelago: Sexuality and Nation in Indonesia*. Princeton: Princeton University Press.

Chun, A. 1996. Fuck Chineseness: On the Ambiguities of Ethnicity as Culture as Identity. *Boundary* 2(23): 111–38.

Fridae. 2011. http://www.fridae.com/aboutus/ (accessed on 13 October 2011).

Gopinath, G. 2005. *Impossible Desires: Queer Diasporas and South Asian Public Cultures*. Durham and London: Duke University Press.

Grewal, I. 2005. *Transnational America: Feminisms, Diasporas, Neoliberalisms*. Durham and London: Duke University Press.

Gupta, A. and J. Ferguson. 1992. Beyond Culture: Space, Identity, and the Politics of Difference. *Cultural Anthropology* 7(1): 6–23.

Jackson, P. 2003. Gay Capitals in Global Gay History: Cities, Local Markets, and the Origins of Bangkok's Same-Sex Culture. In *Postcolonial Urbanism: Southeast Asian Cities and Global Processes*, eds. R. Bishop, J. Phillips and W.-W. Yeo. 151–66. New York and London: Routledge.

Kelly, J. D. 1995. The Privileges of Citizenship: Nations, States, Markets, and Narratives. In *Nation Making: Emergent Identities in Postcolonial Melanesia*, ed. R. Foster. 253–73. Ann Arbor: University of Michigan Press.

Lee, K. Y. 1998. *The Singapore Story: Memoirs of Lee Kuan Yew*. Singapore: Singapore Press Holdings.

———. 2000. *From Third World to First: The Singapore Story, 1965–2000*. New York: Harper Collins Publishers.

Lian, K. F. 1999. The Nation-State and the Sociology of Singapore. In *Reading Culture: Textual Practice in Singapore*, ed. P. Chew. 37–54. Singapore: Times Academic Press.

Manalansan, M. 2000. Diasporic Deviants/Divas: How Filipino Gay Transmigrants Play with the World. In *Queer Diasporas*, ed. C. Patton. 183–203. Durham and London: Duke University Press.

People Like Us. 2011. http://www.plu.sg/society/?p=39 (accessed on 13 October 2011).

Phelan, S. 1997. The Shape of Queer: Assimilation and Articulation. *Women and Politics*, 18(2): 60.

Ratti, R. ed. 1993. *A Lotus of Anther Color: An Unfolding of the South Asian Gay and Lesbian Experience*. Boston: Alyson Publications.

Statistics Singapore. 2010. Singapore Residents by Age Group, Ethnic Group and Sex, end June 2009. http://www.singstat.gov.sg/pubn/reference/mdscontents. html#Demography (accessed on 13 October 2011).

Tan, C. H. 1989. Confucianism and Nation Building in Singapore. *International Journal of Social Economics* 16: 8–16.

Chapter 12: "We're the gay company, as gay as it gets"

Alvord, S., Brown, L. and Letts, C. 2004. Social Entrepreneurship and Societal Transformation: An Exploratory Study. *Journal of Applied Behavioural Science* 40(3), 260–83.

Anonymous. 2010. LGBT History in Singapore. *Wikipedia*. http://en.wikipedia.org/wiki/LGBT_history_in_Singapore (accessed on 15 September 2010).

Banks, J. 1972. *The Sociology of Social Movements*. London: Macmillan.

Berry, C., Martin, F. and Yue, A. eds. 2003. *Mobile Cultures: New Media in Queer Asia*. Durham: Duke University Press.

Branchik, B. J. 2006. Out in the Market: The History of the Gay Market Segment in the United States. In *Handbook of Niche Marketing: Principles and Practice*, ed. Tevfik Dalgic. 211–40. New York: Best Business Books, Haworth Reference Press.

Casson, M. 1982. *Entrepreneur: An Economic Theory*. London: Edward Elgar.

Castells, M. 2000. *The Rise of the Network Society*. Malden, MA: Blackwell Publishers.

Cho, A. 2006. Politics, Values and Social Entrepreneurship: A Critical Appraisal. In *Social Entrepreneurship*, eds. J. Mair, J. Robinson and K. Hockerts. 34–56. Basingstoke, UK: Palgrave Macmillan.

Crane, A. and Matten, D. 2010. *Business Ethics: Managing Corporate Citizenship and Sustainability in the Age of Globalization*. New York: Oxford University Press.

Dart, R. 2004. The Legitimacy of Social Enterprise. *Nonprofit Management and Leadership* 14 (4), 411–24.

Davis, L. 2008. *End of the Rainbow: Increasing the Sustainability of LGBT Organizations through Social Enterprise*. California: NESsT Publications.

Defoe, D. 1965. *The Life and Adventures of Robinson Crusoe*, edited with an introduction by Angus Ross. Harmondsworth: Penguin, 1965.

Drayton, W. 2002. The Citizen Sector: Becoming as Entrepreneurial and Competitive as Business. *California Management Review* 44 (3), 120–32.

Emerson, J. 2003. The Blended Value Proposition: Integrating Social and Financial Returns. *California Management Review* 45 (4), 35–51.

Etizioni, A. 1973. The Third Sector and Domestic Missions. *Public Administration Review* 33, 314–23.

Fejes, F. 2002. Advertising and the Political Economy of Lesbian/Gay Identity. In *Sex and Money: Feminism and Political Economy in the Media*, eds. Eileen R. Meehan and Ellen Riordan. 196–208. Minneapolis: University of Minnesota Press.

Fridae. 2010. *About Fridae. Timeline*. http://www.fridae.com/about/timeline.php (accessed on 30 July 2010).

Gill, R. 2009. Creative Biographies in New Media: Social Innovation in Web Work. In *Creativity, Innovation and the Cultural Economy*, eds. Andy Pratt and Paul Jeffcutt. 161–79. London: Routledge.

Gobé, M. 2001. *Emotional Branding: The New Paradigm for Connecting Brands to People*. New York: Allworth Press.

Grenier, O. 2006. Social Entrepreneurship: Agency in a Globalizing World. In *Social Entrepreneurship: New Models of Sustainability*, ed. Alex Nicholls. 119–43. Oxford: Oxford University Press.

groyn88. 2010. Section 377A of the Singapore Penal Code. In *Knol: A Unit of Knowledge*, http://knol.google.com/k/section-377a-of-the-singapore-penal-code# (accessed on 8 September 2010).

Gudelunas, D. 2005. Online Personal Ads: Community and Sex, Virtually. *Journal of Homosexuality* 49 (1), 1–33.

Heng, R. 2001. Tiptoe Out of the Closet: The Before and After of the Increasingly Visible Gay Community in Singapore. *Journal of Homosexuality* 40 (4/3), 81–97.

Hogan, S. 1999. To Net or Not to Net: Singapore's Regulation of the Internet. *Federal Communications Law Journal* 51 (2), 429(1).

Howkins, J. 2001. *The Creative Economy: How People Make Money from Ideas*. London: Allen Lane.

Jackson, P. and Sullivan, G. eds. 2001. *Gay and Lesbian Asia: Culture, Identity, Community*. New York: Harrington Park Press.

Kawasaki, K. 2004. Cultural Hegemony of Singapore among ASEAN Countries: Globalization and Cultural Policy. *International Journal of Japanese Sociology* 13, 22–35.

Koe, S. 2006. KABP Survey on HIV and AIDS amongst MSM in Singapore. *The Act* 34, 18–21.

Leadbeater, C. 1997. *The Rise of the Social Enterprise*. London: Demos.

Lim, E.-B. 2005. The Mardi Gras Boys of Singapore's English-Language Theatre. *Asian Theatre Journal* 22 (2), 293–347.

Maffesoli, M. 1996. *The Time of the Tribes: The Decline of Individualism in Mass Society*, translated by Don Smith. London: Sage.

Martin, F., Jackson, P., McLelland M. and Yue A. eds. 2008. *AsiaPacifiQueer: Rethinking Genders and Sexualities*. Illinois: University of Illinois Press.

Media Development Authority. 2002. *Creative Industries Development Strategy: Propelling Singapore's Creative Economy*. Singapore: Ministry of Information, Communication and The Arts.

Mueller, E. 2002. Connecting Gay Asia: Fridae.com, an English-Language Portal for Gays and Lesbians, Celebrates Its First Birthday. *The Advocate*, 30 April, 24 (1).

Mulgan, G. 2006. Cultivating Invisible Hand of Social Entrepreneurship. In *Social Entrepreneurship: New Models of Sustainable Social Change*, ed. Alex Nicholls. 74–95. Oxford: Oxford University Press.

Munoz, S. 2010. Towards a Geographical Research Agenda for Social Enterprise. *Area* 42 (3), 302–12.

Nicholls, A. ed. 2006. *Social Entrepreneurship: New Models of Sustainable Social Change*. Oxford: Oxford University Press.

Nicholls, A. and Cho, A. H. 2006. Social Entrepreneurship: The Structuration of a Field. In *Social Entrepreneurship: New Models of Sustainable Social Change*, ed. Alex Nicholls. 99–118. Oxford: Oxford University Press.

Offord, B. 2003. Singaporean Queering of the Internet: Toward a New Form of Cultural Transmission of Rights Discourse. In *Mobile Cultures: New Media in Queer Asia*, eds. Chris Berry, Fran Martin and Audrey Yue. 133–57. Durham: Duke University Press.

Ong, A. 2006. *Neoliberalism as Exception: Mutations in Citizenship and Sovereignty*. Durham: Duke University Press.

Ouellette, L. and Hay, J. 2008. Makeover Television, Governmentality and the Good Citizen. *Continuum* 22 (4), 471–84.

Phillips, R., Watt, D. and Shuttleton, D. eds. 2000. *De-centring Sexualities: Politics and Representations beyond the Metropolis*. London: Routledge.

Pol, E. and Carroll, P. 2004. *An Introduction to Economics and the Creative Economy*. Wollongong NSW, Australia: Innovative Planet.

Prabhu, G.N. 1999. Social Entrepreneurial Leadership. *Career Development International* 4 (3), 140–45.

Pratt, A. 2009. Situating the Production of New Media: The Case of San Francisco (1995–2000). In *Creative Labour: Working in Creative Industries*, eds. Alan McKinlay and Chris Smith. 195–209. London: Palgrave Macmillan.

Price, D. C. 2003. Singapore: It's In to be Out. Got Pink Dollars to Spend? Then Head for the Lion City. *Time Asia*, August, 18–25.

Prince, C. J. 2002. Rolling Out the Red Carpet for Gay Consumers. *The Advocate*, February, 27–30.

Prystay, C. 2007. Singapore Swing: The City's Gay Balancing Act. *The Wall Street Journal*, 10 August, http://online.wsj.com/article/SB118667829527493165.html (accessed on 8 October 2010).

Rodan, G. 1998. The Internet and Political Control in Singapore. *Political Science Quarterly* 113 (1), 63–89.

Rodan, G. 2003. Embracing Electronic Media but Suppressing Civil Society: Authoritarian Consolidation in Singapore. *The Pacific Review* 16 (4), 503–24.

Schumpeter, J. A. 1936 [c1934]. *The Theory of Economic Development: An Inquiry into Profits, Capital, Credit, Interest, and the Business Cycle.* Translated from German by Redvers Opie. Cambridge, Mass.: Harvard University Press.

Sender, K. 2004. *Business, Not Politics: The Making of the Gay Market.* New York: Columbia University Press.

Smith, C. and McKinley, A. 2009. Creative Industries and Labour Process Analysis. In *Creative Labour: Working in Creative Industries*, eds. Alan McKinlay and Chris Smith. 3–28. London: Palgrave Macmillan.

Streitmatter, R. 2004. *Sex Sells! The Media's Journey from Repression to Obsession.* Boulder, CO: Westview Press.

Tan, K. P. and Lee, G. J. L. 2007. Imagining the Gay Community in Singapore. *Critical Asian Studies* 39 (2), 179–204.

Valor, C. 2006. Why Do Managers Give? Applying Pro-social Behaviour Theory to Understand Film Giving. *International Review on Public and Non Profit Marketing* 3 (1), 17–28.

Weiss, M. L. 2006. Rejection as Freedom? HIV/AIDS Organizations and Identity. *Perspectives on Politics* 4 (4), 671 (1).

Yue, A. 2006. The Regional Culture of New Asia: Cultural Governance and Creative Industries in Singapore. *International Journal of Cultural Policy* 12 (1), 17–33.

———. 2010a. Interview with Stuart Koe. 29 June, Singapore.

———. 2010b. Interview with Sylvia Tan. 29 June, Singapore.

———. 2011. Doing Cultural Citizenship in the Global Media Hub: Illiberal Pragmatics and Lesbian Consumption Practices in Singapore. In *Circuits of Visibility: Gender and Transnational Media Culture*, ed. Radha Hegde. 250–67. New York: New York University Press.

Index

Absence, 169
activism,
   HIV/AIDS, 7
   lesbian, 21, 87, 90
   LGBT, 1, 4–5, 15–16, 25, 101, 164, 200, 209
Adorno, Theodor, 155
Ahmed, Sara, 149, 154
Ah qua, 7, 219n1
Althusser, Louis, 39
Anglo-American perspective, 83
Ann Siang Hill/Road, 123, 125–26, 131, 133
Army Daze, 169
Au, Alex, 4, 55, 63, 89, 97, 101, 110, 112, 133,
   169, 199, 214n3, 214n7, 215n9, 217n4
Autopsy, 169, 172
AWARE (Association of Women for
   Action and Research), 20, 59–69, 154

Beautiful Boxer, 169
Benjamin, Walter, 165, 218n5
Bi, Kenneth, 169
Boat Quay, 123, 125
Bogdanovich, Peter, 166, 218n6
Boo, Junfeng, 162, 168–69
Box, The (sauna), 134
breast binding, 16–17
Bugis Street, 7, 31, 118–19
Bugis Street (film), 167–68
butch, 4, 10, 13, 16–18, 201, 207

Café Vienna, 138–39
censorship, 176–79, 184–85, 219n1, 220n4
   media, 8, 22–24, 38, 104, 111, 158, 161–70,
     200, 213n7
   theatre, 12, 102, 183

Censorship Review Committee (CRC),
   178–79, 185
Cheaters, 24, 177–80, 184
Children and Young Persons Act (CYPA),
   48–50
China, 35–36, 43, 190, 198, 202, 208, 217n1,
   220n6
Chinese Singaporeans, 40, 189–90, 194
Cholodenko, Lisa, 23, 175
Chua, Beng Huat, 1–2, 4–5, 12–13, 18, 61,
   94, 99, 151
Church of Our Saviour, 61, 65
citizenship, 103–7, 153, 195
   cultural, 18–22, 29–43, 71–81
   legal, 71–73
   sexual, 19, 21
   spatial, 59
civil society, 1–2, 8, 19–20, 59, 61–65, 68–69,
   104, 209, 220
colonialism, 6–7, 11, 13, 21, 30, 35, 98, 103,
   156, 166, 200, 216n3
coming out, 7, 10–11, 21, 40, 76, 80, 91,
   93–94, 172
communitarianism, 12
compulsory heterosexuality, 19, 30, 33, 37,
   40–42, 178
cosmopolitanism, 19, 21, 98, 100–4, 107–13,
   153, 217n2
creative industries, 2, 9–17, 21, 102, 198–99,
   205–7, 210–11
creativity, 8, 15–18, 95– 96, 100–4, 107–9,
   169, 179, 185, 201–7
crisis, narrative, 36, 106
Cut, 169
Cut Sleeve Boys, 169

deviant/deviance, 11, 18, 22, 29, 62–63, 69,
    78, 94, 105, 152, 156–58
Diamond Health Centre, 135
Duggan, Lisa, 152

economic development, 4, 100
education, 5, 19–21, 37–42, 59, 63, 67–69,
    91, 94, 99–100, 110, 190–92, 203–10
election, 37
enforcement, passive, 20, 45–46, 54–58, 108
Esplanade, 121–22, 180–83
ethics,
    business, 203
    gay, 15–16, 170–71
    political, 159
    social,14, 167, 219n2
    work, 12
eugenics, 32, 41

Facebook, 23, 29, 95, 147
Fanon, Frantz, 35, 39
femininity, 76–79
feminism, 21, 60, 62, 66, 72, 84–85, 90
Florida, Richard, 9, 101–2
Floyd, Kevin, 149, 155
Focus on the Family, 62–63
Forever Fever, 169
Fort Road Beach, 122–23
Foucault, Michel, 15–16, 29, 35, 42, 89, 159
Free Community Church, 146
Fridae, 3, 25, 192–94, 197–212

gay,
    cruising, 7, 15, 22, 119–28, 133–35, 147, 188
    doing, 13, 15–17, 95–96
    entrepreneurs, 8, 22, 25, 129, 141, 193,
        198, 201
    saunas, 15, 23, 52, 111, 128–35, 143,
        188–89, 201
    venues, 117–47
George, Cherian, 59, 113, 151
Glass Cathedral, 11–12
global city, Singapore as, 21, 97–114, 163
global gay, 11, 15, 84, 88, 90, 93–96, 204,
    216n6
globalization, 15, 22, 85, 98–99, 103, 109, 168
Goei, Glen, 169

Hangar, The (bar), 137–38
Happy (club), 144
Harvey, David, 153, 155
heartlander, 111
Heng, Ivan, 13, 169
heteronormativity, 4, 6–11, 21–23, 37, 67,
    71, 76, 81, 91–93, 149, 152, 162–63,
    168, 177
HIV/AIDS, 10, 31–34, 49–50, 55–56, 63, 67,
    89, 154, 199–203, 210–11
homonationalism, 23, 149–59
homonormativity, 2, 12, 23, 152–59
homosociality, 163, 212
Hong Lim Park (Hong Lim Green), 3,
    120–25, 209
human rights, 1, 6, 18, 33, 59, 107, 199

illiberal pragmatics, 2–11, 17–19, 81, 87,
    108, 120, 161, 163, 192, 196, 198
impossible presence, 162–73
Indian-Singaporeans, 24, 188–96
IndigNation, 3, 146, 162, 203–4, 211
Infectious Diseases Act, 55
Internal Security Act, 39
Internet, 8, 22–25, 29, 38, 43, 87–90, 147,
    188, 192–95, 199–210

Jalan Kubor, 119

karaoke, 89, 135, 141, 143
Katong Fugue, 169, 172
The Kids Are All Right, 23–24, 175

Lau, Josie, 61–65
Le Bistro (bar), 136
Lee, Hsien Loong, 40, 45, 102
Lee, Kuan Yew, 8, 30–37, 40, 43, 89, 104,
    109–11, 149
legislation, anti-sodomy, 35, 103–4, 108;
    see also Section 377A
lesbian, 175–85
    Asian, 3, 17, 83–96, 193
    nightlife, 9, 16–18, 130
    performing arts, 24–25, 184–86
    "sexually challenged women", 64
    transnational identities, 2, 83–96, 193, 212
LGBT, 1–4, 8–25, 59, 87, 120, 163, 175–76,
    198, 203–4, 207–12, 216n6, 219n1, 220n2

Liang Po Po The Movie, 169
Lian, Teng Bee, 169
Lim, Max, 129–33
Locust, 169
Lo, Jacqueline, 184
Loo, Zihan, 23, 162, 167–71
Lucky 7, 168, 174
Lume, Kan, 23, 162, 170

Marmota (disco), 140–41
masculinity
    and gay men, 78–80, 140, 156, 199,
        219n13
    and nationality, 11, 21, 36–38, 40–42, 169
    lesbian, 16–17, 92
media,
    control, 8, 23–24, 38, 66, 192, 220n3
    new, 22, 25, 29, 198–99, 206, 212, 220n3
    social, 18, 23, 25, 43, 147, 201–4
Media Development Authority (MDA), 9,
    23, 38, 162, 175–82, 205
MediaCorp Raintree Pictures, 161, 218n2
military, 20–21, 37, 40, 71–81, 104
Military Security Department, 79
Ministry of Education, 38–39, 67–69
Miscellaneous Offences (Public Order
    and Nuisance) Act (MOPOA), 51–56,
    215n9–n10
Money No Enough, 169
Moo, Joash, 10
morality, 32, 62, 179, 209
Mother, 169, 172, 219n11
Mox Bar and Café, 145–46
multiracialism, 3, 5, 18

National Council of Churches of
    Singapore, 65
nationalism, 105, 114, 152–55, 194, 208
    compulsory, 149, 155
National Library Board, 23, 150, 159
National Service, 11, 20, 71, 74–78, 80–81
nation-building, 23, 40, 71, 75, 89, 151, 155,
    157, 159, 196
Nation Party, 3–4, 32, 197, 211, 213n1
negative dialectics, 155–59
neoliberalism/neoliberal, 2, 8–9, 12, 19,
    25, 33, 84, 87, 109, 151–53, 155, 198,
    211–12

neo-Victorianism, 33–34, 37, 40–43
newspapers,
    Chinese-language, 38
    English-language, 60, 65, 149–59, 218n6

Pebbles Bar, 136–38, 141
Peculiar Chris, 11, 34
penal code, 1, 35, 154
People Like Us, 3, 7, 39, 89, 193, 200,
    220n10–n11
pink,
    dollar, 3, 103, 112, 141, 163, 197–98
    dot, 95, 209, 211, 216n6
    tourism, 22, 201, 221n5
Pleasure Factory, 167–68
politics,
    identity, 15, 84, 153, 163
    queer, 15, 21, 27–37, 96–113, 163
    sexual, 1, 152, 154
postcolonial, 1–4, 17, 19, 29, 31, 34, 37,
    84–95, 98, 107, 150–54, 157, 159, 208
pragmatism, 15–18, 81, 87, 91, 95, 108, 151,
    161, 198
prosecution, 7, 20, 46–57
prostitution, homosexual, 30, 166–67
Puar, Jasbir, 152–53, 155
public housing, 6–7, 20, 41, 91–92, 99, 105,
    110–11
public indecency, 215n9–n10
public toilets, 49, 53, 55, 121, 128, 215n9–n11

queer,
    Asia, 2, 4, 25, 93, 207–8
    cinema, 18–25, 163–73
    complicity, 2
    rights, 97, 103, 106–9
    space, 112
    theory, 18, 164
    world-making, 156–59

racialised, 22–24
Rairua (sauna), 132–33
Rajagopal, K, 169
Raw (sauna), 133
RedQuEEn, 90, 200
religion, 14, 40, 59–69
Rice Rhapsody, 169, 172–73
River Valley Swimming Pool, 122, 128

Sa'at, Alfian, 13, 31, 40
Saint Jack, 158, 166–70, 218n6–n8, 218n10
same-sex marriage, 62
Section 377A, 6, 23, 35, 49, 53–54, 61, 87,
     89, 161, 184, 216n3
Sen, Ong Keng, 169
sex education, 59, 63, 67–69, 162, 210
shame, 15–18, 33–34, 94, 154, 156
SiGNeL, 192–93, 220n13
Silly Child, 24, 176–77, 184
Singapore Armed Forces, 73, 106
Singapore Film Commission, 161, 218n2
Singapore International Film Festival, 166,
     169–70
Singapore Tourist Promotion Board, 166
social enterprise, 197–212
social movement, *see* activism
Solos, 23, 162, 164, 168–71, 173, 219n12
sovereignty, 21, 105–7, 113
Spartacus (sauna), 120, 129–31
Spivak, Gayatri, 89
Stonewall (post), 5–6, 10
Straits Times, The, 60–68, 154–59, 193
Stroke (sauna), 131
subjectivities,
     lesbian, 84–87, 90–91, 95
     sexual, 84–86, 94–95, 106, 191

Taboo (club), 143–44, 201
Tanjong Pagar Road, 142–44
Tanjong Rhu, 162, 168
television, 22–25, 38, 179
Thailand, 3–4, 83–84, 128, 198, 208, 216n4
theatre, 12, 89
Thio, Su Mien, 62–67, 217n8
Thng, Victric, 169
Threshold, 162, 168

Tong, Goh Chok, 88, 99
transgender/transexual/transvestite,
     4–7, 10–11, 18, 31, 63, 77–78, 118–19,
     167–69, 213n2
transnational, 19, 21–24, 83–96, 98–99, 105,
     109–12, 162–63, 188, 195
Treetops Bar, 138–39
Turnbull, Mary Constance, 30, 36–42,
     150–51, 217n3
Tutu, Desmond, 66

Uekrongtham, Ekachai, 167–69

values,
     Asian, 12, 32, 34, 36, 89, 151, 169, 190–91
     family, 8, 12, 21, 67–68, 89, 92, 179, 199, 209
     hierarchical, 7
     homonormative, 12
     masculine, 38
     national, 71–72
     Western, 191
Victorian England, 31–37, 41
Vincent's (bar), 141

Wedding Game, The, 169
Williams, Linda, 164–67, 170, 218n5
Women Who Love Women, 168
World Health Organization (WHO), 78,

Yan, Olivia, 176–77, 184
Yellow Fever, 169
Yeung, Ray, 169
Yonfan, 167–68
Yu-Beng, Lim, 170–71
Yue, Audrey, 1–27, 87, 95, 98, 108, 163,
     197–212, 217n7, 221n6